PRIME
OF YOUR
LIFE

PRIME OF YOUR LIFE

by Joe Michaels

with the assistance of
Bill Logan and Wendy Ruoff

Facts On File, Inc.
119 West 57th Street, New York, N.Y. 10019

PRIME
OF YOUR
LIFE

First Printing 1981
Printed and bound in the United States of America

Prime of Your Life was produced and prepared by
Quarto Marketing, Ltd.
212 Fifth Avenue,
New York, N.Y. 10010

Library of Congress Cataloging in Publication Data

Michaels, Joe.
    Prime of your life.

    Bibliography: p.
    Includes index.
    1. Aged—United States—Life skills guides.
I. Title.
HQ1064.U5M52   305.2'6'0973   80-21205
ISBN 0-87196-478-3

INTRODUCTION .

The Prime of Your Life? What, you might want to ask, am I trying to tell you—that the old years are the best years? No. Well, not exactly. What I am trying to tell you is that the onset of those so-called old years don't automatically signal the end of an enjoyable, useful and rewarding life— whatever your age, the Prime of Your Life really is *now*. This book is designed to help you make your elder years the best years, but ultimately it is up to you to squeeze from life all it offers at the moment, this moment.

This was a revelation to me not too long ago—about four years ago, to be somewhat more precise. At that time two things happened. I began to think of what I would do as an elder because the time was approaching; I was in the last three years of my fifties and starting to think that I had done very little planning for the future. It occurred to me, in a desultory kind of way (desultory reflections having been a lifelong habit), that I really should start thinking about what my income would be; how I would manage the problem of two teenaged sons with college still ahead of them; how I would fare on a shrunken income; and what I would *do* with myself when NBC said, "Sorry friend, but it's time to do the watch-and-faithful-employee-now-about-to-enjoy-the-lei- sure-he-never-wanted bit." The second thing was that our program director came to me and told me about a new program the network was starting, a program about the elderly that was to be called "The Prime of Your Life."

His attitude was very diffident, which, in the TV business, seemed an unusual approach to take when asking someone if he would like to cohost a new program. It was, I quickly realized, as though, while he wanted to let me know that he thought I would be good on the program, he was fearful that I might assume he was also telling me, "Look old boy, you're ideal for this program because you're, ah—well, let's face it, you're, ah, well, getting up there, aren't you?"

And I was—am, for that matter. Because I had already been thinking about that very thing, it didn't disturb me. What *did* disturb me was that I knew absolutely nothing about whatever it is people should know about getting old and being old and—it sounded silly, but I knew what I meant—doing it well.

So, I started to read. It was, let me tell you, awful. My first book was Bob Butler's *Why Survive? Being Old in America.* Dr. Robert N. Butler is the founder of the National Institute on Aging, where much important research on the subject is being done. He is much more than that, though. He is one of the first medical men to devote himself to aging, a subject most doctors have historically found as attractive as a poverty-stricken patient. But he's much more than *that,* too. To those who have become involved in gerontology, Butler has been guru, leader, friend, confidante and sharer of whatever he has to offer. Today he is increasingly optimistic, but when he wrote his devastating attack on American attitudes towards the aging, he was just plain mad, and he wasn't looking for good news. Neither was anybody else I read. Anger, I guess, was the mood of the people who wrote about aging in the 1970s—justifiable anger, let me hasten to add. Old people were being treated very badly. They still are. I once wrote in an editorial that the worst crime one could commit in this country was to be old and poor. But as somebody else once wrote in another context, there's a new wind blowing.

It is not something that can be examined like a laboratory

specimen. But it is something that can be felt. We can, for example, feel it when we see politicians hastening to defeat proposed changes in the social security laws that we don't like. People at the senior centers tell me that at election time the would-be office holders flock around like pigeons after bread crumbs, promising, promising, promising.

And our attitudes are changing. Now, we are more likely to demand where once we used to plead or, worse still, to simply accept whatever was given or denied us. We want to *do* things. We are flocking to colleges and universities and being wooed by them, for as our younger countrymen and women are having fewer children, the country's institutions of higher learning are turning to us to fill the empty seats in those hallowed halls. They woo us to come and be educated—please! They offer courses at lower rates or no rates at all. College presidents importune state legislators to make special provision for us. So let's all take advantage of these benefits—each one will enable us to turn these present moments into the prime of our lives, *now*.

When a couple of college professors got the notion that they could help fill those empty classrooms of summertime by introducing short courses for older people, they didn't have a clue as to what the result would be. We can see the result now, though. All over the country, restless elders, hungry for fun and knowledge too, are traveling from school to school absorbing information on everything from local history to folk music and, with all that, having the enjoyment of meeting new people in new places—new places as far away as Scandinavia. Think of it. That's a revolution we're talking about here! And if you're in the 75 and up age group, you're no longer taken in by the self-fulfilling myth that you are debris, simply waiting to be swept up and disposed of, incapable of learning or enjoying—and if you could, learn to what purposes? The old, as a generation ago even they would have said of themselves, are fit for nothing but to wait for the inevitable disintegration in decent quietude. No more!

No, today we are learning and traveling and politicking—yes—and working and contributing. Companies are beginning to recognize the value and worth of the experience and dedication that we bring to what we do. They are thinking of innovative ways to keep us on the payroll—shared jobs, part-time jobs. And retirement looks less attractive to many, though not to all.

Most important is the rise in self-esteem. In researching this book I met and questioned people from 65 well up into their eighties. Some were still working for profit, some were volunteering for fun. They were going to school, starting new careers, transforming hobbies into part- or even full-time endeavors, and some were just enjoying. What these special people had in common was a self-knowledge, visible in their eyes, in their bearing. They were successful people. Not necessarily in the accumulation of goods and money because to many of them, wiser now with the years, the knowledge has come that success is not measured by the envy or awe with which others view them, but by the fulfillment of their own values. These are people who, with all their years, await each tomorrow with anticipation, not resignation.

This is not to say that America is the New Nirvana of the elderly. It is not. I found ample material for continued indignation, and some of it is set out among these pages. But there are plenty of people doing things and plenty of information about how to do them. The new day for the elderly is not yet here in full. But its dawn is here, and it is worth getting excited about.

Joe Michaels

CHAPTER
1

SECURITY

PLANNING FOR FINANCIAL SECURITY

Planning for financial security involves looking into several different matters. If you're young enough, you'll want to know which employers offer the best pension plans, and if you're nearing retirement, you'll want to know how you can best handle your private pension. You'll also want to know about individual retirement plans, social security, life insurance, saving, investing in securities, annuities, time deposits, collecting as an investment technique and your home.

PENSIONS

Working for a small company where everyone knows each other and the atmosphere projects a pleas-

1

ant kind of mutual dependency sounds delightful. The dehumanizing influences so often found in big corporations are absent. Unfortunately, these small companies also quite frequently lack an adequate pension system and often have none at all.

ARMED FORCES

The best possible pension system is offered by any branch of the armed forces. For example, if you stay in the service 20 years, you are eligible for half-pay, not at 60 or later, but immediately. And if you stay for 30 years, you collect 75 percent of your top pay for the remainder of your life. And at this stage, a little basic arithmetic informs you that if you joined at, say, 18, fresh out of high school, you can retire at only 48, still eligible, remember, to use your acquired skills to get a civilian job and draw social security in due course on top of your military pension. Twice yearly, pension benefits are *indexed,* that is, increased to keep up with the cost of living. There are also other advantages, such as inexpensive medical care.

GOVERNMENT

Working for federal, state or local government will provide you with much better retirement benefits than any private concern. For one thing, in many cities and states, you can also retire early and go to work for a private company, thus becoming eligible for both the government-paid pension and social security from another job. Again, chances are that the job will be indexed. Also, in most government plans the pensions are substantially higher than those paid by private companies.

COMPANY PLANS

Company plans are better than none at all—much better, in fact. But they differ in many ways. Some are *integrated*, which means that they discount from their own final pension your social security, thus decreasing a pension's value. With some plans the company makes all the payments up to a certain level of income. With others the company takes out your share right from the beginning. There are also other things in company plans to be examined when you look for employment with retirement in mind.

Aspects Of Company Plans

It sounds independent and dashing to be unconcerned with the future, to wander happily to and fro wherever your whim takes you. But there is a price tag on being footloose and fancy-free. The price tag is usually a low pension or none at all. To become part of most company pension programs, you have to become *vested* in that plan. This means that you must stay with the company for a certain period of uninterrupted employment before you become eligible to receive any pension benefits. Some companies vest you in their retirement plan after eight years. In most cases it is 10 years. Considering that the typical American male stays with one employer on the average of 4.6 years and the typical American female an average of 2.8 years, it is not surprising that most people never do collect on pensions from companies.

Remember, though, that one-fourth of all private pension plans require some employee contribution; even if you are never vested in your company's plan, the amount you've contributed (plus interest) must be refunded when you leave.

If you have the future in mind, as you should for

your own protection, show interest in a company that makes payments on the first $7,000 or $8,000 of your salary without contribution from you. Other benefits may be more important still. Does the company have a pension plan whereby you can, for a minimal payment, continue receiving the medical benefits offered to employees? Are the company's benefits to the surviving spouse generous? No company plan will offer anything remotely as generous to lower- and middle-pay workers as it does to the happy folk ensconced in the executive suites, but the pension plan where you work or may go to work is vital to you. Make it a point to ask about it. Your company must employ people to report to you on its plan. Most will be happy to tell you all they can about how the pension applies to you and what it offers.

If you're nearing retirement or changing jobs, you might want to consider an option that enables you to use your pension as a way of coping with inflation. I'm talking about the private pensions that allow—indeed, often encourage—you to collect your money in a lump sum. The disadvantage of doing this, of course, is that you won't have money left in your pension guaranteeing you payments for life upon retirement. Also, if you take a lump sum, you'll have to pay the 50 percent maximum tax on earned income, which could be substantial if you expect to be in a high tax bracket in retirement. The often compelling advantage in taking a lump sum payment stems from the fact that, with very few exceptions, private pensions are not indexed. So, in times of inflation, your pension goes down in value as the rate of inflation goes up. What you can do, therefore, is to put that portion of your lump sum payment that was contributed by your employer (money that you personally contributed is not eligible) into an Independent Retirement Account (IRA) Rollover Account, thereby allowing it to grow while deferring taxes until you start withdrawing (which you cannot do before you reach the age of 59½ without incurring a tax penalty, except in the case of death or total disability). IRA Rollover Accounts are similar in most aspects to ordinary IRAs (see next section). In subsequent years you can add to your IRA Rollover if you have earned income and are not covered by any other pension plans. However, this is not advisable since your Rollover will then lose its *portability*, or the ability to roll the IRA over into the pension fund of another company that allows you to do so. You can, however, set up regular IRA accounts independent of your rollover account. It is important to remember that you must start an IRA Rollover within 60 days of receiving your lump sum distribution or else you forfeit the opportunity to do so and will have to pay the income tax.

An important point to remember is that the financial institutions that qualify as trustees for IRA Rollover Accounts are anxious to capture your assets. You should therefore consult an accountant to determine whether it is wise for you to roll over your lump sum. If your accountant advises against it, consult him or her as to the best, or least costly, way to handle the taxes on a lump sum distribution. The options are: (1) the portion of the fund attributable to contributions made before 1974 can be treated as a long-term capital gain, with the remainder treated as ordinary income eligible for 10-year averaging ; or (2) the entire amount can be treated as ordinary income with 10-year averaging.

PRIME-OF-YOUR-LIFER

Sylvia Alpert

Sylvia Alpert was left a widow with a small daughter while in her early thirties. She had no money and no skills. Just courage and basic intelligence. Oh, yes—and the ability to see her world as it really was without self-pity. But why talk for her? I asked her about those first days of self-dependence.

JM: Did you have plans?

SA: Most definitely. I made my plans 30 years before because I knew that aging was inevitable, and I wanted to make sure that I put myself in a position where I would not require any financial assistance from anyone. So I knew what I had to do was to get a job that gave me a pension and just keep working so that I could collect my social security and my pension. That was the reason I stayed in the union. [She's talking about the International Ladies' Garment Workers Union.] I was also active in the union. So when the time came, I was ready, financially ready. Because I was a member of this union, it automatically entitled me to Blue Cross, Blue Shield, Major Medical and unlimited medical care at the union health center, which is the biggest problem for somebody that's aging.

JM: Does that give you a sense of security?

SA: More than that. I feel wonderful [with a little laugh] because I don't have to worry about paying for anything and all the money that I get belongs to me. I get social security and a pension, and I'm living in a public housing project which limits my rent to 25% of my income, so, that 75% is for me.

JM: You must have done something besides work.

SA: Oh, I had other interests, too. The union had a studio in the Village so I started with art there, and I've been doing painting and sculpture, working in all media.

JM: And then it came time to stop. What's it been like?

SA: Great. Just great. In the morning I go to the Henry Street Settlement. We have a woman's group, drawing, sketching, ceramics, and then I'm also a member of a folk dance group there. It's been very, very good because I'm studying Hebrew and music there. So, I'm leading a very busy, fulfilling life. We also have a folk dance group which takes to the various nursing homes to perform. We dance for them. We have one who recites poetry. One who sings. As I said, I'm learning music. I play the recorder.

JM: You keep very busy?

SA: Yes. But I have time at night occasionally to watch something good on TV. But the best part of it is that I'm doing what I like.

JM: Would you describe yourself as a happy person?

SA: I would say that—yes. I would say that I never knew such peace of mind as I do now because I'm free from pressure and worry.

JM: You don't miss working at all, then?

SA: Heavens, no. That's a dirty word.

Mrs. Alpert's happiness is based on an investment, but it is not one of stocks, bonds or property. She learned to do something she liked. She planned on getting into a line of work where she would have a pension, and she planned to live in a place where the rent would be minimal. So far as we know, she has no bank account to speak of, but she has put a daughter through college who is now a mother herself. She depends on no one, though,Lord knows, her pension and social security together add up to little enough. Mrs. Alpert

is, by any rational definition, a successful person.
The lesson should be clear. What you decide to
do with your life should be determined with your
retirement years in mind.

INDIVIDUAL PENSION PLANS

If you work for a company that has no retirement
plan or if you are self-employed, there is no longer any
reason for you to be without pension protection. The
IRA and Keogh plans allow you to take care of yourself.

The *Individual Retirement Account* lets employees
not covered by pension plans salt away 15 percent or
$1,500 of their annual income (whichever is less) tax-
free. If you're married and your spouse qualifies, together you can put as much as $3,000 yearly into your
IRA. The funds must stay in the account until you are
59½ years old. Then you can begin taking them out at
any rate you please. Only when you withdraw the
funds do they become taxable, though you must begin
to take them out by age 70½.

Not all IRAs have equal yields as investments, nor
are they equally secure. Your account could take any
of the following forms: a bank or savings and loan account, an annuity administered by an insurance company or credit union, common stocks, bonds, mutual
funds or the specially created U.S. Individual Retirement Bond. It's even permissible to invest in real estate or collectibles, but regardless of the form your investment takes, you must hire an IRS-approved
trustee to oversee it. Banks, savings and loan associations, insurance companies, big brokerage houses and

credit unions have officials qualified to serve as trustees.

U.S. Individual Retirement Bonds are the very safest investment. Bank and savings accounts are nearly as safe and may provide a higher rate of return. Credit unions and insurance companies are usually safe bets also. A mutual fund requires some research to determine what its investments are and how much its rate of return has fluctuated in the past. Stocks, bonds, real estate and collectibles are more speculative. They can provide bigger returns—or bigger losses.

Generally speaking, the more control you choose to exercise over your IRA the more expensive it will be to keep. It costs nothing to invest in U.S. Individual Retirement Bonds. You should compare the charges that different banks, savings and loan associations and credit unions make to maintain an IRA, but such charges are usually small. Insurance company charges vary widely, from eight percent to 90 percent of first-year investment. If you want to maintain a stock portfolio, on the other hand, and change it at your will, you'll probably incur both brokerage and trustee fees every time you make a transaction.

A tip for those investing in bank accounts or annuities: when deciding where to put your money, compare not only charges and interest rates but also methods of compounding interest. It can make quite a difference to your future plans whether your interest rate is compounded quarterly, daily or continuously.

Individual Retirement Accounts have become so popular since their introduction in 1975 that today many companies, particularly small ones which decided that regular pension plans were too rich for their corporate blood, sponsor IRAs and even contribute to the employee's plan. If your company has no information on IRAs, try your local bank or life insurance company. They'll naturally push their own product, but they usually have experts qualified to outline all the options available to you. Your accountant is another good source of information.

As the IRA is to the employees without pension protection, so the *Keogh Plan* is to self-employed people like doctors, shopkeepers and small businesspeople. Investment and withdrawal rules are the same as for IRAs, but under the Keogh Plan you can contribute as much as 15 percent, but no more than $7,500, to your account each year, tax free. The "catch" is that you must cover both yourself and any regular workers you employ. You contribute to their pensions at a percentage rate equal to your own.

An important point for free-lancers and moonlighters to remember is this: even if part of your income is covered by a pension plan, you can put some or all of your uncovered income into an IRA. The same rules apply as for any other IRA account, but in calculating the maximum 15 percent contribution allowable, you include only the uncovered portion of your income. You can turn your moonlight earnings into a retirement nest egg.

SOCIAL SECURITY

The social security concept was already legally established almost all over Europe when our own Social Security Act was finally signed into law in the late summer of 1935. Initially, it covered only workers who had reached the age of 65, but by no means all of them. Farm workers and domestics, among the most in need, were excluded. Continual changes in the law have increased the number and type of people covered. And today social security payments are indexed, which, as I explained earlier when talking about pensions, means that when the cost of living goes up, so do social security payments.

WHO IS ELIGIBLE?

To begin with, 93 percent of everyone 65 or over in the United States is either drawing social security payments, is entitled to them on retirement (not everybody retires at age 65) or is the spouse of someone entitled to such payments. The figure is larger than it looks because three percent of the over 65 group are not eligible because they draw pensions from other sources, such as the railroad system, or from their work in federal, state or local government. Still another category of ineligible workers consists of those receiving military pensions. The system also covers workers who become disabled before they are eligible for retirement and dependents of a worker who dies of a disability before reaching retirement age. There are some limitations in all cases.

To be eligible for retirement benefits, you must have spent at least one-quarter of your working life in qualified jobs. The government figures you can work for about 40 years from age 21. So 10 years of covered employment qualifies you for full benefits. Older workers get a break, however, because the present system of retirement benefits didn't come into existence until 1951. If you turned 21 before then, you'll only have to work a quarter of the time between 1950 and your 62nd birthday to be eligible. For example, say you were 21 in 1940 and will turn 62 in 1981. To qualify for retirement benefits in 1981, you need only have worked one-fourth of the last 31 years (see Tables 1 and 2 on p. 12 and 13).

Table 1

QUARTERS OF COVERAGE NEEDED FOR
FULLY INSURED STATUS

Year of Birth	No. of Covered Quarters Required
1913	24
1914	25
1915	26
1916	27
1917	28
1918	29
1919	30
1920	31
1921	32
1922	33
1923	34
1924	35
1925	36
1926	37
1927	38
1928	39
1929 or later	40

Table 2

Work credit for retirement benefits	
If you reach 62 in	Years you need
1976	6¼
1977	6½
1978	6¾
1979	7
1981	7½
1983	8
1987	9
1991 or later	10

Source: Social Security Administration

To receive disability benefits, however, if you're over 30, you must have worked not only one-quarter of your working life but also one-half of the last 10 years before you became disabled. Rules for survivors' benefits are more lenient. To compute work credit for survivors' and disability benefits (see Table 3 on p. 14).

Table 3

Work credit for survivors' and disability benefits		
Born after 1929, die or become disabled at	Born before 1930, die or become disabled be- fore 62 in	Years you need
28 or younger		1½
30		2
32		2½
34		3
36		3½
38		4
40		4½
42		5
44		5½
46		6
48		6½
50	1979	7
52	1981	7½
54	1983	8
56	1985	8½
58	1987	9
60	1989	9½
62 or older	1991 or later	10

Source: Social Security Administration

Calculating just how "long" you have worked is simple, if not exactly logical. Long ago, companies reported worker income quarterly, so the government computed work time by quarter-years. Now companies usually report annual figures, but the government still calculates quarterly. The number of quarters you are allowed to claim for social security purposes is determined by dividing your total wages for the year by a standard minimum amount. (In 1980, for example, it was $290.) If you've earned four or more times that amount, you get four full quarters of credit. If you've earned less, you get less credit. For all wages earned before 1978, when the law changed, you get one quarter's credit for each $50 of wages paid, up to a maximum of four.

WHAT ARE MAXIMUM PAYMENTS ALLOWED?

Originally, social security contributions from the worker and the employer were based on wages up to no higher than $3,000 yearly. But this figure has been going up steadily because it is tied to the cost of living. The figure rose from $25,900 in 1980 to $29,700 in 1981, and it will continue rising in future years (see Table 4 on p. 16). While this means that both worker and employer put more in, it also means that the worker gets more out. And, as I mentioned earlier, social security payments are now indexed. Because severe inflation skyrocketed the cost of living in 1980, payments were increased by 14.3 percent. This jump resulted in increased benefits for more than 100 million recipients of social security. It brought the average monthly check in 1980 to $330; the minimum to $153, from $133.90; and the maximum at age 65 to $653, from $572 (see Table 5 on pg. 17).

Table 4

MAXIMUM AMOUNT OF ANNUAL EARNINGS
COUNTED FOR BENEFITS AND
CONTRIBUTIONS

	Prior to the 1977 amendments	Present law
1977	$16,500	$16,500
1978	17,700	17,700
1979	18,900	22,900
1980	20,400	25,900
1981	21,900	29,700
1982	23,400	31,800*
1983	24,900	33,900
1984	26,400	36,000
1985	27,900	38,100

*This is the estimated figure resulting from the automatic provisions that increase the maximum benefit and contribution base in accordance with increases in average earnings. All increases for the years that follow are automatic.

Table 5

Examples of monthly social security retirement payments for workers who reach 62 before 1979 (effective June 1980)

Benefits can be paid to a:	Average yearly earnings after 1950 covered by social security						
	$923 or less	$3,000	$4,000	$5,000	$6,000	$8,000	$10,000*
Retired worker at 65	153.10	316.40	372.20	431.60	487.80	606.30	671.80
Retired worker at 62	122.50	253.20	297.80	345.30	390.30	485.10	537.50
Wife or husband at 65	76.60	158.20	186.10	215.80	243.90	303.20	335.90
Wife or husband at 62	57.50	118.70	139.60	161.90	233.00	227.40	252.00
Wife under 65 and one child in her care	76.60	167.40	263.80	364.70	406.80	454.80	503.80
Maximum family payment	229.70	483.80	636.00	796.30	894.60	1061.10	1175.60

*Maximum earnings covered by social security were lower in past years and must be included in figuring your average earnings. This average determines your payment amount. Because of this, the amount shown in the last column generally won't be payable until future years. The maximum retirement benefit generally payable to a worker who is 65 in 1980 is $653.80 (effective June 1980).

Source: Social Security Administration

HOW TO ESTIMATE YOUR BENEFITS

Since the system became indexed in 1978, it has become very complicated to estimate your own benefits. The best thing to do is call your local social security office. They'll have their computer do it for you. If you're a dedicated do-it-yourselfer, call and ask for the pamphlet *Estimating Your Social Security Retirement Check*. The method explained in the pamphlet isn't quite up to date, but Social Security Administration officials say it will still bring you within $10 or $15 of your estimated benefits. Keep in mind, though, that the exact amount of benefits due to you cannot be figured until you actually retire and make an application for them because all your earnings up to the time you make an application may be considered in figuring your benefits.

If you retire at age 62, your benefits will be 80 percent of what they would have been had you remained at work until 65. The logic here is based on how long you are expected to live, or what is known as actuarial tables, and the amount is reduced in order to equalize over the long term what an early retiree would receive in payments as compared to another worker who stayed on until 65. According to the actuarial tables, an average worker probably gets more social security by retiring at 62. On the other hand, if you come from a long-lived family and like your work, it's probably more sensible to stay on until 65.

Here's one final piece of advice on how to ensure that you will receive in benefits all that you're entitled to. To do this, every three years you should check the official social security earnings credited to your account and compare that figure with your own records. The Social Security Administration has a simple form (OAR-7004) that you have to complete and return to them to get this information. (Call your local social security office for the form.) This is important because social security computers do on occasion record such information incorrectly. And if this happens, it's your responsibility to notify the Social Security Administration of any errors and have them rectified.

CAN YOU WORK AND COLLECT AT THE SAME TIME?

After age 72 (70 beginning in 1982), you can earn whatever you like and your retirement benefit will not suffer. Between ages 62 and 72 (70 beginning in 1982), however, there are prescribed earnings limits that you can't pass without incurring a penalty equal to $1 in benefit reduction for every $2 over the limit! The limit is most stringent ($3,724 in 1980) for people between 62 and 65, less so ($5,000 in 1980) for those between 65 and 72. The limits rise each year with the cost of living. This limit is compensated for, in part, by a percent increase in benefits for every year after 65 that a person continues working. The increase is set at 1 percent annually, until 1982, when it becomes 3 percent.

Such restrictions may seem to favor the wealthy, since income from stocks, bonds, savings and other investments is not counted as "earned." A person with investments that net, say, $4,000 per year could still collect the full retirement benefit at 62, while another person with no investments won't be able to *earn* more than $3,724 without suffering a penalty. This apparent inequality is offset by the system's preretirement contributions limits. In 1980, for example, no earned income above $25,900 is allowed for figuring contributions. Any earnings above that amount won't produce any further retirement benefit. This way, lower-income people will receive a retirement benefit that is proportionally higher to their preretirement income than the benefit received by people who make more than $25,900.

Remember, too, that if your job earns you significantly more than the penalty limit for your age group, you'll probably still come out ahead if you keep working. Say you're making $12,000 on your 65th birthday in 1980. That's $7,000 above the limit, so you'll receive $3,500 less in social security benefits. If you were in the average $330 benefit category, netting $3,960 annually, your annual benefit would be reduced to only $460. Considered broadly, though, which would you rather have, $12,000 taxable *plus* $460 tax-free or only $3,960 tax-free? Since the tax on your $12,000 is not likely to be much higher than $1,600, you'll end up making $10,860 instead of the $3,960 from social security alone.

HOW DO YOU GET YOUR BENEFITS?

To get your social security benefits, you have to make an application. You should first notify your local social security office a few months before you intend to retire. You should certainly notify them as soon as you reach the retirement age you select, that is, from 62 to 65. Be sure to collect all the personal documents you have, including such things as proof of age and marriage, social security card and last income tax return. If you're not sure about what you must bring with you, or if you don't have one of these documents, call the social security office and ask exactly what you need.

HOW SECURE IS THE SYSTEM?

In 1977 there was a deficit in the social security fund that frightened a lot of people. In addition, as younger workers watch their contributions go up and up along with inflation, many have begun to wonder whether they will ever be able to recover what they have put in and whether there will be anything left when it's their turn to collect.

To make the system more secure, Congress decided in 1977 to substantially raise payments into the social security fund. The financial experts (who have been pretty accurate up to now) say without equivocation that the steps taken in the past few years have solidified the fund, certainly up to about 2025. If present calculations are accurate, rate increases will produce a surplus through the first 25 years of the new plan, which will offset later deficits. After 2025 there may have to be a new rise in payments or a decision to use the government's general funding as a source. (Our system differs from others in that it is not funded from general revenues but from the money paid into it by employers and employees.) The reason for such a rise is a decrease in the birth rate, resulting in fewer workers paying in while the number of those over 65 continues to grow.

In the long run, however, with so much of the country paying into the fund and facing dependence, how could a democratic government let the system go under? It doesn't make sense.

LIFE INSURANCE

Years ago an insurance man came to see me and my wife about getting our various kinds of insurance into proper order. He wasn't very successful, partially because we were young and foolish in our mutual conviction of immortality, but also because he had a habit of using the expression "hanging crepe," presumably a euphemism for death. So every time he wanted to point out that it was quite possible either or both of us might die and thereby create a financial situation that should be faced in advance, this gentlemen, who had a long, undertakerish face, would start by saying, "I don't want to hang crepe, but . . . ." After the fifth or sixth crepe-hanging, my wife and I were close to illness from suppressed laughter. We never did hear properly what the poor man had to say and certainly didn't buy any additional insurance from him.

The irony of all this is that the insurance agent really didn't have to keep punctuating his sales pitch with that unfortunate expression. For, as you probably know, not all insurance programs are designed solely for death protection purposes. The agent could have emphasized the saving features of certain kinds of policies.

Although insurance companies these days put together elaborate documents designed to convince you that their plan is most certainly the best there is, don't be overly impressed. Basically there are only two types of life insurance: cash value insurance and term insurance. And as explained in the following sections, all life insurance policies fit into one of these two categories.

TERM INSURANCE

Term insurance is *pure* insurance. It pays a fixed death benefit if and only if the policyholder dies within a set term. It has no savings value, cannot be borrowed against and expires after the set term. When you're young, however, term insurance is the cheapest kind of protection. Usually, it is both renewable and convertible. *Renewable* means that the policyholder has the guaranteed right to buy another policy for the same term as his or her previous policy when that policy runs out. Since premium rates are geared to a person's age, the rates will rise every time the policy is renewed. Generally, term insurance is not renewable after the age of 65 or 70. Some policies, nevertheless, are renewable up to age 100. It's very difficult, however, to start term insurance after the age of 65 or 70 and even if you can, you may not want to since the price will probably be as great as that of cash value insurance. *Convertible* means that you can trade in your term policy for a cash value policy without having to prove you're healthy.

LEVEL TERM INSURANCE

This kind of protection pays a fixed benefit over the whole term. The most typical policy is for a five-year term. If you have a $10,000 policy on this basis, the full $10,000 will be paid to your beneficiary if you die at any time within the five-year period. When it comes to renewing the policy, you can usually decrease the size of the death benefit without any "red tape," but to increase the amount you'll probably have to give new medical verification of your health.

DECREASING TERM INSURANCE

This is typically a young person's kind of insurance. It is very inexpensive, but the death benefit it pays decreases yearly over the length of the term. A young family that either expects its income to grow rapidly after a few "lean" years or has large initial expenses that decrease over time (a mortgage, for instance) will probably want to look into decreasing term insurance. Such a family reasons that as more cash is freed for independent investing, less insurance protection is needed.

GROUP TERM INSURANCE

Many companies offer this sort of term insurance to their employees. In general, it's cheaper to buy than ordinary level term insurance because the insurance company writes one policy to cover the whole group and only presents one bill. Sometimes the employer will pick up the whole cost of the insurance. When the employer doesn't, the cost to you will often be gauged by figuring an *average age* for all employees and charging one price for all. If you're younger than the average age, you might be better off seeking coverage elsewhere, but if you're older than the average, you'll be getting a break. Older people will pay less than they would if their actual ages were figured; younger people will pay more.

Not only companies have group term insurance. Clubs and associations may also have group policies for their members. Some retirement clubs, like the American Association of Retired Persons (AARP), have group policies specifically geared to the needs of older people. For more information on this program, contact AARP, 1909 K Street, Washington, D.C. 20049.

CASH VALUE INSURANCE

Cash value policies combine insurance protection and a savings plan. For this reason the premiums are higher than those for term insurance. They are so high, in fact, that many companies regularly over-charge their policyholders, returning the excess amount each year in what they call a "dividend." The *face value* of your policy, that is, the amount you originally insured yourself for, remains the same over the years the policy is in force, but its allocation changes. During the first year the policy is all insurance, but as you continue to pay premiums over the years, the amount of insurance decreases while the cash surrender value of the policy increases. Say you contract for $10,000 of cash value insurance at age 35. By age 60, your death benefit will have been reduced by, say,

$4,940, but the cash surrender value will have increased to $5,060. This means that you can cancel the policy and receive the full cash surrender amount. You can also borrow against the policy, using the cash surrender value as security.

As savings instruments, cash value policies are usually no more efficient that ordinary bank savings accounts. Then why should you choose a cash value over a term policy coupled with an independent savings account? Your choice should in large part depend on how advantageous a premium rate you can obtain. In general, however, cash value policies have two advantages over ordinary savings accounts. First, they compel you to save regularly and encourage you not to raid your savings, since if you take the cash surrender value, you lose the policy. Second, they provide a tax advantage because income tax on the "inside interest," which is calculated into the cash surrender value, is deferred until you terminate the policy. Even then, you can deduct the cost of protection from the amount on which you have to pay tax.

Of course, advocates of term insurance will point out that you could better that tax break by simply investing the money you save on premiums in a long-term savings account, which may earn substantially more than either a regular savings account or a cash value policy. Your decision will have to be based on a careful study of premium rates, cash values and savings interest rates available.

ORDINARY LIFE POLICIES

Also called "straight" or "whole" life policies, they charge a standard premium for your whole life or until you reach 100, whichever comes first. Premiums are higher for ordinary life than for term insurance, but lower than for other forms of cash value insurance.

But the fact that these policies will keep charging

you until you're 100 doesn't mean you have to keep paying. Most retirement-age people should consider ways to *stop* paying ordinary life insurance premiums. There are three alternatives: you can take the policy's cash surrender value, convert the ordinary life into a paid-up policy or buy an extended term policy.

The *cash surrender* option will give you an immediate lump sum. You can use the money to make other investments, if you're thinking of your survivors' security, or you and your spouse may wish to spend it for some shared pleasure like a big vacation or the downpayment on a camper. Remember, though, that when you take the cash surrender value, you lose all the policy's insurance protection.

If you expect to live many more years but don't want to give up the policy's protection, you can buy a *reduced paid-up* policy with the cash surrender value of your ordinary policy. Say your $10,000 ordinary life policy will yield over $5,000 cash surrender value. That amount will buy about $7,500 of paid-up insurance. The benefit will be smaller, but you'll never have to pay premiums again. Assuming your health is good, you could make up for the lost coverage in just a few premium-free years.

If your health is *not* good, the *extended term* option may be for you. You can convert your ordinary life policy into a fixed term policy for the same face value and never pay another premium. If you have a $10,000 ordinary policy, you can trade it for a $10,000 extended term policy. The term is negotiable depending upon the amount of cash value built up in the insurance when you convert. If the policyholder dies within the term, the beneficiary gets the full amount; if he or she dies *after* the term expires, the beneficiary gets nothing.

LIMITED PAYMENT LIFE POLICIES

Like an ordinary life policy, this kind of protection "matures" when you reach 100 years of age. Only then is the whole face value equal to the cash surrender value. The difference between the two policies is that a limited payment policy arranges premium payments so that the policy is paid up after a given length of time. A 20-payment life policy is fully paid up after 20 payments, but the premiums are correspondingly large. Another common form of limited payment insurance is life paid up at 65. This policy prevents you from paying premiums after you retire, but it is much more expensive than ordinary life insurance.

ENDOWMENT POLICIES

Premiums are quite high for endowment policies. Not only are they limited payment plans, but they also mature as of the date of the last payment. In other words, when the policy is paid up, its full face value becomes payable to the policyholder. If you have a $10,000 endowment policy that is paid up at age 65, you will be able to draw the full $10,000 at that time, either in a lump sum or by reinvesting it in a monthly annuity for life.

RETIREMENT INCOME POLICIES

These are the only policies whose premiums are higher than those of endowment policies. The reason is that the policyholder contracts for a lifelong annuity but may take the projected amount of the annuity as a lump sum. Thus, though the policy may have a face value of only $10,000, if the policyholder elects a lump sum payment, he or she will get as much as

$16,000. This is because the monthly sum, multiplied by average life expectancies at 65, may yield a figure much *higher* than the policy's face value.

EMERGENCY SAVINGS FUND

This is the kind of thing we'd all rather not have to think about, but if we are going to be even reasonably cautious about the future, we must. Financial experts have their own formulas for what is needed. These range from an emergency fund equal to three or four times whatever retirement income you need on a monthly basis to two and a half times what you need on a yearly basis. For most of us, any such formula is obviously too arbitrary. There is no single answer; we all have different circumstances.

You must think in terms of emergencies, though. Once you have done so, look at your investments in terms of liquidity, that is in terms of how readily you can convert your investment monies to cash. A bank savings account has liquidity value, and if you don't already have such an account, you might want to consider opening one for an emergency fund. However, because of low interest rates, make sure that you keep in the account only as much as you think you'd need in an emergency. Unless Congress lets bank deposit interest rates go much higher than is currently permitted, it simply does not make sense to keep any more money in a bank account than you absolutely feel you may need. Having decided what that sum is, then make very sure to place it in an insured savings institution.

U.S. SAVINGS BONDS

The federal government doesn't raise enough

money from taxes and commercial treasury offerings, so it raises more, directly from the people, by selling U.S. savings bonds. Patriotic though such an investment is, it may not be the wisest place to put your funds. Under a new law effective November 1, 1980, savings bond interest will rise to a maximum of eight percent. But if you cash the bond within five years of the date of purchase, you'll suffer an interest penalty. If you had $500 to invest in November 1980, you could put it in a 30-month savings and loan account at 12 percent interest. A 2½-year bank savings account offers 11.75 percent interest. Clearly, the special savings accounts available from banks and savings institutions offer more attractive rates of return and tie up your money for a shorter time.

The new law is a provision that could make savings bonds attractive in the future, but it's too early to tell what effect it will actually have. Under the new law the Secretary of the Treasury can raise savings bond rates a maximum of one percent every six months, with the approval of the President. It'll no longer take an act of Congress to change the rates. But whether the Secretary will exercise his right to raise rates and whether or not he'll also have the right to lower them again is as yet unclear.

The government began to offer two new series of bonds, the EE and HH, in June 1980. These have a one percent higher interest rate than their predecessors, the E and H series. The EE bonds are offered in denominations from $50 to $10,000 and pay 7.5 percent with an additional .5 percent bonus at maturity; HH bonds come in $500, $1,000, $5,000 and $10,000 denominations only and yield 7.5 percent interest with no bonus. The bonds also differ in the way their interest is paid: the EE bonds, known as *accrual bonds,* pay interest in a lump sum when they're cashed; the HH bonds, known as *current income* bonds, yield interest monthly.

The government is doing what it can to keep savings bonds attractive. If you bought E bonds prior to the November rate change, you'll get the one percent increase anyway, computed from the date it went into effect.

To try to make you keep your money in savings bonds, the Treasury is offering a special tax deferral deal for those who convert their mature E and EE bonds into HH bonds. You'll be able to roll both principal and interest from the E or EE right into a new HH without having to pay tax on the accrued interest. You'll pay it only when the HH matures. This option has the added advantage of offering you the immediate monthly income of the HH bonds. Unless you really need that added monthly income, however, you're probably best to pay the tax on your savings bond interest and put both the principal and your net interest into a higher-yield savings account.

INVESTING IN SECURITIES

Retirement age is no time to find yourself locked into long-term low-yield investments. You should begin looking for opportunities that combine high yield with maximum liquidity. When you stop working, you'll be dependent on income from your investments to supplement your pension and/or social security checks, so it's good to plan early to get out of, for example, a stock that's yielding only two percent in dividends and into an investment that will give you more income. If this generates more money than you need, you can dispose of the excess by giving it in gifts to your heirs. The more you can give them before you die, the less death tax will be taken from your estate.

Just how you decide to combine high yield with maximum liquidity in your investment program depends on your time and resources. It's easiest and safest to simply put funds in high-yield savings accounts at your bank or savings institution (see the section on "Time Deposits"). Even if you're forced to withdraw your money early from a high-yield savings account, you'll still get both principal and a portion of the interest you contracted for. Other investments are either more complex, more risky, or both, but if you've got the time and money to spare, you could get higher yields.

The investments discussed in the following sections are listed roughly in order of increasing risk. (See *Sources for Further Information* to find out more about any of the investment topics discussed.)

U.S. TREASURY BILLS, NOTES AND BONDS

U.S. treasury bills, notes and bonds are just as secure as U.S. savings bonds, but they can yield a much higher interest and have the advantage of being exempt from state and local taxes.

Treasury bills have maturities of three months to one year, treasury notes range from two to 10 years and treasury bonds have 10- to 30-year maturities. Treasury bills have paid very high rates during 1979 and 1980, twice passing the 14 percent mark. In general, bills pay a higher rate than either notes or bonds, but they also have a higher minimum investment. While the minimum for the longer-term securities varies from $1,000 to $5,000, the minimum for bills is $10,000. Treasury bills have the added advantage of state and local tax exemption, which may not mean much if you live in rural Oregon, but if you live in a city such as New York where the combined state and local tax bite is sizable, the break can mean a substantial saving.

There are two ways to buy a treasury bill (commonly referred to as a T-bill). One is to do it yourself. This has the advantage of eliminating all charges for the transaction, but it takes some effort. First, you must find out when your local Federal Reserve bank plans to auction T-bills. Then you must appear in person with a certified check, or send one by registered letter, which must arrive before the date of the auction. Next, you should put into your safe deposit box the statement the Federal Reserve gives you and keep it there until the bill comes due. Everytime you reinvest in a T-bill, you have to repeat the process.

The other way is to buy your T-bill through your bank or broker, whose charges tend to range from $25 to $50 per bill on orders under $100,000 (there is generally no fee for an order over that amount). The charge may be worth it not only for the convenience, but also because the Federal Reserve will not buy back your T-bill should you need cash before it comes due. On the other hand, your broker or bank will maintain a market in these bills. You may take a loss if prevailing interest rates are higher when you need to liquidate, but at least you do have liquidity.

As long as interest rates remain high, treasury obligations will remain a popular form of investment. For retirement-age people, however, the longer-term treasury notes and bonds have some drawbacks. Though notes and bonds pay rates almost as high as the shorter-term bills and distribute their interest in semi-annual checks, they cannot be cashed before maturity. You may be able to predict accurately your financial needs six months into the future, but two to 30 years is quite another matter. Say, for example, you must raise cash quickly on a five-year treasury note that you've held for only three years. You'll have to sell it though a stock broker on the open market, where it could fetch little more or even less than you paid for it.

There are other kinds of securities issued by federal agencies and backed by the government, but these are mainly for sophisticated investors. They may pay rates slightly higher than treasury obligations but are less easily negotiable if you need to cash them before maturity. Ask your broker about them.

MORTGAGE CERTIFICATES

One new kind of government-backed security that may be of particular interest to retired people is the GNMA Pass-Through, or Ginnie Mae Pass-Through. It has a high minimum investment—$25,000—but since it is tied to mortgage rates, it offers a high rate of return. Sold through your broker, a GNMA Pass-Through represents participation in a pool of government-insured mortgages. Even if the borrowers default on the mortgage, the government will pay the full principal and interest due. The novelty in this kind of security is that it pays back both principal and interest in a monthly check. It therefore gives you very high cash flow—more monthly money in your pocket—though you should remember that once you receive your last check, your participation is at an end and there is no remaining principal to recover. The mortgages on which these pass-throughs are based are 30-year mortgages, but since they are often prepaid, the average length of investment is from 10 to 12 years. You can sell your participation on the open market, though full return of principal is guaranteed only if you hold the security to maturity. A GNMA Pass-Through offers dependable monthly income and, unlike an annuity, allows you the option of selling or holding until maturity.

MONEY MARKET FUNDS

Many investors are unable to put their money in treasury bills because they can't afford the $10,000 minimum. An interesting alternative that is growing

increasingly popular is *money market funds,* which
offer comparable interest rates with minimum investments as low as $1,000. While they are not insured by
the government, these funds buy treasury bills, notes
and bonds, as well as the debt securities offered by
big corporations and banks. They buy only top-rated
securities, so the chance of default on them is very
small. (Investors who feel nervous about a fund that
diversifies into corporate debt may be interested in
the money market fund sponsored by the American
Association of Retired Persons [AARP]. It invests only
in government securities. It too is uninsured, but the
government securities in which it invests have the full
backing of the government. The interest paid may be a
little lower than that of other money market funds, but
this could be a small price to pay for peace of mind, on
which it is hard to put a price tag. For more information on this, write the AARP at 1909 K St., N.W.,
Washington, D.C. 20049.) The particular portfolio a
fund chooses will affect the return you get. As long as
interest rates remain higher than the rates offered for
passbook savings accounts, money market funds are a
good place to put your money.

These funds have the added advantage of making
your money available whenever you choose. If you
need all or part of your investment for an emergency
expense, say, you can withdraw it without interest
penalty. Many funds have a check-writing privilege,
which will let you write checks on your account as
long as they're for $500 or more.

The reason that only money market funds are able
to offer the flexibility they do is that they represent a
large pool of investors. Money market funds are a kind
of mutual fund (see next section), but unlike many of
the mutual funds that buy stocks or bonds, money
market funds usually don't charge sales commissions.
(Funds that don't charge commissions are called *no-
load* funds; those that do are called *load funds.*) Thus,

the fee for keeping your account will usually be quite
low, but shop around because fees and rate of return
on investment vary from company to company. Also,
be prepared to move your money back into bank accounts if the rates offered by money market funds
drop below the pass-book level. You can track your
fund's performance in the *Wall Street Journal.* The
performance of the leading funds is compared
monthly in the "Fund Watch" column of *Money* magazine.

MUTUAL FUNDS

Companies that represent a large number of investors who have pooled their capital are called *mutual
funds.* These companies invest in stocks, bonds, options, gold and other opportunities. Minimum investment is usually no more than $1,000 and you can with-
draw your money without penalty whenever you like.
They're always more risky than bank accounts or investments tied to the money market, but depending
on the individual fund's objective, they may offer the
chance of a better return for only slightly greater risk.
Each mutual fund specifies in its prospectus just what
its investment objectives are. Some funds characterize
themselves as "growth" funds, which means that they
may buy undervalued stocks and wait for their value
to appreciate over the long term. If you're an older
person of limited means, the more agressive of these
may be too risky for you; on the other hand, the more
conservative ones may provide too slow a capital appreciation to be of maximum value to you. "Income"
funds may be more attractive to the older investor because they try to maximize dividend and interest income while protecting the client's principal. Nevertheless, every mutual fund has an advantage over
direct, individual investment in stocks or bonds (or

any other investment medium) because it pools the capital of many investors and can thus afford a diversified portfolio. This means that if one of the stocks the fund buys turns out to be a turkey, for example, the net effect of the loss will tend to be canceled by the rise in value of other stocks in the fund's portfolio.

When you join a mutual fund, you abdicate the choice of specific investments to the fund's managers, who are experienced professionals in their fields. The important decision you make is which fund to put your money in. To make this kind of investment work for you, you'll need to keep a close watch on financial markets. For instance, you will probably decide against putting your dollars into a stock fund if the stock market as a whole is declining. You'll also want to compare the specific features of various funds by looking at the prospectus of each. Some funds are *load funds*, which means that they add a sales charge of about 8.5 percent to the price of buying a share in the fund; others are *no-load funds*, which have no sales charge and only a small annual fee for managing your money. Some funds are really a "family" of different funds, offering everything from money market to stock to bond funds. Such companies may make it very easy for you to switch your money from one type of fund into another, allowing you to take advantage of changes in the investing climate.

Two services offered by some funds are of particular interest to older people. If you're eligible to start an IRA or Keogh account (see the "Individual Pension Plans" section), you can often do so by investing in a mutual fund. This option may be of even more interest to you if you choose a mutual fund group that allows easy transfer between its different member funds. The Internal Revenue Service (IRS) puts a limit on the frequency with which you can move your IRA account from one investment into another, but this limit doesn't apply to money shifted within a single mutual fund group. You could, therefore, go from the money market to the bond market to the stock market, as quickly and as often as you like, without violating the rules for retirement accounts.

Another service offered by some mutual funds lets the investor withdraw a fixed monthly amount, regardless of what rate the fund is returning. The monthly payments will usually consist of both principal and interest, but just how much of your principal is being eaten up will depend on how well the fund is doing. As long as your fund is paying a better rate of return than passbook savings accounts, you'll be maintaining just as high a cash flow but with better investment yield.

Load funds are sold by brokers; no-load funds are bought directly from mutual funds. You can check the progress of your fund daily in the *Wall Street Journal*. A monthly survey of leading funds appears in *Money* magazine, and *Forbes* does an annual review of the performance of all leading funds.

STOCKS AND BONDS

When you invest in stocks and bonds as an individual, you take greater risks. If you were smart enough to guess that the stock of Genetech—a company specializing in products such as synthetic insulin, made by genetic engineering—would shoot up when it was first traded, you could have made a lot of money. Those who bought the stock when it was first offered paid $35 per share. On October 13, 1980, the first day the stock was publically traded, it shot up as high as $89 per share before closing at around $79. If you had bought at the offering and sold immediately, you could have made a fortune. What if you held on to your stock? As of mid-November it was trading at only around $47, still a profit but not nearly as spectacular as it might have been. But the market can go just as quickly in the other direction. In October 1980, for instance, the stock of Dome Petroleum, a solid company in a strong industry, fell 20 points in a few days on reports of Canada's plans to nationalize part of its oil industry. High-rated bonds from reputable companies and municipalities shouldn't vary so widely, but even so apparently secure an investment as New York City bonds were jeopardized in 1975 when the city nearly defaulted.

If you intend to invest in stocks and bonds, you need three things: considerable available capital, the ability to leave that capital invested for a long enough period of time to show results and good advice. If you can answer the first two questions "yes," next find a good stockbroker. This doesn't mean simply showing up at the local office of a brokerage firm and asking for one. You may well get a good broker that way, but you'll certainly get a less experienced one. Most brokerage houses keep brokers who haven't yet built up a full roster of clients on an "on-call" list to pick up the customers who come in off the street. You'll be sure to get an experienced broker if you look for one who is recommended to you by someone who has used him or her. Family friends or your accountant may be able to make a recommendation. If you do choose to take the "on-call" broker at the local office, ask him or her for references from a few satisfied customers. The broker should be happy to comply. But remember: your broker will advise you, but the choices—and the responsibility for them—are your own.

REAL ESTATE

There are advantages to investing in real estate. All expenses you incur are tax deductible, and if you buy improved property, for investment purposes, you can take a deduction for annual depreciation in the building's usefulness. But the expense of investing in real estate is high, as is the risk. If you buy an investment property, you'll need the services of, at least, a lawyer, a real estate broker, a surveyor or engineer and an accountant. In general, you should only consider real estate investments in an area where housing values are rising rapidly and steadily. Above all, avoid buying sight unseen any land offered by hucksters over the telephone or at testimonial dinners. These two sales techniques are the favorites of shady operators.

While the ability of the individual to diversify properties and to manage sizable holdings is limited, there are opportunities to pool funds with other investors, thereby permitting purchase of more and larger properties than would ordinarily be possible on an individual basis, as well as leaving the management details to experts. Participation in such arrangements generally requires a minimum investment of around $5,000. One way to obtain information on such funds is via the tax shelter department of multiservice investment firms.

ANNUITIES

Most annuities are sold by insurance companies. The advantage to an annuity is that it pays a monthly income for life, even if the amount paid out eventually exceeds the amount you put in. The disadvantage is that it pays a fixed income: in a period of high inflation, the money you put into an annuity loses purchasing power rapidly. Assume, for example, that in 1980 you contract for an annuity to begin paying you $200 a month in 1990. If inflation runs at 10 percent each year, your $200 income in 1990 will only buy what $100 would have bought in 1980. Worse, you'll continue to receive the same fixed sum for the rest of your life, as it continues to decline in value! For this reason many experts are cautious about recommending annuities. Still, if a guaranteed lifetime income is important to you—say, you're in excellent health but have limited independent means—you might consider an annuity worthwhile and a good supplement to an IRA or Keogh account.

There are basically three kinds of annuities: deferred annuities, immediate-pay annuities and variable annuities. In general, a *deferred annuity* presents the greatest inflation problem. You buy the annuity—whether with a single lump sum premium or a number of monthly premiums—some years before you want to start getting your checks. The longer the gap between the date you pay and the date you start to receive checks, the worse the effect of inflation will be. The best kind of deferred annuity is the single-payment variety. Though sales and other charges may amount to four percent of your investment, interest yield is often comparatively high. These interest earnings will be tax-deferred until you begin to draw on the annuity. The deferral may in some cases offset your inflation loss. Deferred annuities bought with multiple payments usually offer lower interest earnings.

Whereas a deferred annuity is generally more suitable for younger people, an *immediate-pay annuity* is basically designed for those of retirement age. They work this way: you give the insurance company a lump sum, and the company in turn guarantees you a set monthly income for life. A deferred annuity can be converted into an immediate-pay annuity on retirement.

The *variable annuity* represents an effort to come to terms with inflation losses on fixed annuities. It pays a varying check, depending on the fluctuations of the stock market. If the market beats inflation, you do fine: if it doesn't, you don't.

It's not strictly true that if you buy an annuity and

die young, the insurance company will automatically pocket your money. Although the *individual life annuity* does indeed behave this way, options are available that guarantee some benefits to your survivors. Of course, the options cost more.

If you do decide to buy an annuity, shop around. Premium rates vary widely, as do sales and other charges.

TIME DEPOSITS

For many years banks and savings institutions have offered a variety of time-deposit savings accounts, requiring small minimums and length of deposit from 90 days to 10 years. The rates they offer are fixed by law. Traditionally there has been a .25 percent differential on the rates savings and loan associations could offer as opposed to rates banks could offer—savings and loan rates being higher. Under a new law signed by President Carter in March 1980, the differential will be phased out by 1986.

This change has been far overshadowed, however, by the market-rate time deposits first made available in June 1978. *Certificates of deposit* (CDs), based on the yield of treasury bills, generally have higher minimums than ordinary savings accounts, but as long as money market interest rates remain high, they also pay greater rates. As of November 1980 the highest interest available on an ordinary time-deposit account was 7.5 percent (for a six- to 10-year deposit). At the same time, CDs were offering interest rates between 11.75 percent and 14.166 percent. The rates offered change every one or two weeks, depending on the kind of treasury obligation they're based on, and once you make your deposit, you are guaranteed the rate prevailing on that day. This guarantee helps you if interest rates drop, but it can hurt you if they rise. You can't withdraw your funds early from a six-month or

30-month CD without suffering a substantial interest penalty.

The six-month CD offers the highest interest rate available, but it also has the highest minimum: $10,000. Banks and savings institutions pay the same rate on these CDs. In an effort to attract investors, some banks and savings and loan associations offer special deals. They will allow you to deposit a lower minimum, usually $5,000, then "lend" you the additional $5,000 at one percent interest. This device allows you to meet the $10,000 minimum requirement to make a six-month CD. You thus get an interest on your $5,000 only one percent less than that of the six-month CDs, for which you must deposit the whole $10,000.

A few banks offer check-writing privileges on six-month CD accounts, though strictly speaking, these again amount to money "loaned" you by the bank at one percent interest. They give you the money, deduct one percent of the interest rate, and pay you interest only on the total amount remaining.

Two and a half year (30-month) CDs have a much lower minimum, usually $250, but they tie up your money for much longer and offer interest rates generally a couple of points below those of six-month CDs. The 2½-year CDs offer an attractive interest rate, but you must be able to do without your money for that long a period. On these accounts, savings and loan associations can still pay .25 percent more than banks.

COLLECTING

Most everyone has heard of the money to be made in collectibles. I was told years ago by an extremely wealthy man that he had advised his chauffeur at the time the employee's first born came into the world to buy a full sheet of every issue of U.S. stamps. If he had done so, the man told me, in the years from the child's birth to his entry into college, the stamps would have appreciated in value enough to have paid the boy's entire tuition! Of course, for every story of this kind, there's an opposing tale: baseball card enthusiasts who paid $3,300 for a 1952 Mickey Mantle baseball card in 1979 saw its value drop $1,600 by 1980.

To collect for investment purposes alone is advisable only in the stamp, coin and arts/antiques markets. Even then you should know the field very well before you speculate. Values in these fields have steadily appreciated, in general, but individual items may rise or fall. Also, sales commissions are often high. You can find out the retail value of any American coin by consulting *A Guide Book of United States Coins*. Stamp values are listed in *Scott's Standard Postage Stamp Catalogue*. Both are available at bookstores and hobby shops or from your local library. To find the value of other antiques or collectibles, you'll probably need to get an appraisal. The *Time-Life Encyclopedia of Collectibles*, a sixteen-volume series probably available at your library, has brief articles on many kinds of collecting. Each article contains an addenda, listing relevant books, museums and collectors' organizations.

The more ephemeral collectibles—things like bubblegum cards, beer cans, political buttons and radio premiums—are seldom good investments, though they can be a pleasure to collect. Buying and selling takes place within a close-knit collector's community. The people who make money on such collections are those who have a long-standing love of this field. If you have a passion for, say, old barbed wire, pursue it by all means. Even if you don't make a profit in cash, you'll have a collection you're proud of.

YOUR HOME

If we assume that housing values remain at or close

to recent values with inflation added, then there's money in them thar bricks! First, there is a one-time exemption from capital gains of up to $100,000 if you are over 55. If your children are grown and if you're rattling around in your house, you might want to sell, perhaps taking a portion of the money you receive to buy a home more suited to your current needs or a condominium or cooperative (see Chapter Three for a discussion on condominiums and cooperatives). With the remaining money you can make a conservative investment to add to your income for living.

You might also acquire more income by selling your home directly, taking the mortgage yourself and, for the years remaining to you, becoming a renter at a specified amount. Another alternative, depending on the zoning laws, would be to retain a part of your home and rent out the remainder. With the right tenants this arrangement can be very comforting as well as profitable for aging people. (See Chapter Three for further discussion and other ideas about what you can do with your home.)

SOURCES FOR FURTHER INFORMATION

Pensions

If you have questions about your pension plan, contact the following organization:
Pension Rights Center
1346 Connecticut Ave., N.W.
Washington, D.C. 20036
(202) 296-3778

A monthly newsletter offering useful information about IRAs and Keogh plans is available for $18 per year from:
NROCA Newsletter

P.O. Box 12066
Dept. Q
Dallas, Tex. 75225

The following book will answer most of your questions about IRAs:
Unthank, L. L., and Behrendt, Harry M. *What You Should Know About Individual Retirement Accounts* Homewood, Ill.: Dow Jones-Irwin, 1978.

Social Security

A forthright book by a former commissioner of the Social Security Administration that will tell you everything you want to know about social security is:
Ball, Robert M. *Social Security, Today and Tomorrow*. New York: Columbia University Press, 1978.

For a helpful book that explains how you can roughly estimate your social security retirement benefits, contact your local social security office and ask for:
Estimating Your Social Security Retirement Check.

For more information on how your earning might affect social security payments, contact your local social security office and ask for the booklet:
You Can Work and Still Get Social Security Checks.

Life Insurance

Consumers Union recently published a useful comparative guide to insurance policies, premiums and benefits entitled *The Consumers Union Report on Life Insurance: Planning and Buying the Protection You Need*. It is available for $5 plus 50¢ postage from:
Consumer Reports Books
Dept. R5-03

P.O. Box 350
Orangeburg, N.Y. 10962

A detailed, comparative guide to the rates charged by
different insurance companies for all kinds of policies
is A.M. Best Co. annual *Flitcraft Compend*. Find it at
your library or order it for $12 from:
A.M. Best Co.
Ambest Road
Oldwick, N.J. 08858

Another publication of the A.M. Best Co. is *Best's Life
Insurance Reports*. It compares the strength and relia-
bility of over 1,400 insurance companies. It's available
at most libraries.

Investing

A good general introduction to all kinds of investing
and financial planning is:
Quinn, Jane Bryant. *Everyone's Money Book*. New
    York: Delacorte Press, 1979.

U.S. TREASURY BILLS, NOTES AND BONDS

If you're interested in learning more about buying
U.S. Treasury bills, notes and bonds yourself, ask your
local commercial bank for the address of the Federal
Reserve bank nearest you and write requesting the
following publications:
*Information About Treasury Bills Sold at Original Is-
    sue.*
*Information About Treasury Notes and Bonds Sold at
    Original Issue.*

MORTGAGE CERTIFICATES

For more detailed information on Ginnie Mae Pass-Through mortgage certificates, write your local Merrill Lynch brokerage office for the following publication:
Merrill Lynch Explains Pass-Throughs.

MONEY MARKET FUNDS

For a list of 95 money market funds that gives addresses, toll-free telephone numbers and minimum investment requirements, write to:
Investment Company Institute
1775 K St., N.W.
Washington, D.C. 20006

MUTUAL FUNDS

For a list of no-load mutual fund members that specifies the kind of investment and objectives of each as well as the minimum investment that may be required, write to:
No-Load Mutual Fund Association
Valley Forge, Pa. 19481

For a listing that gives the same type of information for both load and no-load funds, write to:
Investment Company Institute
1775 K St., N.W.
Washington, D.C. 20006

STOCKS AND BONDS

Helpful publications on investing in stocks and bonds are available from the New York Stock Exchange.

Free orientation pamphlets include *How to Get Help When You Invest* and *Ten Questions to Ask Before You Buy Stocks.* Listings of nationwide brokerage firms and an investor's bibliography are also available free. *The Investors Information Kit,* offered for $2.50 postpaid, includes explanations of stocks and bonds and tells how to read financial statements. Order these publications from:

New York Stock Exchange
Publications
11 Wall Street
New York, N.Y. 10005

An excellent introduction to stock market investing is:
Rukeyser, Louis. *How to Make Money on Wall Street.* New York: Doubleday, 1974.

ANNUITIES

An annual publication of the A.M. Best Co., the *Flitcraft Compend,* has a section that compares the annuity payment rates of the major life insurance companies. Your library should have a copy, or order one from A.M. Best Co. (see p. 46 for address).

Canadian Sources

Canada, Department of Health and Welfare. *Your Old Age Pension: A Program of the Government of Canada.*
This pamphlet contains general information on the Old Age Security pension. It should be read before filling out an application. If more detail is needed, contact one of the Income Security Programs offices listed at the end of the pamphlet. It and any other

pamphlet distributed by the Department of Health and Welfare are available by writing to:
Dept. of Health and Welfare
Information Directorate
Brooke Claxon Building
Turney's Pasture
Ottawa, Ontario K1A 0K9

Canada, Department of Health and Welfare. *Old Age Security, Guaranteed Income Supplement, Spouse's Allowance.*
This publication contains tables of rates in effect from October to December 1980.

Canada, Department of Health and Welfare. *Federal Services:Senior Citizens.* Catalogue no. IC24-3/1-1975.
Brief descriptions of social programs for the elderly are provided.

Canada, Department of Health and Welfare. *Your Canada Pension Plan.*
This publication contains general information on the Canada pension plan that began in 1966. It should be read before filling out an application.

Death Benefits: Canada Pension Plan
Disability Benefits: Canada Pension Plan
Survivors' Benefits: Canada Pension Plan
Retirement Pension: Canada Pension Plan
Youths 18–25 Years of Age: Canada Pension Plan
This series of pamphlets distributed by the Department of Health and Welfare describes basic benefits, qualifications etc.

If you have problems in obtaining your pension, write to:
Pension Review Board
473 Albert St.
Ottawa, Ontario K1R 5B4

For military pension information,contact:
Dept. of Veterans' Affairs
VA Building
Lyon and Wellington St.
Ottawa, Ontario K1A 0P4

For information on life insurance benefits,contact:
Dept. of Insurance
140 O'Connor St.
Ottawa, Ontario K1A 0H2
or
Bank of Canada
Special Services Division
Dept. of Insurance

WORKING

American attitudes toward work are changing. That is the conclusion we have to draw from a poll done by Louis Harris for the House Select Committee on Aging in 1978. Quite plainly, most people want to continue working. This was not always so, but the poll makes it equally clear that a majority of those who did retire wouldn't have done so if, to paraphase an old saw, they had known then what they know now.

We are not talking about a renewal of the work ethic here because it is not always the American workers' desire to continue working that motivates them to do so. For example, the eagerness of those workers who have a generous, indexed pension to retire as quickly as possible attests to that. No, rather it is fear of poverty that motivates them. People see pensions being eroded and their standards of living tumbling. Large numbers of retired people are seeking jobs, usually at a lower level than those they formerly held. Even larger numbers are turning to part-time work, which is becoming more attractive now that an older person can earn up to $5,000 yearly without reducing his or her social security payments.

Opportunities for part-time work are good; those for full-time work are not so good. But there are ways of dealing with this. People facing retirement are learning new skills, some in the many community colleges that have been springing up across the country, some in programs created under the 1978 Comprehensive Employment and Training Act (CETA) and some in subsidized schools that train people of all ages in useful skills. There are lots of things most younger Americans simply do not want to do, such as small machine repairs; in many neighborhoods you can wait for months to get an appliance repaired. Now many older people are training themselves in these skills and becoming self-employed.

One important step forward is the law that forbids an employer, under most conditions, to discharge an employee until the age of 70. The law's existence is important, but it's too soon to say whether or not it has had any measurable effect on the nation's economy.

The following sections discuss all these topics in greater detail.

WORK ATTITUDES

Polls are a basic tool in American life, whether one is selling a politician or a new soap. It's fashionable to scorn this country's obsession with what people think, desire and do, but that attitude would quickly change after a short working stay in a third world country where even the most basic statistics are not to be had. What people feel is always of importance but especially when it comes to work, which, after sleep, takes up the greatest portion of their time. The 1978 poll (which I mentioned earlier), paid for by the pension advisory firm of Johnson and Higgins and conducted for the House Select Committee on Aging by Louis Harris is an extremely important study, not only to a congressional committee with legislation in mind but also to private businesses, which have a rapidly increasing number of older employees.

Among the more important findings of this poll are strong indications that the resentment said to be felt by young workers against older ones may not really exist, at least not in the work place. The majority of current workers say they don't believe that older workers should be forced to retire and make way for the young. It's instructive to note, however, that among employers 46 percent think that older workers should be forced to stand aside. Could it be that the so-called resentment of the younger workers is actually an expression of what some employers wish were true?

There are stories without number about older workers being forced out, usually under some pretext that carefully avoids mention of that filthy word "age." Despite denials by employers, current and retired workers are overwhelmingly convinced that there is discrimination against older workers. Eighty percent of today's workers think so, while only 15 percent do not agree. The retirees themselves are a bit more tolerant: 75 percent feel that discrimination in the work place is a reality, while 20 percent disagree. Only a little more than half of employers agree there is discrimination, however, and we think it should be a matter of substantial concern to American business and industry that their workers suspect their intentions toward older workers so vehemently.

To complete this brief and partial survey, there is now a slight majority, 51 percent, of current workers who would like to stay on after retirement age. And of those who have retired, for whatever reason, 53 percent now think it was a mistake and would have stayed on had they known what they were facing. But as that figure on employer attitudes indicates, it is not easy for older workers to stay on. They are not wanted. Employees are convinced that there is discrimination. And for those who do come back, it may be very difficult to get the same kind of work they once had or to match their old salaries.

Here I'm obviously not talking about self-employed professional people, who are for the most part masters of their fate, if not captains of their souls. But it is ridiculous for anyone to contend that age discrimination does not exist for those who work for others. It exists in private industry; it exists in government programs. In a paper written for the Public Affairs Committee, Irving Dickman offers figures to show that discrimination against the older worker actually begins at 45, not 65. He points out that in 1969, there were less than 600,000 people over 45 among the unemployed. In 1975 the figure was over 1.5 million. The population has gone up and unemployment has gone up, but not by that much. If further proof is needed, another study in the late 1970s showed that 70 percent of the workers who had exhausted their unemployment insurance were over 45, and 45 percent of these were over 55.

Can agism be fought? Yes. But only if the victims have the will and the energy to go to court over it.

WORK AND THE LAW

The Age Discrimination in Employment Act of 1967 prohibits discrimination against would-be workers because of their age. Period. An amendment to that law, passed on January 1, 1979, says that an employer cannot forcibly retire people before age 70. This amendment, however, does not apply to employees of very small firms; employees in a truly supervisory capacity whose benefits, exclusive of social security, are over $26,000 a year; and tenured college professors. Even there there is discrimination. Federal employees have what we all should have: that is, whatever their age, they cannot be fired unless it is demonstrated that they can no longer do the job.

So the law is there. But as I have indicated earlier, employer enthusiasm for it is, overall, not great. This is ironic because those employers who have approached the subject with an open mind have discovered that older employees are more conscientious about their work, are absent from work less frequently and are a less disturbing element in the work force because they are no longer restless about lack of advancement and are generally happier in what they are doing.

What can you do about the discrimination that, regardless of the law, is there? You can sue. (See *Sources for Further Information.*) Companies try to conceal attempts to get rid of older workers by structuring their organization charts to eliminate jobs and, of course, the people holding them. There have been large suits—in one, for example, Standard Oil of California had to pay $2 million to 160 older workers they had rid themselves of in this way. Other cases even involve individuals who successfully fought discrimination.

PART- OR FULL-TIME WORK

The Harris poll (referred to before) indicated that most older workers prefer part-time work. The reasons for their choices are not clear, but it would seem that while some fear the psychological effects of idleness,

others—particularly in the lower income brackets—
think they must work to make ends meet. Of course,
there are exceptions (see box on p.57).

The Harris poll indicates that those who wish to
work full time are usually people who have been in a
profession or are self-employed. For others, part-time
work is usually more desirable. Remember that with
the upward change in how much you can earn and still
remain in full possession of your social security rights
(see the section titled "Can You Work and Collect at
the Same Time?" in this chapter), such work becomes
more and more attractive.

WHAT CAN YOU DO?

If you have left your full-time job, or if you really
want to do something different, you might take a tip
from the businessman turned groundskeeper (see box
on p.57). Are you good at something? Do you have a
hobby? Have you noticed, for instance, that if you return a small appliance like a lawn mower or snow
blower to the manufacturer for repairs, it can take
months before it comes back? Have you known people in your neighborhood who take care of their own
lawns only because the professionals are simply too
expensive for them? The same is true for gardening (I
live in the country and have a thumb as brown as the
earth itelf).

Many men and women are good at these tasks and
have the knack of repairing anything from a toaster to
a tractor. Look around your community and you'll
probably find that there are many jobs to be done. Are
you good at carpentry? If you can repair your own
chairs, you can repair chairs for other people, too.

Is there some kind of work you would like to do but
don't have the skills for? There are opportunities ga-
lore here. In some cities and towns the high schools

offer opportunities for you to work at something new. Where they don't, you should encourage them to do so; our schools (and too many of our teachers) are underutilized. Other organizations, public and private, give courses in a host of things—some free, some almost free. Have you thought of your local community college and the courses it offers? With the drop in younger student enrollment, colleges are increasingly anxious to fill empty seats. Many make special provisions for older students, and just about all of them will, at the very least, allow you to take courses that have not been filled up and to do so without charge. (For more detailed information on educational opportunities, see Chapter Two.)

At institutions throughout the country, there is a host of useful things you can still learn, from jewelry making to office work. If you have the initiative, you can get part-time work. It's really up to you. And speaking of office work, there is a permanent shortage of office workers, according to the head of Mature Temps, an organization that specializes in placing part-time help with businesses. Nor is it necessary to be able to type, take dictation or run some complex office machine. This gentlemen says that you can probably do more than you think. If you can balance a checkbook, you can do bookkeeping. If you can talk clearly and pleasantly, there are survey companies that may need someone like you. Mature Temps has offices in 11 cities throughout the country (see *Sources for Further Information*) and claims that in the world of office work there is no shortage of work, only of workers.

PRIME-OF-YOUR-LIFER

Harry Lapow

Harry Lapow was a package designer who gave up his own business to work for a large corporation. A mistake. He was forced out at age 64, and he was "mad as hell." He said to himself, "By God, I've got to do something about this. I've got to do something, not only for myself, but for other people like myself. We really don't want to quit. We don't want to retire. I've been down to Florida. I've seen what happens on the beaches there. All these people sitting around."

Mr. Lapow had a hobby. He had taken up photography while in his 40s, using a second-hand camera given to him by his wife. He didn't just play with that camera; he studied the craft and became expert at it. Now Harry Lapow is a professional photographer (we're skipping over a lot of Harry's work and heartache to come to this point). He has a book to his credit and can look back at the people who forced him out and say, "I really should be thankful to them because they pushed me into something that is marvelous. I have nobody to report to. I do my own thing, and fortunately for me, it seems that my work is appreciated. And that's good."

We are not all as talented and as energetic as Mr. Lapow, but many of us have talents we have never dreamed of using: a groundskeeper of a retirement community chuckles over the failure of its residents to invite him to their get-togethers. What amuses him is that in his previous job as vice-president of a Midwestern corporation he had more social prestige and today probably has more money than the people who leave him out of their social life. He is secure enough to be untroubled by this and is happy in working with plants and other growing things.

Throughout the country there are many employment agencies that specialize in work for the elderly (see *Sources for Further Information*). Opportunities are springing up in other areas, too. Government has some, among them the Green Thumb program, which has a limited number of jobs in rural areas and smaller communities (see Chapter Two for detailed information about this and other such government programs).

THE FUTURE

The greatest number of job openings for older people will be self-help jobs—healthier older people helping their less healthy peers. It has been predicted that there will be a need for some 300,000 such people in the next few years. In my opinion, to have older people helping other older people is the soundest way to get the job done. Anything else is derogatory and condescending.

An encouraging note for those who find themselves getting older in the latter part of the 1980s, and certainly in the 1990s, is that age discrimination will probably decline steadily. The country will have used up its stock of young workers, those born during the so-called baby boom that followed World War II, and if the jobs needed to be done are going to get done at all, older workers will be called upon to do them.

Sources for Further Information

Work and the Law

If you have questions regarding your legal work status or any general queries regarding age discrimination and the law, write to:
Age Discrimination Project
American Association of Retired Persons
1909 K St., N.W.
Washington, D.C. 20049

Part- and Full-Time Work

The following book lists employment agencies located throughout the country that specialize in work for the elderly:
Tenenbaum, Frances. *Over 55 is Not Illegal*. Boston: Houghton Mifflin, 1979.

Mature Temps, the employment agency that specializes in placing part-time office workers in businesses, has offices in Baltimore; Boston; Chicago; Dallas; Houston; Los Angeles; Philadelphia; San Francisco; New York City; White Plains, N.Y.; and Washington, D.C. They say that they'd be happy to answer any questions you may have. Check your telephone book for their number.

In the past two years a new association has been formed to help employment agencies specializing in placing seniors to improve their services and to assist those who wish to start up such an agency in their own

community. For further information write to:
Thomas Bradley
Association of Employment Services for the Elderly
National Council on the Aging
1828 L St.
Washington, D.C. 20036

With the increase in employment agencies that specialize in placing older people, the part-time and full-time job market is becoming more accessible. Most of these agencies are nonprofit and don't charge a fee. To find the nearest such agency in your area, call your local office on the aging. You'll find the phone number under the state government listings in your telephone book.

Canadian Sources

If you have problems with age discrimination on the job, contact:
Canadian Human Rights Commission
Ottawa/Hull
(613) 995-1151
or their regional office listed in your phone book

Civil Liberties Association
229 Yonge St. Suite 403
Toronto M9B 1N9

For information on employment, contact:
Dept. of Employment
Phase IV Place du Portage
Hull Quebec K1A 079

Canada, Department of Employment and Immigration. *Unemployment Insurance: UI and You: When You Reach 65.* Catalogue no. LU2-76/1980.
This publication explains the special one-time benefit you may receive upon reaching 65 if you are still working.

RETIREMENT

Is it good or bad to retire? Almost everyone is now familiar with Dr. Alex Comfort's witticism on the subject. He wrote, "Two weeks is about the ideal length of time to retire." The remark was made in an otherwise fine book, *A Good Age*, which is full of sound advice to elderly and near-elderly folk. However, based on my contacts with people who have retired, retirement isn't necessarily something to be hated.

TO RETIRE OR NOT TO RETIRE

When I first became directly involved with the problems and concerns of aging (in our New York program, which has the same title as this book), I had definite preconceived notions about retirement. Like Dr. Comfort, I thought it was simply bad. I thought that people would wither and blow away like dried-up autumn leaves once they stopped working. Any work. Many authorities still feel this way. Their reasoning goes like this: people have spent their entire adult lives, 40 years or more, with a definite task to do seven or more hours a day. Then someone comes along with an alluring smile and says, "You've done your share. Go and rest now. You deserve to have long pleasant days of leisure in the golden years of your life." But, those authorities ask, how is that possible? How are people whose habits have been formed over a lifetime simply going to throw them aside at 60 or 65 and suddenly enjoy the fruits of their life of work even if they can afford it, which is often not the case?

I agreed with the authorities who said this was not possible. This, you must understand, was based on my own reasoning—not on observation.

But let us reflect. Those authorities get pleasure from what they do. Leaving their work would proba-

bly be a terrible blow to them. Being told they must
stop doing what they enjoy so much would be the
same as telling them what we all fear to hear—"You
are no longer wanted. You are no longer needed. You
are useless!" How many egos can survive that kind of
condemnation from someone or something with the
power to make it stick? Very few, I think. And those
few only with a lot of support.

So what we arrive at, it seems, is that people who
very much like doing what they do dread retirement.
It may well be deadly for them. On the other hand,
people who have spent a lifetime working on a production line at a task they feel to be tedious and unre-
warding and people who have done hard manual labor
and who have long since passed the age when such
labor gave them a feeling of strength and well-being
may indeed welcome retirement. They often blossom
when they quit work. For example, you'll find few ex-
auto workers who are not happy to have a union contract that permits them to get out while still in their
fifties with a decent pension to provide the where-
withal to make retirement possible.

But even when I discovered that there were people
for whom retirement was a good thing, I still looked
around for rules, and there were people who agreed
with my grave determination that, at any rate, there
must be structure—tasks to do, or even pleasures to be
pursued. My first interviews with a number of people
who had reached retirement age and were not working provided me with comfortable evidence that I was
on the right track. Well, it wasn't quite that simple.
Actually, the pleasure part didn't enter into my first
theory on a structured retirement. People who retire, I
thought, should do something meaningful. Preconceived theories are not very difficult to substantiate—
you just go out and find the right kind of evidence. I
did. I interviewed men who had been in business and
who now worked as volunteers, some on an executive

basis and some more directly involved. One fine man told me about his work at a hospital, where he works with people who have very serious physical problems. He does it on a regularly scheduled basis. Good! That fitted into my retirement theory very well. But I kept coming across individuals who simply refused to fit into my retirement theory at all. One of these was a lady named Sylvia Alpert, whom you read about at the beginning of this chapter.

Okay then, a retirement activity doesn't have to be something that is helpful. But preconceptions do not die easy deaths. If it isn't helpful, then it certainly must be worthwhile, I decided. Really? No, not really! (See box on p. 64 .)

So you don't necessarily have to keep on working in order to be content. And you don't necessarily have to be doing something utilitarian. And clearly you can be quite pleased with your existence without studying the harp or dance or something on that order.

However, structure did still seem to be important. And with almost all my other theories on successful retirement in tatters, I thought I could cling to that very important concept. Structure, as illustrated in the retired school principal's daily activities. But this cherished concept of mine was also to be shattered (see box on p. 65).

So that was the end of my theories about retirement and what we must do. We are each of us individuals, and we each have different emotional needs. There are people to whom a useful, working career is so important that if they are denied it at age 65 or even older, they wither away and die. There are people who must be doing something whether they are paid for it or not, preferably for others or for the community. There are people who require a neat, structured existence at the very least if they are to be happy. And there are people who are happy doing nothing at all. There are some important facts about retirement and things to consider when facing it. But one of the most important questions—and one that I have neglected up to now—is, Can you afford to retire? Only you know what kind of person you are. Only you can say what your needs are—now, as well as later. The following sections will help you determine them.

PRIME-OF-YOUR-LIFER

Mr. T

A friend introduced me one day to her uncle, a retired teacher and school principal in a small South Carolina town, one of the very first black people to become principal of an integrated school. A tall, fine looking man, he still had the firm, confident stride of an athlete, and I simply could not believe that he was 78 years of age.

And what did he do with his time? To tell the truth, not very much—and that "to tell the truth" represents my reluctance to admit it, not his. Mr. T. told me that he gets up at about 7:00 each morning, makes his own breakfast (his wife is dead, and he lives alone in his house) and then does a bit of gardening. He likes to garden. After a couple of hours of that, he has a light lunch and goes down to the barbershop. If you're from a small town, you're probably nodding your head at that one. Barbershops are a great center for gabbing and gossiping, much as the late lamented general store and its stove used to be.

An hour or so of that and it's home, probably for a little more work around the house—houses are very good at taking up any stray moments you may have—and then a light dinner, a couple of hours of television and so to bed. Another successful day ended. Successful? Yes, successful!

PRIME-OF-YOUR-LIFER

In a restaurant where I was having dinner one night before going to teach a class, a prosperous-looking, rather elderly gentleman sitting at an adjoining table looked over at me several times and asked if I was the Joe Michaels of television. When I told him I was, he started telling me about his son, of whom he was very proud. He told me that he had held onto his own business for some years because of that son. He had been afraid the young man wouldn't be able to make it in business on his own in that big, cruel world out there, but he had been wrong. His son is "very successful. He's doing just fine," the gentleman told me.

And how about the gentleman himself? I wanted to know. What did he do? From what he had indicated, once his worries about his son's future were over, he had retired. "Yes, I'm retired," he told me placidly. So, what did he do to keep himself occupied? What—I couldn't resist—did he do to give his life structure?

"Nothing."

"Nothing?" I exclaimed.

"No, I watch your program to see the pretty lady who does it with you [he was talking about my cohost Ponchietta Pierce], and I watch you, too, of course [that last thrown in somewhat hastily, but appreciated nevertheless]."

But what, I wanted to know, did he do to keep occupied?

"Not much," the gentleman said comfortably. "I like to take my meals out and look at pretty women. I'm not too old for that. Sometimes I go to a show or see friends, but nothing much, nothing in particular."

Did he enjoy himself?

"Very much," he said with conviction.

And by the way, if he didn't mind my asking, how old was he?

"Seventy-five."

I paid my bill, and we shook hands. I went on my way to class thinking, 75! I would have believed him if he had said 60—and a comfortable, secure-looking 60 at that.

CAN YOU AFFORD TO RETIRE?

It is Wednesday afternoon, February 28, 1979. The members and staff of the U.S. House of Representatives Select Committee on Aging have gathered in Room 345 of the marble-clad old Cannon Building in Washington, D.C. to hear the first public presentation of what is probably the most important study of the attitudes of aging Americans yet compiled. The study is the work of pollster Louis Harris. It was commissioned by a pension advisory firm, Johnson and Higgins, and a very pragmatic study it is. The subject matter is retirement and pensions—how people feel about these things, what they anticipate, how they are getting along on what they have.

Some of the major points are brought up as the session goes along, but none is more important than a single sentence from the Committee's chairman, Claude Pepper, still forceful, vital and as concerned today at 78 as he was in a previous incarnation as Sen. Pepper 30 years ago. "Inflation," says Rep. Pepper, "is the number one public enemy of the elderly." He goes on, "It eats away at their fixed incomes, and to the extent that they are entitled to cost of living raises in pension plans such as social security, the increase trails the double-digit increases in the cost of health care, food, energy and housing."

As I'm writing this book in 1980, the inflation erosion of income (in the area of 14 percent for the nation at large) is more threatening than at the time Rep. Pepper made his remarks. In light of this single fact, and regardless of your desires, it is only practical in considering whether you can afford to retire to ask yourself these questions: where do I stand financially? How much do I spend? What will I need? And how much will I actually have?

WHERE DO YOU STAND FINANCIALLY?

To answer this question, you must take the trouble to sit down and do some calculating, and it can be a pretty painful experience finding out how little you have to show for the time you've worked. Still, if you are going to consider retirement before you are forced to do so, then you need a merciless assessment of your financial state of health. It should start with your current status. Where does the money come from?

Making a chart such as this one can be useful:

Present Financial Status

Salary or salaries or, in
place of above, _____

Professional income _____

Worth of home less
mortgage _____

Savings _____

Dividends from stocks
and/or bonds _____

Surrender value of
insurance _____

Other income _____

Total _____

Having added up what you have, put down what
you owe: mortgage still unpaid, unpaid portions of
loans, debts, unpaid taxes and so forth. No need to
draw up a chart here, our unpaid items are clear
enough to all of us.

On the positive side, there may be items not mentioned here, such as annuities, money you expect to
inherit, whatever. The important thing is to be totally
honest. If you do not know what your house is worth
now, ask a real estate dealer you know and trust or
possibly the bank that holds your mortgage. The important thing is to know.

HOW MUCH DO YOU SPEND?

What are your current expenses? For neat and
thrifty folk who have carefully kept to budgets all their

lives, this presents no problem. For most of us, though, budgets are reproachful reminders of past good intentions, reluctantly conceived and quickly dropped. Still, it's important to know. Completing a chart such as the following will help you to determine present expenses:

Present Expenses

Housing	_____
Food	_____
Clothing	_____
Entertainment	_____
Tuition	_____
Laundry	_____
Utilities	_____
Transportation	_____
Automobile	_____
Payments on debts	_____
Taxes	_____
Medical care	_____
Miscellaneous	_____
Total	_____

Again, some of these things may have no meaning for your family in which perhaps there were no children or the children are grown and the question of tuition does not arise. Or there may be payments not listed here—our family, for instance, pays for having a special kind of water purifier, required because of the soil where we live. The important thing is to get everything down.

WHAT WILL YOU NEED IN THE FUTURE?

This requires the most painstaking care of all. Some
of it you can do for yourself, but if you still need advice, it's available (see *Sources for Further Information*). Planning is also required. If you hope to retire
soon, then do several things first: is the car over the
hill? Get a new one or a really sound second-hand one
now, while your earnings are still on the high side.
The same thing is true for such things as refrigerators,
stoves, lawn mowers—I'm sure you get the idea. Anything you anticipate needing after retirement that will
be fairly costly should, if possible, be bought before
you retire and your income suffers the shrinkage
nearly every retired person faces. On the other hand,
now is the time to break once and for all that old
American custom of buying things "on time." One
thing you do not need for your retirement is a bunch of
interest-loaded debts.

The next step is to work out how much you're going
to need in retirement and compare that figure with
your present expenses. Most authorities claim that in
retirement you'll need substantially less than you now
make. The figures are vague, though. Calculations of
how much you would need to maintain your present
scale of living vary from two-thirds to 80 percent of
your current income. To my mind, whatever that figures comes out to is meaningless. You are the best
judge of what you will be comfortable living with. But
certain things are obvious. If, for example, you are currently working in some kind of office, your clothing
bills should be lower in retirement. Obviously, if you
are a factory worker, this will not be the case. If your
present work requires you to do a fair amount of non-
reimbursible spending to keep in touch with the right
people, that too can be reduced—so, entertainment
expenses will be reduced, although you'll still want to
see a movie or attend the theater. Perhaps you take a

train or drive your car to work now. You won't have to do that in the future. On the other hand, medical expenses, which we discuss in Chapter Five, will almost undoubtedly grow, and you should plan for this. If advice, or a lot more detail, seems desirable, there are a number of organizations that can help (see *Sources for Further Information*). Some have programs of their own. If you work for a large company, the chances are increasingly good that it will have an advisory program of its own for potential retirees. Ask about it.

There are a lot of questions, most of which you and your spouse must ask of one another. Questions like, Do we intend on staying in our present home? If not, do we want to move elsewhere, perhaps somewhere closer to the children, perhaps to someplace cheaper? Would it be wise to get rid of our house and rent? Or buy into a condominium or cooperative? How about retirement communities? Do they make sense for us? Having decided to retire, what kind of life do we want for ourselves? These are very important questions, and they're discussed in greater detail in Chapter Three.

HOW MUCH WILL YOU ACTUALLY HAVE?

First and foremost, there is Old Age, Survivor's and Disability Insurance (OASDI), better known under the blanket term of social security. At last accurate count (August 1980), it paid $10.5 billion dollars a month to more than 35.2 million people.

A breakdown of the average yearly income from social security for July 1980 looks like this:

Retired worker $3,753.00 (1980)
Retired couple $6,403.80 (1980)

These are averages, remember. Your income could be
as high as $653.80 a month, adding up to $8,061.60 a
year as an individual, or as low as $153.10 a month
amounting to $1,837.20 a year. Obviously, if you're go-
ing to make any plans, you need an idea of how much
you can expect (see the section entitled "Social Security," which appears earlier in this chapter, to find out
how you can estimate your benefits).

What else will you have? If you are one of the lucky
few (about seven million), you may be receiving a private pension. These average $2,204 per person. You
should have been getting regular reports on what you
are entitled to receive upon retirement at various
ages.

Then there are private savings. For most people
over 65, the home is the major part of such savings; 77
percent of all elderly couples and 37 percent of single
elderly people own their own homes. Other savings
don't amount to much for most people. The Social Security Administration figured in 1967 that 55 percent
of people over 65 had less than $1,000 in savings.

And you might also have some annuities, stocks,
bonds, convertible insurance and/or other assets such
as property, gold or collectibles.

As I point out in Chapter Five, you have a right to
Medicare and somewhat greater benefits if you continue to be a contributor under Part B. This covers less
than 50 percent of the medical care you may need, but
it is vastly more than what it used to be. I'll leave Medicaid (also discussed in Chapter Five) out of our calculations since it is available, for all practical purposes, only when all other assets are gone.

So, to summarize the income (both actual and potential) you will actually have:

Part 1

Social security   _____

Pensions   _____

Annuities   _____

Investments (stocks,   _____
  bonds, rental
  properties etc.)

Other income   _____

Part 2

Home or property   _____

Life insurance cash   _____
  value

Antiques, collectibles   _____

Precious metals   _____

Other assets   _____

Remember that the income from assets listed in Part Two is available only if you liquidate them. When you list your grandmother's silver tea set, keep in mind that you have to part with it in order to get the income. Also, of course, Part Two income can be counted only in the year you sell the asset.

When you figure your financial situation, take into account not only your assets, but also the special savings that you will be entitled to as a senior citizen. People over 65 are automatically entitled to *tax savings,* including an extra personal exemption on federal income tax and a 15 percent tax credit on most other income. Social security income, of course, is tax free. Some states also help seniors out on their income and property taxes. And if you're over 55 and sell your house, you get a special one-time tax exemption on the first $100,000 of capital gains. Low-income seniors are also eligible for special supplementary programs like the federally funded Medicaid and Supplemental Security Income (SSI) and locally funded "meals-on-wheels" programs. Older people are also eligible for reduced-price tickets at cultural events as well as special rates for public transportation and some shopping rebates.

SOURCES FOR FURTHER INFORMATION

Canadian Sources

Canada Senate. *Retirement Without Tears: Report of the Special Senate Committee on Retirement Age Policies.*
The effect of demographic trends, inflation etc. on retirement and retirement planning is assessed. The report is available at your local library, or write to:
Canadian Govt. Publishing Centre
270 Albert St.
Ottawa, Ontario K1A 0S9

Retirement: Policies, Pensions and Proposals.
Catalogue no. YC2-304/5-01-1.
Highlights of *Retirements Without Tears* are presented. This publication is available from the Canadian Government Publishing Centre (address listed above).

For information on Retirement Income Funds, check with any district office. For private plans, check with a trust or insurance company.

For information on Retirement Savings Plans, check with any district office. For private plans, check with a trust or insurance company.

DEALING WITH YOUR LEGAL NEEDS

Lawyers were once called "mouthpieces." For most of us, though, they are more like "pinch hitters." A lawyer goes to bat for you when you're afraid someone may throw you a curve. He makes sure your interests are protected in such complex legal processes as forming business partnerships, arranging contracts and closing real estate deals. Such a pinch hitter is particularly useful to older Americans when it comes to estate planning and money management.

ESTATE PLANNING

It's not as hard to decide who should get your worldly goods as it is to figure out how to give them. You can distribute property, directly or through your will, in a bewildering variety of ways, each with its own advantages and disadvantages.

WILLS

Every will goes through probate court to be "proven." This process takes time and money—up to a full year and 10 percent of your estate—but in almost all cases, it's best to grin and bear it. A will gives you maximum flexibility in distributing your assets and provides the most opportunities for reducing death taxes.

Dying without a will (intestate) means that your

property will be distributed according to state law. States that have adopted the Uniform Probate Code will give the surviving spouse the first $50,000, plus half of any amount above that, but other states may give her or him only one-third of the total estate! Your spouse could be left with insufficient funds for his or her remaining years. Dying intestate is even worse if you are single or a widow and have no children or living parents. State laws on distribution of property to siblings and cousins can be quite convoluted; relatives you barely know could end up inheriting a part of your estate. If you have no relatives and no will, the state will get your money.

Unless your will is complicated, a lawyer seldom charges more than $100 to draw it up. The expense is well worth it. Some states won't recognize a handwritten will, and even where they do, irregularities in language or procedure can result in its invalidation.

Your will should tell three things: who will administer it, who will receive your estate and how much each heir will receive. Before you go to a lawyer, consider each of them. The administrator of a will is called an *executor*. Anyone whom you trust—from a bank representative to a relative or friend—may act as executor, so long as the executor is not also named as an inheritor in the will. Your executor must be a good business-person with a stable living situation. It may take him or her several years to dispose of all the estate's business, since the executor must arrange your funeral, liquidate your assets, pay your outstanding bills, hire a lawyer for probate proceedings and supervise and account for your estate's distribution. Banks and trust companies usually charge from two to four percent of the estate's value to act as executors. A friend would usually be much cheaper, but make sure you choose a friend experienced enough to manage your estate efficiently and dedicated enough to give freely of his or her time for your sake and that of your heirs.

Having chosen an executor, you'll want next to consider who gets your money and how much each heir will get. Many people prefer to think in terms of proportions rather than absolute dollar amounts; say 50 percent to the surviving spouse and the rest divided proportionately among the children. After all, you don't know exactly what your estate will be worth at the time of your death. You may choose a dollar amount when you want to limit what an heir will get. For instance, you might leave only a token amount to a wealthy son, leaving more for a younger daughter about to enter college. You may also want to bequeath some personal effects to specific individuals. Or you may want to allow your heirs to divide your mementos among themselves as they see fit, in which case you wouldn't bequeath those items—they would become part of your residual estate (whatever is left after payment of debts and other expenses). Be sure to mention all your heirs in the will; even if you intend to leave them little or nothing. This will prevent an heir from suing to overturn your will because he or she was forgotten.

Figuring the approximate amount your willed estate is worth may help you apportion it to your heirs. Remember, though, you may have assets not covered in your will that your heirs will receive (see the section titled "Other Kinds of Legacies"). Take these assets into account when deciding how much to leave to each heir. Use the following chart to compute the approximate value of your *willed* estate.

Your Willed Estate

Assets

Life insurance (individual   _____
   or group)

Checking and savings
accounts   _____

Pension death benefit   _____

Investments (stocks, bonds   _____
etc.)

Home   _____

Other real estate   _____

Owned business   _____

Personal property   _____

Total Assets   _____

Liabilities

   Mortgage   _____

   Other loans   _____

   Bills due   _____

   Income taxes   _____

   Death expenses   _____

     Funeral   _____

     Probate fees   _____

     Executor's   _____

     Costs of
      liquidating
      estate   _____

  Subtotal   _____

  Total Liabilities   _____

BEFORE-TAX ESTATE
VALUE
(total assets minus total
liabilities)   _____

The value of your estate may, of course, change
greatly over time, as may your ideas about who should
get your worldly goods. You can change your will at
any time, however, providing you explicity cancel the
previous one.

DEATH TAXES

Death and taxes are inevitable, they say, so too are
taxes after death. Federal estate tax plus state inheritance tax can take a sizable chunk out of your estate.
Unless you're wealthy, it's not worth tying your estate
in knots trying to avoid them, but certain deductions
and tax strategies may help to reduce the burden.

Everyone gets a break on federal estate tax. Starting
in 1981, no estate worth less than $175,625 will be
subject to any estate tax at all! Estates worth more can
deduct this amount, called the *unified tax credit*, from
their taxes. Married people get additional relief.
When you die, your spouse will automatically receive
half the estate or $250,000 whichever is greater, free
of estate tax. These two deductions, taken together,
can allow a spouse a tax-free inheritance of more than
$425,000.

These tax breaks are certainly an improvement, but
consider what happens when a spouse who has inher-
ited $425,000 tax-free dies. He or she can take the uni-
fied estate tax credit, but that leaves $249,375 taxable
in the estate. At the present rate, that means a tax of
more than $80,000! To meet this and other problems
associated with larger estates, certain strategies can be
useful. You may want to discuss the following options

with your lawyer: marital deduction trusts, tax-free gifts and assignment of your life insurance. Each of these can reduce your estate taxes, but each also limits the funds available to you while you live. Be sure you've provided for yourselves before you take care of your heirs.

The *marital deduction trust* is of particular interest to widows or widowers who want to avoid a large tax when they die (see example given previously). At least part of the value in the estate over and above the allowed marital deduction should be placed in trust for the children, but with the provisions that all income from the investments (plus principal, in the event of an emergency) goes to the surviving spouse until he or she dies. Either a bank or the surviving spouse can manage the trust. So long as he or she holds to the letter of the agreement, no funds in the trust will be taxable in the estate! The tax savings can be dramatic. Say you leave an estate worth $350,000. You can leave it all to your spouse tax-free, but when the surviving spouse dies, $175,000 of it will be subject to tax (after the unified tax credit has been taken). If that $175,000 had been put in a marital deduction trust, it would not be taxable and there would therefore be no estate tax. That could mean a savings of up to almost $60,000 in taxes.

Rules on *tax-free gifts* can further reduce your taxable estate, but keep in mind that you need to maintain enough funds for your own support. You can give your spouse up to $100,000 tax-free during your life. Also nontaxable are $3,000 worth of *annual* gifts each to spouse, children, other relatives or friends. If you and your spouse join in giving the gifts—to your children for example—you can give each recipient up to $6,000 tax-free every year. The only catch is that to keep their tax-free status, the gifts must be given at least three years before your death.

Under some circumstances it can even be advantageous to give a taxable gift. Say you have a rapidly appreciating asset, such as a successful growth stock or your home. You may save in the long run if you give it to your heirs now, paying the gift tax but avoiding the presumably greater tax on its appreciated value at the time of your death. Use caution when you give your home: you must give it with no strings attached, even if you continue to live in it. Even if you only keep paying the heating bill, the IRS might claim the house still belonged to you and is therefore taxable in your estate.

You can avoid making your life insurance a part of your estate by *assigning* it to an heir. Again, make sure that the assignment form you get from your insurer specifies that the policy is a free gift to the heir. That way it won't be taxed in your estate or the heir's, at least until the heir cashes the policy. If the policy is large, you may incur a gift tax, but it will likely be much less than the eventual estate tax. Of course, you'll only pursue this course if you feel you'll never want to change beneficiaries or borrow against the policy. Once you've given it away, you have no further say in its disposition.

As if federal estate taxes were not enough, all states except Nevada, Georgia and Florida impose an *inheritance tax* directly on heirs. The tax for close relatives runs anywhere from two to six percent of the estate, depending on the state and the person inheriting. Most states provide the lowest rates and most generous exemptions for surviving spouses and children. Distant relatives and friends have a lower exemption and a higher rate. In California, for example, a surviving spouse pays no tax on the first $60,000 of the inheritance and six percent on the amount between $60,000 and $100,000. A friend, on the other hand, gets only a $300 exemption and pays 10 percent even on the first $25,000. A trust is unfortunately no protection against inheritance taxes. Heirs pay tax on the

amount held in trust for them regardless of how long
they must wait to get it.

OTHER LEGACIES

The high cost of probate—as much as five percent of
an estate—encourages many people to take assets out
of their willed estate, even where no tax savings are
anticipated. Often they may also want certain assets to
pass directly to their heirs without the long waiting
period imposed by probate proceedings. Three arrangements are possible: joint tenancy with right of
survivorship, living trusts and beneficiary status.
They are all discussed in the sections that follow.

JOINT TENANCY WITH RIGHT OF SURVIVORSHIP

This is a form of property ownership. Any asset may
be owned in this way, and any two people may be
joint tenants. Generally, though, a married couple
with an estate small enough to escape death taxes are
the ones who'll be interested in this kind of ownership. For them, putting part or all of their assets into
joint tenancy with right of survivorship means that the
assets will pass directly to the surviving spouse, without waiting time or probate costs, regardless of who
dies first. Note, however, that both spouses still need
a will. When the survivor dies, or if both should die
together, instructions should be left for the distribution of his or her, or their, property.

There are, however, some problems with this form
of ownership. If the estate is large enough to be liable
for estate tax, a couple runs the risk of increasing the
tax because joint tenants cannot take a marital deduction trust (see p. 80). If a couple can't prove that each
spouse paid his or her share of the jointly owned property, one spouse may have to take the share as a gift. If

that gift exceeds the $100,000 gift tax deduction, then gift taxes will be incurred.

Joint tenancy can also entangle your estate in unexpected ways. If a marriage of joint tenants is unstable, considerable friction can result since one spouse can't buy or sell an asset without the consent of the other. Moreover, if husband and wife are not absolutely agreed on who should inherit their estate when they both die, some people could be disinherited. All property the survivor inherits is up to the survivor to dispose of. Say you have a joint tenancy with right of survivorship established for you and your second wife. If you die first, she might well be disinclined to include children of your first marriage in her will. If she didn't include them, they'd get nothing.

Community property is *not* the same thing as joint tenancy. A few states—Arizona, California, Idaho, Louisiana, Nevada, New Mexico, Texas and Washington—require that all assets a couple acquired during a marriage be considered jointly owned. Inheritances and property acquired before the marriage may be regarded as separate property, depending on the state in question. In all cases a spouse has the right to will his or her half of the community property to whomever he or she pleases. Separate property may be owned individually or jointly.

LIVING TRUSTS

Unlike joint tenancy, a *living trust* may be of use to wealthy people who wish to avoid probate. Privacy and flexibility are the great advantages. Whereas a marital deduction trust (see p. 80) goes into effect only on your death, a living trust names beneficiaries and goes into effect while you're still alive, often with yourself as trustee. The trust agreement names a trustee to take over on your death. This arrangement allows you to give your money to whomever you please, and since it keeps the estate out of probate, it prevents outsiders from finding out who got what. (Probate proceedings are a matter of public record.) Choose an experienced lawyer to draw up a living trust, since it can become a very complex document, and don't expect to realize maximum savings.

BENEFICIARY STATUS

The third way of giving your property to an heir without entering probate is to name him or her as your *beneficiary*. This form of legacy is available only on the following kinds of assets: insurance policies, checking and savings accounts, government savings bonds and IRA and Keogh plans. Property disposed of in this way escapes estate tax but will be taxed as ordinary income to the heir.

MONEY MANAGEMENT

Once you retire, you'll depend increasingly upon your savings and investments. Wise management of these funds will provide you and your heirs with the most security for the coming years. Sometimes an older person may become too sick or too forgetful—or for that matter, too busy—to manage his or her money efficiently. In such cases you can hire skilled professionals to supervise the funds.

CUSTODIAN ACCOUNTS

You can hire your bank to manage all your income and assets and pay all your bills. If you give the bank a limited power of attorney, it can also decide how to invest your funds, moving them to keep up with changing economic conditions. Such accounts are called "investment management accounts."

TRUSTS

I have talked about forming trusts for saving on taxes and avoiding probate, but you can also use a trust simply as a management tool. You agree to invest a certain sum in the bank's trust fund, which usually consists of a pool of trust investors. The bank deducts a fee for their services, then returns your investment's monthly income to you. You can have your lawyer draw the trust agreement so that the bank pays your bills out of the income. If you have more than $100,000 to invest, the bank should be willing to assign an individual manager to your account. Some experts say that bank trust funds are less efficient money managers than many mutual funds. For an older person interested in steady income, however, the bank offers a conservative strategy which may not show spectacular results but which also doesn't provide a severely fluctuating return.

REPRESENTATIVE PAYEE

Any individual can be named to take charge of paying an elder's bills. Your lawyer can draw up an agreement delegating authority to a representative to receive the older person's income and pay his or her bills. Any signer of the agreement, including the elder, can revoke it at will.

GUARDIAN

The guardian of an estate has broader powers than a

representative payee. He or she not only pays an older person's bills but also manages the elder's funds to maximize return. Where someone is appointed "guardian of the person," he or she will be responsible for the physical and mental welfare of the older person, arranging for payment of all medical care as well as daily maintenance. A guardian will often be appointed to take care of both the estate and the person.

Not all states use the same terminology for these functions. Some call a guardian a "conservator." Others simply require that a person performing these duties be provided with a "power of attorney." In all states, however, a person must have a court order to act in the capacity of guardian. Your lawyer can explain the particular requirements of your state. Some require that the elder be declared legally "incompetent" before such powers can be delegated; others say only that the petitioner must show that the elder is incapable of managing his or her financial and/or personal affairs.

GETTING LEGAL ADVICE

For all the questions discussed in this section, you need reliable legal advice. Other matters—turning that hobby into a business, dealing with age discrimination at your job or preventing a greedy relative from having you declared "incompetent"—also require legal counsel. If you don't have a lawyer already, ask a friend or associate you trust if he or she can recommend one. Your insurance agent, broker or accountant may know a lawyer skilled in arranging financial matters. State Bar Associations can give you referrals—or put you in touch with those who can—but the attorneys on these referral lists may be young and inexperienced, good for a minor problem but not right for complicated litigation or trust arrangements.

If you can't afford to hire a lawyer at $50 or more per hour, you have several options. Legal clinics, which will handle minor problems for half the cost of private lawyers, now exist in many cities. There are also legal services meant for the poor and elderly poor. Local legal aid societies and senior citizen advocacy groups are among the organizations providing such services. Lists of local and national sources of low-cost legal assistance are included in the ACLU's informative *The Rights of Older Persons*. (See *Sources for Further Information*.)

Sources for Further Information

A pamphlet offering an introduction to retirement legal problems and suggestions about when to consult a lawyer is *You, the Law, and Retirement*, available free of charge from:
Administration on Aging
Publication Dept., Rm. 4146
330 Independence Ave., S.W.
Washington, D.C. 20201

The American Association of Retired Persons offers a useful introductory legal booklet entitled *Your Retirement Legal Guide*. Order it free of charge from:
American Association of Retired Persons
P.O. Box 2240
Long Beach, Calif. 90801

An ACLU handbook prepared by four professors of law offers answers to layman's questions on retirement legal problems ranging from social security benefits to age discrimination and involuntary medical treatment. It also contains a very useful list of local and national agencies offering free or low-cost legal services for older poeple. Find it at a library or buy it at a bookstore for $2.50.

Brown, Robert N. et al. *The Rights of Older Persons.* New York: Avon Books, 1979.

Canadian Sources

If you have problems with legal planning, contact:
Civil Liberties Association
National Office
229 Yonge St. Suite 403
Toronto M9B 1N9

CHAPTER
2

LEISURE

OK. You've definitely made up your mind. You're going to retire. Or maybe you're another type. You just went ahead and did it. It makes no difference. In either case, if you haven't already thought it all out, you must consider what you're going to do next. Unless of course you're the rare type who can contemplate doing absolutely nothing with genuine pleasure. In this chapter I'll give you an idea of the many options that are open to you.

EDUCATION

Have you thought of going back to school? Lots of older Americans are doing it, you know. In fact, two million of us aged 55 or over are enrolled in some kind of formal education program. This doesn't necessarily mean going to college, or even high school. It can be a class conducted in a senior center on how government works. Or a class held in your local library on the mys-

terious workings of the Dewey decimal system. The Y
has courses, school systems have evening classes—almost everyone, it seems, is getting into the education
game. And you are their prime target, which is as it
should be. There is hardly a soul alive who hasn't said
to himself or herself at some time or another, "Gee, I'd
really like to know more about that, if only I had the
time." And you have the time.

Think about it. Education is supposed to give you
the necessary knowledge to make your life fuller,
richer. And yet most people use it solely to "get someplace." Practically the only groups who can use education properly are the rich, who don't have to worry
about "getting someplace," and the elderly, who are
already there.

So why not consider education as a way to enrich
your well-earned leisure time. You can study that subject which always interested you. You can get the high
school diploma you never had, either by going to high
school or by taking correspondence courses. You can
polish old skills or acquire new ones in a community
college. You can get a college degree, if that attracts
you. Or if you already have a degree, get another one.
You can go to classes simply to listen and learn for
yourself, or you can throw yourself into the fray and
compete with the kids.

And don't worry about not being welcome. The
number of institutions of higher education that are
prepared to give you either a break on charges or an
opportunity to study, even for credit, without charge,
is growing steadily. According to the latest figures
from the Institute of Lifetime Learning, about 46 percent of the 3,150 institutions connected with higher
learning give elders some kind of special treatment.
Some of these schools also have special courses in
subjects they believe will be of interest to you. And
don't be backward about taking advantage of these offerings. Colleges need new customers because the old

ones are no longer around. That is, the drop in the
birthrate has now hit the upper reaches of education.
Many of these schools are looking for students, and
they are discovering them by the hundreds of thousands among people like you.

The broadening of educational opportunity at all
levels is one of the more heartening aspects of the senior scene in America today. From weekend seminars
to doctorates, it's all there.

GETTING YOUR HIGH SCHOOL EQUIVALENCY DIPLOMA

Why not get the high school diploma that you were
unable to qualify for all the way back then because
you had to go to work at an early age, or for whatever
reason. Some colleges and universitites will require
you to have that document if you want to enroll in a
program of study that leads to a degree.

A high school equivalency diploma is exactly what
it sounds like, a diploma that is equivalent to one you
would have received if you'd remained in high school.
But you don't have to go back to high school to get the
diploma. You can get the equivalency diploma by taking examinations put together by General Education
Development (GED), an organization of the American
Council on Education. There are examinations in English, mathematics, social studies, literature and natural sciences. According to the Institute of Lifetime
Learning, there are 2,600 GED centers around the
country where these tests are administered. They are
not costly, usually no more than $9 each. You can get
exact information on this opportunity from your local
department of education and probably from adminis-
trators at the local high school as well.

If you need brushing up on any subjects, several
companies put out paper-bound review books that are

excellent and also inexpensive. Barrons, Cambridge and Arco are three of them.

GETTING COLLEGE CREDITS

If you've been thinking that it might be fun, or even useful, to have a college degree but shudder at the thought of plodding through four or more years of school, and so wind up saying to yourself, "Forget it; too much time," then take hope. It might not require any such commitment of your time. You've spent a lifetime acquiring information, and much of it could very well be translated into college credits. Schools like the College of New Rochelle in New Rochelle, New York give credits for life experience. And the idea is picking up around the country. Inquire of the community college nearest you whether this might not apply in your case.

The College Level Examination Program (CLEP) is another way you can get some college credits without actually attending college. For example, if you've been studying a specific subject on your own or have acquired learning in a certain subject by experience, you can take a CLEP test in that subject. It will cost you $20. These tests are given in the third week of every month in centers all over the country, some 900 in all (see *Sources for Further Information*).

LOW- OR NO-COST TUITION

Two million people aged 55 or over are now part of some kind of formal education program. Millions more (nobody knows exactly how many) take courses on a more informal basis. According to a new report of the Institute of Lifetime Learning, 22 states now have legislation requiring reduced tuition for elders or in some cases no tuition at all. Another 13 states have policies calling for the same thing, mandated by executive power. This doesn't mean elders are excluded in the other 15 states by any means. In all of them there are institutions of higher learning that make provisions for older people to receive educational opportunities at reduced cost or at no cost at all (see *Sources for Further Information*).

Not all states run these educational programs in the same way, so you should make inquiries (at your state department of education or at the institution covered under the program) about the requirements for admittance. But to give you an idea of what to expect, here are some of the major differences. First, there is the definition of what constitutes eligibility. This is simply a matter of age. Some states say you are eligible at 60, some at 62 and others at 65. Sixty-two is the most common, followed by 60.

You'll also have to decide whether you are interested in moving toward a degree or not. If you are, you'll want to take courses that give credit. In such courses you will play a full role in the activities of the class: taking exams and quizzes, making recitations and receiving grades. If you're not interested in getting a degree, then you'll want to take courses that are offered for audit only. In this case you'll attend when and if you want to, listen and take notes, if that seems desirable, but you will not be allowed to participate in the activities of the course. Many people, interested only in learning and not in proving anything to anyone, will find this quite satisfactory.

Many states have an additional qualification—the "space available" clause. This means that if you're not paying full tuition or are taking courses on an audit basis, you must wait until registration is complete. After that, you may attend a class that's of interest to you if there is still room.

SPECIAL PROGRAMS

Are you interested in college-level programs directed specifically at your age group, created to deal with your problems and particular interests? They exist in any number of shapes and forms. You can attend the courses at the Institute on Aging at Portland State University in Portland, Ore. and not only take the regular subjects but, if you like, get counseling on how to appproach a new career. There is a community college near Minneapolis, the North Hennepin Community College in Brooklyn Park, that offers courses to several hundred people over 55 on matters of particular concern to older people. Many states are becoming involved in gerontological courses, but California and New York probably do more than any of the others. To find out if any of the colleges in your area have such programs, contact your state department of education.

NEW APPROACHES

Education is learning no matter how you approach it. And today there is an enormous variety of different approaches for you to choose from. In the following sections some of the main types are discussed.

ELDERHOSTEL PROGRAM

Elderhostel is an education idea that is booming. Maybe "exploding" would be more accurate. It certainly has come a long way since Martin Knowlton and David Bianco thought of it back in 1975. Their notion was to provide a week of classes for older people in the relaxed atmosphere of one of five New Hampshire colleges. Cost would be extremely low. Living would be simple—housing in college dormitories, ordinary

college fare and a week of unpressured learning during which, they hoped, elderly students would discover that the juices still flowed, that they could learn
and enjoy the process and that they were not simply
old crocks to be left standing empty on some mantlepiece until they fell apart from sheer age.

The founding fathers were overly optimistic and
overly cautious at the same time. They did not suddenly rediscover the Fountain of Youth (mental) for
their few students that first summer. But they opened
up intellectual doors to literally thousands of people,
many of whom had never cared much for learning but
discovered that learning, presented this "new way,"
introduced them to a new world—indeed for some, a
new way of life.

The new way continues as it did that first summer.
There are three subjects, and a lecture period of one
hour is held on each subject every day. The courses
are given by regular members of the faculty and can
cover anything from subjects of local interest to excursions into the depths of philosophy. Only one subject
is barred—aging.

Pressure? Competition? There is none, no quizzes,
no exams, no marks. Not even compulsory attendance.
Just the pleasure of learning, which, by the way, is not
confined to the elderly students. Those teaching them
have, in turn, discovered that elders often carry the
wisdom and wit of their years. That's the only equipment they must bring with them to the classes. There
are no educational requirements.

I used the word "exploding." Judge for yourself.
From that tiny beginning, with five enrolled students,
the Elderhostel program now has more than 20,000
participants, and calculations are that the figure for
1981 will be 30,000 to 35,000! From five New Hampshire colleges, the number of participating institutions
has soared to well over 300, located all over the
United States and Canada. But even that is too limit-

ing for the now boundlessly ambitious people who run the nonprofit institution. So many people were taking summer courses (many of them spending eight or 10 weeks touring schools and tasting learning) that now Elderhostel is currently operating the year round.

But even this is only the beginning, says Michael Zoob, Elderhostel's vice-president and chief promoter. Already in the works are Elderhostel programs abroad. Hostelers will spend several weeks with British instructors in several English universities. Or they will be able to do the same, but with American instructors, at a folk school in Denmark, Sweden or Finland. Two-week Elderhostel programs in Mexico under the auspices of several American universities are now available. And that reminds me to mention that a Spanish-language program is now available in California.

Elderhostel thinks it's wrong that only people who are relatively well educated should get involved, so it is in the process of making arrangements for programs to be run in conjunction with certain trade unions. Perhaps signing up in a group will inspire more self-confidence in some. Still another idea is an Elderhostel gift certificate. Hopefully a grateful child, remembering the education for which his or her parents once paid, will return the favor in some small measure. The possibilities, as you can see, are almost endless—and almost endlessly joyous.

Costs are never joyous, but they are still low. When the idea was conceived, the federal government provided a grant that enabled Elderhostel students to have their week for only $60. But now the government is out, and inflation demands its due. The price for a week, everything included, is now about $140. Michael Zoob, who is buoyantly optimistic, says that the cost remains a tremendous bargain. How much less, he wants to know, would it cost you just to eat and entertain yourself at home?

The only important requirement other than the ability to pay the fee is that if two people attend together, one must be 60 or over. To this I would add that anyone interested should be pretty vigorous. Few of the colleges have elevators, and there is usually a fair amount of walking required.

What kind of people will you be meeting if you decide to participate in this program? Well, the average hosteler is about 68, though there are hostelers well into their eighties. They are mostly middle class, but not too many are rich; a survey showed that 50 percent had annual incomes of less than $12,000. And not all are educated. Mr. Zoob's mother worked in a factory all her life. Last year he and his wife gave her and his mother-in-law a week's hostel trip, and she soon became a confirmed hosteler.

One final note: there almost certainly are colleges, particularly community colleges right in your own area, that run similar programs. I have written so much on Elderhostel because it is the largest and most ambitious, but there are other programs involving study and sometimes travel, too. Some are more advanced, directed primarily at the older student seeking a degree. One of the most unusual is The Bridge at Fairhaven College in Bellingham, Wash. There older students, 31 in all, live in The Bridge dormitory for up to two years, taking regular college courses. But since they are on campus, the age gap is narrowed. There are projects deliberately designed for that purpose. By the way, it is possible to audit courses here, too; the student 60 or over is not required to take courses only for credit. The small apartments for seniors are comfortable and the price is minimal, about $200 per month for a one-bedroom apartment.

COLLEGE AT HOME

A concept now spreading for those who don't want to go traveling around or who must stay home or who are too—what shall we call it—shy to face a campus full of youngsters is contract learning. This is a method whereby the student (with faculty advice) plans an educational program, deciding what it will accomplish in how long a time, what will be read and what assignments will be performed—possibly even outside work fitting in with the program, such as an internship or field work. When planning for the program is complete, the student signs an agreement, which in effect is a learning contract.

This approach to learning was pioneered at the Empire State College, which is part of the State University of New York. It is for students of all ages who cannot or do not wish to attend college on a campus. A large number of these students have been people over the age of 60.

There is a nationwide network of such institutions, which is called the University Without Walls. Your state department of education can put you in touch with the one closest to you.

SHORT COURSES

No matter what your interest is, you can probably find a course in that subject at an institution quite close to you. For example, there are weekend courses for hobbyists interested in subjects such as leather work or jewelry making. And these types of workshop programs are often expanded for those whose interests are more serious.

Some courses are conducted outdoors, such as a three-day workshop on ecology. During this course the participants live on a 500-acre wildlife sanctuary

in Connecticut, in rustic but comfortable surroundings. Or if that sounds too far-removed and you'd like
something more closely connected with your everyday life, there are once-a-week evening sessions held
in various places on the relationship between seniors
and the realities of politics. They are often taught by
officeholders or professional politicians and may feature as a field trip a visit to the state capital when the
legislature is in session.

Interested in historic sites? There are short field
trips to such places led by historians. There are also
courses on small-business management. Well, I'm
sure you get the picture. No walls here either. (See
Sources for Further Information.)

OTHER PROGRAMS

If for any reason you are not inclined or are physically unable to attend a college or university, you
might be interested in studying at home by taking correspondence courses. Under this system you'll receive your course work and return your assignments
by mail. You can take individual courses in subjects
that interest you or take courses that will lead to a degree (see *Sources for Further Information*).

If you already have some type of higher education
and are interested in learning from your peers, or possibly in bringing your knowledge to them, you can do
this at the Institute for Retired Professionals (IRP). It
was created by Hy Hirsch some years ago at the New
School for Social Research in New York City. This in
itself is appropriate since the New School is the first
institution of higher learning in the country completely devoted to adult education.

The IRP courses are the creation of the student
body, which is now a rather large group of people
(about 600), most but not all of whom have at least one

degree and are extremely interested in remaining vital and in learning. They teach one another in a classroom situation. They do papers and assignments.
(George Carrel, a retired engineering executive and
an old friend with a broad knowledge of psychology,
philosophy, languages and Lord knows what else, told
me his discovery of the IRP has proved one of the
most exciting experiences in his life.) Students pay a
fee of $275, which entitles them to take any other
courses offered by the New School, and these are ex-
traordinary in their number and breadth. The Institute
has attracted the attention of retired professionals in
other cities. There are more than 15 IRP spinoffs in
cities across the country, and the number is going up
(see *Sources for Further Information*).

Do you feel a trifle uneasy about getting into a college scene after many years of work and with perhaps
comparatively little education? At Fordham University's Lincoln Center Campus in New York City there
is another type of institution called the College at 60.
The name refers to the address, not the average age of
the student body, most of whom are actually older
than that. First the college tests the applicants. If they
are accepted, the college then has them take a number
of courses carefully geared not only to their interests,
but also to sliding them smoothly into college life.
These courses are taught at a level about high school,
but not quite up to college demands. After two years
students can move into the hurly-burly of Fordham's
regular course structure.

I asked one student, Harry Gabel, a 68-year-old retired garment manufacturer with practically no previous formal education, how it felt to compete with
thousands of quick-minded, bright-eyed youngsters.
He looked at me querulously and said, "Didn't they
tell you?" "Tell me what?" I asked. "Mr. Michaels,"
he said, "in my senior year I was president of the student body at Fordham." Some competitor!

SOURCES FOR FURTHER INFORMATION

Getting College Credits

If you want to know what subjects the College Level Examination program covers or if you want any other information about the program, write for the free *Bulletin of Information for Candidates* at the address given below:
College Level Examination Program
P.O. Box 592
Princeton, N.J. 08540

Low- or No-Cost Tuition

To find out what institutions in up to three states offer low- or no-cost tuition, write to:
Institute of Lifetime Learning National Retired Teachers Association/American Association of Retired Persons
1909 K St., N.W.
Washington, D.C. 20049

Elderhostel Program

To learn more about the Elderhostel program and to obtain a copy of its catalog, which lists all the schools, their locations and the courses offered, write to:
Elderhostel
100 Boylston St.
Suite 200
Boston, Mass. 02116

Short Courses

A fine book that offers many examples of workshop or weekend courses and short courses of all types is:

Cross, Wilbur, and Florio, Carol. *You Are Never Too Old to Learn*. McGraw-Hill: New York, 1978.

To find out what types of short field trips and short courses on various subjects are held in your locality, write to:
Old Americans Project
Adult Education Association of the U.S.A.
810 18th St., N.W.
Washington, D.C. 20036

Other Programs

For information about the type of subjects you can take through correspondence courses and for general information about the program, write to:
Frederick H. Jackson, Director
Committee on Institutional Cooperation
Suite 130
820 Davis St.
Evanston, Ill. 60201

For more information about IRP, write to:
Institute for Retired Professionals
New School for Social Research
66 W. 12th St.
New York, N.Y. 10010

Universities that sponsor similar programs include Brooklyn College (N.Y., N.Y.); Delaware; Duke (Durham, N.C.); Harvard (Cambridge, Mass.); Hofstra (N.Y., N.Y.); Nova College (Fla.) and California (Berkeley, Los Angeles, San Diego and San Francisco).

For more detailed information on the whole gamut of

unconstructed approaches to education, here is an excellent book:

Gross, Ronald. *The Life Long Learner.* Simon & Schuster: New York, 1977.

For information on all kinds of educational programs for the elderly, write to the following organizations:
Adult Education Association of the U.S.A.
810 18th St., N.W.
Washington, D.C. 20036
This association is specifically interested in education as a lifelong process.

National University Extension Association
Suite 360
One Dupont Circle
Washington, D.C. 20036
This is an organization of professional educators. It has many services, including the courses made available by its members, and information on correspondence courses.

American Association of Community and Junior Colleges
One Dupont Circle
Washington, D.C. 20036
Since more courses are offered by these two-year colleges than by four-year schools, they are of particular interest. They can also tell you specifically what is available in a community college in any locality. This could be important if you are considering moving upon retirement.

Clearinghouse on Adult Education and Life-Long Learning (ADELL)
% Informatics, Inc.
6000 Executive Blvd.
Rockville, Md. 20852

Telephone: (301) 770-3000
The telephone number is included because the Clearinghouse will also answer by phone your questions
about anything involving adult education.

The National Home Study Council
1601 18th St., N.W.
Washington, D.C. 20009
The Council puts out a free booklet called *Directory
of Accredited Home Study Schools.* You can get it by
writing to them.

Canadian Sources

For information on your province's education programs, write your local government office.

VOLUNTEERING

There has long been a stigma attached to volunteering in this country. It runs along the lines of "anything
that is worth doing is worth getting paid for." And
then there's the old saw, "the workingman is worthy
of his hire."

The origin of this stigma, I suspect, goes back to the
early days of the trade union movement and indeed
has clung to trade union thinking to this very day.
Trade union leaders saw volunteerism as a device to
take paying jobs away from people by putting unpaid
volunteers in their place. The fear was legitimate, but
it's out of date. Today, volunteerism has many aspects,
and there are many programs. Some are creations of
government and are national in scope. Some are special projects, conceived locally, sometimes with government funding, sometimes not. There are volunteer
programs that you can participate in if you need

money to supplement your income while you're giving your time and skill to people; there are others that you can work on if you don't need to supplement your income but would like to be reimbursed for costs to and from the work place. In the sections that follow, examples of all these types of volunteer programs are discussed.

We become increasingly interdependent as our population grows and ages. I believe this is a good thing. Perhaps it will help melt some of the frigidity that seems to be a sorry by-product of a generally prosperous society. It is only under stress that we come together, care for one another and take care of one another. As an example, I'm sure many of you will remember Britain in World War II. People didn't have much. Rationing was the rule. Then there were the air raids, which increased interdependence among people. You watched out for your neighbors, they for you. If a bomb hit, everyone rushed to the rescue. If someone wanted to make a bit of a party, people shared their rations. The famous British reserve vanished. American G.I.'s were amazed at how talkative and friendly people were, and not just in the pubs. There was a we're-all-in-this-together spirit. Everyone was a volunteer.

And when the war ended, so did the spirit. The generosity, the give and take, the camaraderie, the readiness to share were over. A visitor returning three years after the war ended saw a London that was back to normal. It seemed a shame that this one happy by-product of war had to vanish with peace.

I believe we are slowly coming to the realization that unless we help each other voluntarily, without pay or with only the amount really needed by those who cannot afford to give their time for nothing, we cannot survive in decency. It seems to me that the increase in volunteers throughout the country shows that this is so.

As we grow older, giving—not money, but ourselves—the abilities, the skills and, if you like, the wisdom we have accumulated over the years can be a joy.

ACTION PROGRAMS

Most programs in which government participates have been consolidated under a single agency called ACTION. The following sections describe some of the ACTION programs. (If you'd like more information on any of them, contact one of the offices listed in *Sources for Further Information*.)

FOSTER GRANDPARENT PROGRAM

The key word is love. Everyone needs it, to give it as well as to receive it. Since on the receiving side the need is most poignant among children, and since children of older folk have usually long since gone their own adult way, this program is inspirational. John Corbin, a retired contractor in Washington, D.C. can attest to that. *The Washington Post* did a story on the joy this 80-year-old man brings to the handicapped children he has been spending several hours with each weekday morning since last year. Mr. Corbin raised 12 children of his own. He retired seven years ago, and last year he lost his wife. Coming to the Hospital for Sick Children each day relieves the loneliness of his life these days.

He is untypical in two ways. Most of the Foster Grandparents are women, and Mr. Corbin is probably a bit more comfortable financially than most. But in other ways he is like the 16,880 other Foster Grandparents who are giving their help and affection to 46,500 children in all the states, plus the Virgin Islands, Puerto Rico and the District of Columbia.

They spend two hours a day with each of two children (a total of 20 hours a week), helping in a multitude of ways. They play games and read stories with some, help feed and dress others and assist with speech and physical therapy. This work can take place in various kinds of homes for children who are disturbed, handicapped or retarded.

Some Foster Grandparents are assigned to hospitals and some to homes where they can help teach parents how to deal with their own children. There are even some working in institutions where children in need of correction have been placed. They are taken to the place where their services will be rendered and are reimbursed for whatever expenses may be incurred on the job. Personal liability and accident insurance during this period are provided, along with hot meals and a modest stipend.

To participate in this program, you must be in good health, 60 years of age or over and have an income at or below the poverty level defined for your state. To find out what the cut-off line is, call the ACTION toll-free telephone number: (800) 424-8580. There is a 40-hour training and orientation period and, if necessary, additional training may be given during the program.

SENIOR COMPANION PROGRAM

Gerontologists are becoming increasingly convinced that the people best qualified to help keep elderly persons out of institutions are other older people. That is what Senior Companions do. They spend 20 hours a week with other elderly persons who need help to function at home.

There is a 40-hour orientation and training period. Like Foster Grandparents, Senior Companions must be 60 years of age or over and, although it varies from state to state, are expected to have low incomes. A modest stipend and transportation or an allowance for transportation are provided. Senior Companions also receive a daily hot meal, accident and liability insurance while serving, a yearly physical and periodic in-service training during the working period.

PEACE CORPS

The Peace Corps is still the glamour program for volunteers—and don't say, "Oh, that's just for kids who can go on safaris in the African jungles." There are now over 5,600 Peace Corps workers in 60 different countries, and while it is true that most of them are young, quite a few are over 50—330 at last count. And there is no age limit. Nor should there be. Knowledge and wisdom count here.

I said this is still the glamour program in government, but this is true only to a degree. The program was created during the Kennedy Administration, a short-lived period of innocence when Americans, secure in the belief that one sharp people-to-people stroke would smash the artificial barriers that separate one people from another, happily volunteered to share their famed know-how with the developing world. But in reality the changes that the Peace Corps people make are the slow ones, the imperceptible ones that make no mark on world politics. For example, they explain how to balance a diet, clean a wound, make a fish pond or plant a tree. Not very thrilling stuff, but oh so important.

To become a member of the Peace Corps, you need skills that are translatable into the everyday needs of others. You must be healthy and able to adjust to people whose ways are different from yours. You must be prepared to live among people in a foreign country and adapt to them rather than expecting them to adapt to you. You must be prepared to quickly immerse yourself in their culture, their customs and their history and to look upon them with respect. Although you don't have to be married to become a Peace Corps member, if you are, you and your spouse must go as a team. One without the other is not acceptable. There is a short but quite intensive training period. If you are a quick learner, you can be taught to qualify for a training area that is quite different from the area in which you already have experience, but of course, previous knowledge in a certain field is a big help.

The usual assignment period is 24 months. You will be provided transportation and an adequate, but hardly generous, allowance for food, clothing, shelter and whatever travel your job may require. It will not enable you to live in the local Hilton. At the end of service with the Peace Corps, you'll receive $125 for each month of service. This is intended as a lump sum to provide for readjustment to life at home. Comprehensive health insurance and a $10,000 life insurance policy are included.

VISTA

The acronym stands for Volunteers in Service to America. I think of it as a kind of domestic Peace Corps, and I think that is reasonably accurate.

VISTA workers go to areas within the country that need a certain type of help. They work with the poor, the culturally deprived and the physically or mentally handicapped. As a VISTA volunteer, you would work for a year in such an area, receiving a 10-day orientation plus as much skill-training as the job might require. You might be asked to help with legal aid, with a drug abuse program, in a day care center or with people in correction programs. Your skills might be useful in a ghetto or on an Indian reservation.

A VISTA worker's rewards are of the spirit—the organization pays for monthly living costs plus $75 for everything else. The readjustment stipend is $50 for each month served.

VISTA workers make an important contribution to their less fortunate fellow Americans, and the organization has attracted quite a few elders; about 500 at present are over 55.

RETIRED SENIOR VOLUNTEER PROGRAM (RSVP)

In many ways RSVP may be the most satisfactory of the government-sponsored programs so far as you're concerned. It is volunteerism, pure and simple; basic expenses, such as carfare, are all you'll get. And what do you give? The words come from New York Director Gertrude Leyendecker, and they're better than any description I could provide:

> The premise is that volunteer opportunities should be provided for older people so that they can continue an active involvement in the community. And since for many older people, volunteering has never been part of their cultural background, they do need some assists along the way. They need to have someone help them to locate volunteer opportunities, someone to help them become familiar with the place where they are going to volunteer. And very often they are much more comfortable in volunteering if they do it with a group of their peers, so in many of our programs the volunteers go in a group.

If you have anything at all to offer, from a specific skill to a receptive ear, there is a place in RSVP for you. One lady simply sews for patients in a hospital. Many tutor children who have learning problems.

Many contribute time to libraries, service centers, museums, the courts—you name it, if society needs it, RSVP volunteers will provide it. They work from one day a week on up.

What RSVP volunteers do for those they serve is clear enough. What do they get out of it? Gertrude Leyendecker says, "I think it gives them a heightened sense of self-esteem, a feeling that they're doing something worthwhile. They are making a contribution to the lives of others."

OTHER PROGRAMS

Other branches of government are also involved in areas of particular interest to seniors. So are some private or volunteer organizations, usually in partnership with the government as sponsor of a program. Let's take a look at some in both categories. (See *Sources for Further Information* to find out more about each of the following programs.)

SERVICE CORPS OF RETIRED EXECUTIVES (SCORE)

Are you a retired businessman or businesswoman who'd like to be of help to those who want to start a new business and know nothing about how to go about it? If so, then you might want to consider working for SCORE. The organization was started by the Small Business Administration to help ensure that money they lent to people wanting to start small businesses wouldn't be lost through simple ignorance.

The counselors in SCORE are totally unpaid. They come in four days a week, and the expert knowledge they have to offer is—well—encyclopedic. To qualify as a SCORE counselor, you must submit an application describing yourself and your business experience to your local SCORE chapter. (See *Sources for Further Information* for addresses to write to.) SCORE's admissions committee, composed of members, will vote on your application. Relevant experience and communications skills are what they like to see.

GREEN THUMB

This program is not as well known in urban areas as other programs because it's mostly a rural operation. It helps provide work for the 55 and over age group, dealing with applicants at or below the national low-income level established annually by the U.S. Department of Labor. In 1980 the figure for an individual was $4,738 a year, and less for farmers.

The Green Thumb program began in 1964 and its first project was to make the nation's highways more presentable. A worthy task in itself, but now over 15,000 workers are doing much more—insulating homes, restoring parks, driving fire engines, cutting wood and so on. These are hardworking people, as you might expect, since the sponsor for this Department of Labor program is the National Farmers Union.

If you're interested in working for this program, you'll have to put in a 20- to 24-hour week, and you'll be paid the minimum wage for your area.

SENIOR AIDES

Age discrimination is theoretically illegal. The actuality, as you may know, is that it's not only real but is also a problem that occurs before the age of 65. It just gets worse as one gets older. Senior Aids was created in 1968 to fight age discrimination.

PRIME-OF-YOUR-LIFER

Harry Weiner

Harry Weiner had made a success out of a pat-
ent for slicing machines that he had brought from
Germany in the early 1930s. Later in life he sold
his factory, but when his wife died (and with his
children leading their own lives), Harry had serious problems. SCORE was his salvation. It gave
him the opportunity to share with others the accumulated wisdom of all those years in business.

Here's how he put it when I asked what it had
meant to him: "Everything. I think I gave quite a
bit to the community at large, but not nearly as
much as I got back—personal satisfaction of helping somebody. When you're able to tell someone
something, and they pick up their heads and give
you that look of wonderment in their eyes, as if to
say, 'Why didn't I think of that, it's so simple?' it
communicates back to me. And I love it."

And why shouldn't he?

The program is sponsored by the National Council
of Senior Citizens, which considers age discrimination a prime enemy. Funding comes through the U.S.
Department of Labor. If you're unemployed, 55 or
over and have an income at or below the Labor Department's national low-income figure, then you can
be hired to work on any number of community projects. Over 7,000 Senior Aides are now working on
projects such as helping out in town libraries, serving
as resource people for the unemployed and the handicapped, doing paralegal work, driving buses and acting as instructors and repair workers. And in this program some of the Senior Aides are handicapped
themselves. For example, a blind lady maintains contact with shut-ins (those who cannot get around

alone), and a lady who must use a wheelchair comes to
help people who can't get around at all with writing
letters and handling problems.

SENIOR COMMUNITY SERVICE PROJECT

This program, funded by the Department of Labor
and sponsored by the National Council on the Aging,
is intended to help people between the ages of 55 and
62 supplement their incomes—because it is this
group, between the age periods when work can be
hard to get and social security is not yet available, who
need financial and other help the most.

In 1980, if your income was below $4,738, or $6,263
for a family of two, you may have qualified not only to
work in a variety of community programs, but also to
get training for new skills—or sometimes a first skill if
you've never had the advantage of possessing one before. Fifty-five is the minimum age, but despite the
target levels there is no upper limit. A 20-hour average
workweek is what the program aims for. Wages are at
the local or federal minimum level, whichever is
higher. The mean age of those in the program is 64.7
years. About 1,000 people are now enrolled, but the
numbers change quite frequently.

COMMUNITY MUTUAL-HELP PROGRAMS

Mutual-help volunteer programs are being organized in communities throughout the country. To give
you an idea of the range of these programs, here are a
few brief examples of some. (To find out if you have
any of these programs in your community, check the
telephone book.)

There are Reach Out programs in many places. For
instance, the Distributive Workers Union (District 65)
in New York City has an extremely active program in

which retirees help one another, contributing their
own skills to help their fellow retirees through workshops or counseling on the telephone those who may
be homebound.

PRIME-OF-YOUR-LIFERS

Irving Geldman and *Hattie Karthan*

Irving Geldman got so disturbed when he was
forcibly retired at 65 that he decided to do something about it—for others. He went back to school
in order to get some counseling skills to supplement previous experience as a personnel manager, and then got a voluntary organization called
People Management, Inc. to teach older people
how to look for jobs.

Hattie Karthan lives in New York City, in
Brooklyn's Bedford-Stuyvesant section—not an
easy place to live. But despite her 79 years, a bad
heart and arthritis to boot, this plucky, lovely lady
decided that something could be done to preserve the block where she lived and the beauty of
the old section of the city of which it is a part.
Others have contributed a lot since, but it was
Hattie who got the neighbors to clean up the
block, to heckle the city until, by dint of their
sheer cussedness and persistence, the authorities
agreed to help by cleaning out rubble-filled lots
and eventually by contributing trees. Trees! People said there was no way that trees would be
able to survive in Bedford-Stuyvesant. Hattie
Carthan didn't believe it either, so to ensure that
they did survive, she came up with this idea:
bring trees and children together so that each tree
would be a child's responsibility, its special care
and later its special pride, too. There are tree-

lined blocks lending additional grace to the distinguished old brownstones in much of this area today. And there is one ill old lady who learned how to organize because she felt she had to, who got children involved in order to save the trees—this lady and the Tree Corps she created.

An organization filling a vitally important social and personal need is the Council of Widows-Widowers. Bereavement and the loneliness and loss that go with it are clearly a major problem for the elderly. The Council helps people in this situation by bringing them together to provide companionship and consolation to each other. If no chapter exists in your locality, you might want to think about starting one.

Counties are now starting their own programs. In Nassau County in New York the county Department of Senior Citizen Affairs and the schools have joined in a novel and interesting program. They are trying to break through the age barriers between the young and the elderly, so sadly typical of our day, by having seniors teach about aging to youngsters from kindergarten all the way through high school. The teaching program is being supplemented by a variety of imaginative programs that hopefully will introduce older people to the young, creating understanding and bridging the gap.

Bell Telephone has been operating the Telephone Pioneers program since 1911. Members must have at least 18 years in the communications business. Fittingly enough, the first member was Alexander Graham Bell himself. Of the 540,000 members, 205,000 are retired. They contribute some marvelous things to the community at large. Telephone Pioneers have taken the handicapped as their particular interest; for example, they have invented over 100 devices to help handicapped people function. One such device is a small box that attaches to a touchtone telephone and lights up the letters so that people with hearing difficulties can communicate by telephone using a simple code. As volunteers, Pioneers also help care for other elderly people in institutions and for the homebound.

As part of its retirement program, the Equitable Life Assurance Society has started a program encouraging former employees to use their executive and office skills to help charitable and voluntary organizations perform tasks from clerical work to accounting, as these skills are ones that such organizations may well not be able to afford.

Maintenance Central for Seniors in Detroit, aided by a grant under Title III of the Older Americans Act, helps older people with low incomes to get home repair work done economically so that they can remain in their homes. This is a successful, locally controlled project where community people do what needs to be done and do it cheaper. Just a small grant, $49,500 with 15 percent matching funds raised locally, has increased the programs funds to almost $2 million.

In East Islip on Long Island there is an interesting variation on the Detroit program—a mutual-help Home Chore program through which those needing minor house repairs that they are not capable of doing themselves can get the work done for a small charge by other elderly craftsmen.

Turn where you like and people who want to be part of what is happening are finding ways of doing it. In some states, Connecticut for one, elderly volunteers have been asked to help get the state's files in order. The state went to a local program called Services Performed With Aging and got 12 volunteers who were happy to be of assistance.

You don't have to be an indomitable old lady, or a person who starts things on his own or one who gets involved with federal or other programs. The opportunities are everywhere. If you go to a senior center, you know they need all the help they can get. So do churches and fraternal organizations. A lot of local volunteer projects are starting to use the words Reach Out. They're good words. Reach out! You are wanted and needed!

SOURCES FOR FURTHER INFORMATION

Action Programs

For more information on any of the ACTION programs (Foster Grandparent, Senior Companion, Peace Corps, Vista and RSVP), write to the program of your interest at the main office in Washington, D.C. or to one of the regional offices given in the following list (or call the telephone number):
Main Office
ACTION
Washington, D.C. 20525

REGIONAL OFFICES

Regional Director
ACTION–Region 1
John W. McCormack
Federal Building
Room 1420
Boston, Mass. 02109
(617) 223-4297/4464

Regional Director
ACTION–Region III
320 Walnut St., 6th Floor
Philadelphia, Pa. 19106
(215) 597-0732

Regional Director
ACTION–Region II
26 Federal Plaza, Room 1609
New York, N.Y. 10007
(212) 264-2900

Regional Director
ACTION–Region IV
101 Marietta St., N.W.
(25th Fl.)
Atlanta, Ga. 30303
(404) 221-2860

Regional Director
ACTION–Region V
1 North Wacker Drive
Chicago, Ill. 60606
(312) 353-7499/7244

Regional Director
ACTION–Region VI
212 North St. Paul St.
Dallas, Tex. 75201
(214) 749-1361

Regional Director
ACTION–Region VII
Two Gateway Center
4th and State Sts.
Kansas City, Kans. 66101
(816) 374-4486/4541

Regional Director
ACTION–Region VIII
1845 Sherman Street
Room 201
Denver, Colo. 80203
(303) 837-2671

Regional Director
ACTION–Region IX
211 Main St.
San Francisco, Calif.
94105
(415) 556-1940/1733

Regional Director
ACTION–Region X
1601 2nd Avenue
Seattle, Wash. 98101
(202) 442-1558/4810

SCORE

To find if there is a SCORE office in your community, look under the Small Business Administration listing in the U.S. government section of your phone book. Or write to:
SCORE
Small Business Administration
1441 L St., N.W.
Washington, D.C. 20416

Green Thumb

Green Thumb
Suite 600
1012 14th St., N.W.
Washington, D.C. 20005

Senior Aides

National Council of Senior Citizens
1511 K St., N.W.
Washington, D.C. 20005
Or contact one of the community service agencies that
currently sponsor Senior Aides at the locations given
below:

ALABAMA

Anniston—East Alabama Regional Planning and Development Commission

Bessemer—Bessemer State Technical College, Senior Citizens Service

Camden—Alabama-Tombigbee Rivers Regional Planning and Development Commission

Decatur—North Central Ala. Regional Council of Governments

Dothan—S.E. Ala. Regional Planning and Development Commission

Mobile—South Ala. Regional Planning Commission

Opelika—East Ala. Services for the Elderly, Inc.

Sheffield—The Muscle Shoals Regional Council on Aging

Tuscaloosa—W. Ala. Planning and Development Commission

CALIFORNIA

Bakersfield—Mexican American Opportunity Foundation

Fresno—Council of Older Americans

Imperial County—Economic Opportunity Commission of Imperial County

Modesto—Senior Opportunity Programs of Stanislaus County

Monterey—The Alliance on Aging

Oakland—Social Service Bureau of East Bay, Inc.

Oxnard—Mexican American Opportunity Foundation

Orange County—Senior Citizens Program Office

San Diego—Adult Protective Services

COLORADO

Denver—SENIORS!

Pueblo—Senior Citizens Resource Development and Coordinating Agency, Inc.

CONNECTICUT

Bridgeport—City of Bridgeport Department on Aging

Brooklyn—Quinebaug Valley Senior Citizens, Inc.

Hartford—City of Hartford

New Haven—Regional Council of Elected Officials of South Central Connecticut

Waterbury—Waterbury Area Retired Workers Council

FLORIDA

Dade County—Senior Centers of Dade County

Ft. Lauderdale— Areawide Council on Aging of Broward County, Inc.

Ft. Myers—City of Ft. Myers/Lee County

Volusia County—United Way of Volusia County

West Palm Beach—Gulfstream Areawide Council on Aging

ILLINOIS

Belleville—General Studies and Community Services, Belleville Area College

Chicago—City of Chicago Department of Human Resources

Chicago—Senior Citizens Community Programs, Catholic Charities

Kankakee—Kankakee County Housing Authority

Mt. Carmel—Illinois Eastern Community Colleges, Wabash Valley College

Rock Island—NOW Community Action Agency

INDIANA

Evansville—Community Action Program of Evansville

Gary—Gary Neighborhood Services, Inc.

Muncie—Action, Inc. of Delaware County

South Bend—Real Services of St. Joseph County, Inc.

IOWA

Sioux City—Woodbury County Community Action Agency

LOUISIANA

Lafayette—Lafayette Parish Council on Aging

Ville Platte—Evangeline Council on Aging, Inc.

MARYLAND

Annapolis—Anne Arundel County Economic Opportunity Committee, Inc.

Baltimore—Urban Coalition

Baltimore—Constant Care

Baltimore—State Commission on Aging, Senior AIDES Program

Montgomery County—Jewish Council for the Aging of Greater Washington, Inc.

Prince Georges County—County Department of Service & Programs for the Aging

Salisbury—Wicomico County Government

Towson—Baltimore County Aging Programs and Services

MASSACHUSETTS

Boston—Commission on Affairs of the Elderly

Boston—Legal Research and Services for the Elderly

Brockton—Old Colony Elderly Services, Inc.

Cape Cod & Islands—Elder Services of Cape Cod and the Islands

Fall River—Citizens for Citizens

Lawrence—Elder Services of the Merrimack Valley, Inc.

New Bedford—YWCA

New Bedford—Coast Line Elderly Services, Inc.

Springfield—City of Springfield

Worcester—City of Worcester Council on Aging

MICHIGAN

Detroit—City of Detroit Manpower Department

Lansing—Capitol Area for Community Services

Owosso—Shiawassee Council on Aging, Inc.

Pontiac—Oakland-Livingston Human Service Agency

MINNESOTA

Duluth—City of Duluth
Manpower Services
Minneapolis—Central
Labor Union Council

St. Paul—Amherst H.
Wilder Foundation

MISSISSIPPI

Gulfport—South Missis-
sippi Planning & De-
velopment District

Jackson—Mayor's Office,
Allied Service Depart-
ment
Wesson—Copiah-Lin-
coln Junior College

MISSOURI

St. Louis—Cardinal Rit-
ter Institute

NEW JERSEY

Camden—Community
Planning and Advo-
cacy Council of Cam-
den County
Newark—North Jersey
Community Union

New Brunswick—Mid-
dlesex County Eco-
nomic Opportunities
Corp.

NEW YORK

Babylon—Town of Baby-
lon
Buffalo—Erie County
Office for the Aging/
Buffalo AFL-CIO
Council

Mayville—Chautauqua
County Office for the
Aging
New York City—New
York City Department
of Air Resources

Schenectady—City of
Schenectady
Steuben County—Steu-
ben County Economic
Opportunity Program

Troy—Commission on
Economic Opportunity
for the Rensselaer
County Area, Inc.

NORTH CAROLINA

Bryson City—State of
Franklin Health Coun-
cil, Inc., Western Caro-
lina University
Durham—Coordinating
Council for Senior Cit-
izens, Inc.

Fayetteville—Cum-
berland County Board
of Commissioners
Wilmington—The Cape
Fear Area United Way,
Inc.

OHIO

Akron—Greater Akron
Community Action
Council
Ashtabula—Ashtabula
County Community
Action Agency
Columbiana County—
Columbiana County
Mental Health Clinic,
Lisbon

Dayton—Senior Citizens
Center of Greater Day-
ton Area
Marietta—Community
Action Program Corpo-
ration of Washington-
Morgan Counties
Youngstown—Youngs-
town Area Community
Council

PENNSYLVANIA

Butler—Tri-County
Manpower Commis-
sion
Carbon County—Schuyl-
kill Carbon Agency for
Manpower

Erie—Greater Erie Com-
munity Action Com-
mittee
Lancaster—Office for the
Aging

Pittsburgh—Allegheny
County Adult Services

Wilkes-Barre—United
Services Agency Office
for the Aging

RHODE ISLAND

Providence—Adult Education Department,
Providence Public
Schools

SOUTH CAROLINA

Charleston—Charleston
Area Senior Citizens
Services, Inc.

Hilton Head Island—
Lowcountry Senior
Citizen Services, Inc.

TENNESSEE

Chattanooga—Senior
Neighbors of Chattanooga, Inc.
Knoxville—City of Knoxville

Martin—Northwest Tennessee Development
District
Memphis—Senior Citizens Services, Inc.

TEXAS

Austin—City of Austin
Port Authur—Senior Citizens Services, Inc.

Texas City—Galveston
County Senior Citizens Program

WASHINGTON

Tacoma—Pierce County
Community Action
Agency

Tacoma—City of Tacoma
Office of Comprehensive Employment and
Training

WEST VIRGINIA

Fairmont—Marion
County Commission

Wheeling—Children &
Family Services

WISCONSIN

Eau Claire—Eau Claire
City-County Associa-
tion on Aging, Inc.
Green Bay—Curative
Workshop Rehabilita-
tion Center

Kenosha—AFL-CIO
UAW
Milwaukee—Social De-
velopment Commis-
sion
Wausau—Marathon (Co.)
Commission on Aging

DISTRICT OF COLUMBIA

Washington, D.C.—Dis-
trict of Columbia De-
partment of Manpower

Senior Community Service Project

National Council on the Aging, Inc.
1828 L St., N.W.
Washington, D.C. 20036

Canadian Sources

See list of organizations concerned with problems of
the elderly that is included at the end of Chapter
Four.

TRAVEL

If you have a little extra money available, there is
good news for you. Also a tiny bit of bad news. The
good news is that buses, trains, airlines, many popular

resort areas and entertainment and recreational facilities are prepared to give you discounts. The bit of bad news, as you might expect, is that they usually want to give you those discounts under conditions and at times convenient to them, which is not so terrible for people whose vacation time is not tied to official holidays or any particular time of the year.

TRANSPORTATION AND ACCOMMODATION

Here are a few useful hints for traveling in the United States.

The two biggest bus lines, Trailways and Greyhound, are both offering 13 percent discounts for one-way and roundtrip fares for people over 65. To be sure the discounts still apply, call them and ask.

The Amtrak train system also offers discounts for people over 65, with certain restrictions (see *Sources for Further Information*). The discounts offered by many airlines operating within the country are also for people over 65. You should be aware of the restrictions though. Usually an airline will not let you make reservations more than one day in advance, and you won't be able to get discounts on bargain flights. Even with these restrictions, though, this can still be quite a bargain because you'll usually get a one-third discount and can go most places at almost any time.

When you get to your destination, there are many hotels, motels and restaurants that make discount prices available to you. Discounts are usually offered in what is known as the off-season, meaning for instance, that in Southern resorts they will be available only in spring, summer and fall months, when business is not at its peak.

WARNING! Don't be shy. Before you travel anywhere or before you sign for your room or order a meal, ask if there is a discount for senior citizens and be prepared to show proof of age.

Group-trip discounts are something you should look into if you are a member of a club or organization. Travel agents will know about these, not only for domestic trips, but for trips abroad as well. For foreign trips also keep in mind the Elderhostel programs that are just getting under way. (These were discussed earlier in this chapter.)

Then there are the senior organizations. The American Association of Retired Persons (AARP) and the National Council of Senior Citizens (NCSC) have a variety of travel programs, both for trips within this country and abroad as well (see *Sources for Further Information*). Membership in either of these organizations can get you discounts at different hotels and motel chains and reduced rates for renting cars under certain conditions—for example, a car rental company probably won't give you a discount for the cheapest car they have.

ENTERTAINMENT AND RECREATION

When you're on vacation, or at any other time for that matter, do you enjoy going to the movies, theaters, concerts, museums, ballet performances and/or operas? If you're a senior citizen, the chances are that you can get discount tickets for all or most of these events. Some places advertise their discount rates for senior citizens and others don't, so make sure you inquire about this before buying tickets.

If you like visiting the national parks and other government recreational areas and you're over 62, then you're entitled to free admission to any of these areas in the United States. But you have to apply for what is called a Golden Age Passport (see *Sources for Further Information*).

SOURCES FOR FURTHER INFORMATION

Transportation and Accommodation

To get detailed information on the discount plans that Amtrak has available and other travel programs it offers (such as excursions, package plans, escorted tours), write to:
Amtrak
955 L'Enfant Plaza
Washington, D.C. 20024

To find out more about the AARP and NCSC travel programs and on how you can become a member of these organizations, write them at the addresses given below:
American Association of Retired Persons
1909 K St., N.W.
Washington, D.C. 20049

National Council of Senior Citizens
1511 K St., N.W.
Washington, D.C. 20049

To receive the federal government pamphlet *Travel Tips for Senior Citizens*, write to:
Public Information Service
Room 4827A
Department of State
Washington, D.C. 20520

To apply for a Golden Age Passport, write to:
Public Enquiries
National Park Service
Washington, D.C. 20240

Canadian Sources

For information regarding travel and special senior citizens' discounts, contact:
Canadian Government Office of Tourism
Travel Information Services
235 Queen St.
Ottawa, Ontario K1A 0H5

THE ARTS AND SPORTS

There has always been a kind of connection between the elderly and the arts, somewhat condescending in tone—on the order of, "Why don't you get some water colors and take up painting?" This is followed by vague references to Winston Churchill and Dwight Eisenhower, both of whom painted with varying degrees of success. Michelangelo, Titian, Picasso and Matisse all continued to paint well into their later years, but they are not mentioned. The suggestion doesn't have to do with creativity but with keeping old people out of the way, out of trouble and busy doing—well—something.

PAINTING

Older people are interested in painting. Your senior center, your school system and quite possibly your library will offer courses in these areas, and you might yet surprise those superior youngsters with what you learn and can do.

THEATER

Theater is an area, an art that is positively booming in senior circles. All over the country older people are starting theaters—professional, semiprofessional and amateur. They are not interested in doing roadshow versions of what was popular a few years ago on Broadway and aping the youthful stars of those productions. No, indeed. The seniors starting these theaters want to tell their stories—stories about age discrimination; about the problems of Medicare and Medicaid; about mugging and self-doubt, depression, thoughtless youngsters and the nightmare nonsense of stereotyping elderly people. They want to bring the stories to younger people and are doing just that, often with plays and sketches—some serious, some comic— that they write and perform themselves. Like the old actor who "has tuxedo, will travel," they take their plays to schools, churches, clubs, hospitals, nursing homes and institutions of various kinds. (For a sampling of amateur and semiprofessional theater groups and for ideas on how to start your own, see *Sources for Further Information*.)

OTHER AREAS FOR SELF-EXPRESSION

Are you interested in poetry, not just reading it but learning to write it? Then you might want to take a poetry-writing course or read a book on how to write poetry. What about joining a dance group, a chorus or an orchestra? Senior centers and other groups are involved in organizing such activities (see *Sources for Further Information*).

Senior councils for towns in places like Huntington, N.Y. have started their own musical groups for people over 55. There are now groups of people playing both popular music, often the music of the Big Band era of the thirties and forties, and also more ambitious efforts—chamber and symphonic groups. Your music will be highly welcome in the schools as well as senior centers, nursing homes and institutions.

SPORTS

Until recently, older people were encouraged to exercise but to do it very, very carefully. Of course, all exercise should be done with some supervision, but if you're healthy, you can do more than just exercise in a gingerly fashion—you can compete, and seniors are starting to do just that.

Your neighborhood may well have a ski club for seniors as well as exercise classes. There is now a Senior Olympics program in many states, and it is intensely competitive. A comparatively new sports program called the Masters Sports is run in cosponsorship by the President's Council on Physical Fitness and the Amateur Athletic Union. It has competitions at different age levels, starting at 30 and going on to forever, in track and field events, swimming and, more recently, rowing. You compete with other Masters in your own age group. (See *Sources for Further Information.*)

SOURCES FOR FURTHER INFORMATION

Theater

Chicago's Free Street Too Company
59 W. Hubbard St.
Chicago, Ill. 60610
This company is an offshoot of the professional Chicago Free Theater Group. Seven players who did lots of diverse things in the years before they turned 65 now play all over the country.

New Dimension Theater
60 Sargent Drive
New Haven, Conn. 06511
Directed by Marilyn Jo Duchin, this amateur group

consists of seven actors, who hold workshops wherever they are wanted and perform plays, often of their own writing. They are all over 60. I know they are good because they have been on our own "Prime of Your Life" television program.

College Avenue Players
546 Crofton Avenue
Oakland, Calif. 94610
This is a semiprofessional group, which means they will take money when they can get it. They are managed by Stuart Kendell and have on staff four directors and teachers. There are 25 actors, from 55 to 84 years of age. They perform in colleges, senior centers, nursing homes and schools—anyplace in the Bay Area where they can get an audience. They train would-be actors in their workshops at no charge. The College Avenue Players have developed a series of programs for schools, their effort at bridging the intergenerational gap. The actors do sketches in which they play historical figures and do plays about the relationships between old and young people.

New Wrinkle Theater
25 Essex Street
Suite 1
Cambridge, Mass. 02139
Directed by Mark Rider, this group also trains would-be performers and is open to anyone. It is a touring theater of retired people who put on plays about the elderly, and they have been performing since 1975 on over 100 stages in the area.

Barn Players
5165 Mirriam Drive
Mirriam, Kan. 66203
This group of amateurs has its own theater and has performed before more than 5,000 people in six short

plays about the elderly and their problems. They require that anyone wanting to join their classes be 60 or over and "ready to add a little challenge and excitement to your life," not a bad prescription for an interesting existence at any age.

Acting Up
7900 North Nagle Avenue
Morton Grove, Ill. 60053
This group is led by Marcie Telander and is affiliated with the Oakton Community College. They are a company of 10, whose members are 65 and older. They have also made a documentary film called *Acting Up* that offers some helpful suggestions on how to start up your own acting company.

For specific information on how to start an acting company, write to the organization listed below. On request it will send you material on how to start a company and on where funding can be obtained, either from federal government sources or from private institutions in your area that have historically been friendly to such efforts. The organization will also send you a list of reading materials.
Center on Arts and the Aging
National Council on Aging
1828 L St., N.W.
Washington, D.C. 20036

If you don't want to write your own plays right at the very beginning, here are a few books which contain plays that will probably interest you:
Gray, Paul. *Dramatics for the Elderly*. New York: Teachers' College, 1974.
Cornish, Roger N., and Orlock, John. *Short Plays for the Long-Living*. Baker's Plays, 1916.
For a copy, contact Baker's Plays, 100 Chauncey Street, Boston, Mass. 02111.

A list of short plays on a variety of subjects pertinent to aging is available from:
Plays for Living
44 E. 23rd St.
New York, N.Y. 10010

Poetry-writing

Koch, Kenneth. *I Never Told Anybody: Teaching Poetry-Writing in a Nursing Home.* New York: Random House, 1977.

Dance

Dance Exchange
Liz Herman, Director
1443 Rhode Island Ave.
Washington, D.C. 20005

Sports

Masters Sports
Amateur Athletic Union
3400 W. 86th St.
Indianapolis, Ind. 46268

Senior Olympics
5670 Wilshire Blvd.
Suite 360
Los Angeles, Calif. 90036

CHAPTER
3

LIVING

DO YOU WANT TO STAY WHERE YOU ARE?

Do you want to remain in your present neighborhood and in your own home but think that your house is too large for just you and your spouse? Or too expensive to maintain? If so, then there are several options that will enable you to solve this problem. They are all discussed in the sections that follow.

CONVERT YOUR HOUSE INTO APARTMENTS

Converting part of your home into an apartment or even two apartments has a number of advantages. For example, it will not only reduce your expenses, but also produce an additional source of income. Furthermore, it could be reassuring to have other people around. And if you are going to be doing some traveling, you'll have a built-in house sitter, a definite plus in these lawless times!

However, there are some questions you should think about before going ahead with a conversion.

First, do you really want close neighbors in the house? How about children? Pets? Would it be necessary to share some facilities? How would such things as heat and light be paid for? What will conversion do to your taxes? And perhaps most important, what rent will you charge? The rent, of course, must be enough to cover your conversion expenses over a period of time and provide some income. But it doesn't pay simply to decide what you think the new apartment should get for you. Inquire of real estate people about the rents in your area.

Next, consider your community's local ordinances. Zoning laws may prohibit multifamily dwellings, or the local building code may require that major rewiring and replumbing jobs accompany any conversion. In some small communities the building inspector will visit your home, explain the code restrictions and give you an idea of how much your conversion plans will cost. In other areas you can learn the law from the city planning department or city hall, but you'll probably want to have an architect or engineer estimate the costs.

The costs of converting can vary enormously. Say you have a 1,200 sq. ft. two-story home with both upstairs and downstairs plumbing already installed. To convert it into a downstairs apartment for yourself and an upstairs apartment for rental, you may need to do as little as wall off the stairwell, provide a second-floor entrance and install upstairs kitchen facilities. The average cost of this minimal conversion, according to the University of Illinois' Small Homes Council, would be between $4,000 and $5,000 in late 1980. Since the average rent at the same date was hovering around $230 per month, it would take about 17 to 22 months to pay back the costs out of rent alone. Maintenance expenses must be added to your costs, of course, but such expenses are also deductible from your federal income tax. In addition, you get a deduction for "depreciation" on the rental portion of the home. To calculate the depreciation, you figure the value of the rental portion of your home, generally based on the percentage of house rooms included in the rental apartment. Multiply this number by the appraised value of the house, then divide by the number of years of useful life left in the home (usually 25 to 30 years). The resulting figure equals the depreciation deduction you can take for each of these years.

While a conversion that costs around this minimum amount can be both financially and socially rewarding, higher costs make the option much less attractive. Some jurisdictions may require that you bring the whole building "up to code" when you convert only a portion. If you have an old house, you may end up rewiring and replumbing the whole house! Your town may also require that separate utility lines and meters be installed for each apartment. Costs skyrocket when such improvements are made, so be sure to learn your local building code's requirements before you start.

BUILD ANOTHER HOUSE

A home is such a precious asset these days that all possibilities should be carefully explored. For instance, if your property is large enough (again, you have to consult your local authorities about zoning laws), you might give some thought to building another house on it, one that would be smaller and more economical. This could have other advantages. We talked of privacy. With a small house, or bungalow, of your own, you could preserve that privacy. A bungalow would also enable you to rent all of your old house, which will probably leave you better off financially than renting out part of it.

The cost of building a small home may be prohibitive, however, even when you already own the land.

At the end of 1980, costs for material and labor averaged about $60 per square foot nationwide, and usually even higher for homes less than 1,000 sq. ft. If you constructed an 800 sq. ft. bungalow on your own property, you'd probably pay more than $48,000! If you rented your original home, you might get back the cost of constructing a new bungalow within 10 years, but you would have to tie up a lot of capital in the new construction.

This being the case, you might consider cheaper kinds of new housing: mobile homes or fabricated housing. Again, be sure to check your local zoning ordinances since they may prohibit these forms of housing. Mobile home prices averaged only around $19,000 in 1980, and prefabricated housing only $23,000. Mobile home living is discussed in more detail later in this chapter.

HAVE AN ENERGY AUDIT

No matter what you want to do with your present house in terms of staying there or moving, it will be to your advantage to have an energy audit and to make any recommended improvements. If you remain in the house or rent some or all of it, such improvements will save you a considerable amount on energy costs (see Table 6 on p. 142), and if you decide to sell, they will increase the value of the house. Right now, for example, you may be sending quite a bit of money right up the chimney because of a lack of double windows, insufficient insulation in ceilings and walls or a heating unit that does not function at top efficiency. (For example, see Table 7 on p. 143, which shows how improving the efficiency of an oil-fired furnace can save you money.) Don't throw up your hands and say who can afford such things. The federal government provides a tax break for improvements ranging from installing insulation and storm windows to improving the efficiency of your home heating unit. The dollar-for-dollar tax credit amounts to 15 percent of the cost of improvements or $300, whichever is less. In addition, various states have their own laws to assist you in making such improvements.

To give yourself an idea of what energy-saving repairs your home may need, complete the Energy-Saving Checklist (Table 8 on p. 143). Also, while we're talking about energy savings, don't forget your large household appliances. See Table 9 on p. 147 to get an idea of just how much their operation can cost you each year.

CONSIDER A REVERSE ANNUITY MORTGAGE

If you want to stay in your own house but don't want to convert it into apartments or build another house on the property, then you might want to consider a reverse annuity mortgage as a way of providing you with additional income.

Reverse mortgages work in two ways. The simplest arrangement goes like this: you sell your house in return for monthly payments continuing until the full purchase price has been paid, but you are guaranteed the right to live in the house for the rest of your life. A more convoluted system involves your taking out a mortgage from a savings and loan association. As the association sends you monthly "mortgage" checks, it gradually acquires ownership of the house. It gets both principal and interest payment by selling your home when you die.

The advantage to a reverse mortgage is the substantial increased income it provides. "Why keep all that deed equity," the argument goes, "when you can turn it into current income that lets you enjoy the rest of

Table 6

HOW AN ENERGY AUDIT CAN SAVE YOU MONEY

Energy Conserving Action	Annual Dollar Savings (Current Prices)		Volume of Fuel Saved Winter (Cubic Feet)	Cost Estimates Based On	Estimated Costs	Years to Recover Investment	Yield on Investment	
							Present Costs	With Inflation
Install Storm Windows on all Windows	From:	$65	24200	Do-it-yourself	$375 to $420	5.1	20.0%	23.9%
	To:	$80	29900	Contractor	$525 to $570	7.0	14.0%	17.6%
Install 3–4 Inches (R-11) More Ceiling Insulation	From:	$50	18900	Do-it-yourself	$160 to $240	3.8	32.0%	35.4%
	To:	$65	23400	Contractor	$225 to $290	4.5	24.5%	28.1%
Install 5-7 Inches (R-19) More Ceiling Insulation	From:	$65	23100	Do-it-yourself	$290 to $350	4.5	24.0%	28.1%
	To:	$80	28500	Contractor	$350 to $400	5.1	20.0%	23.9%
Install 7-9 Inches (R-22) More Ceiling Insulation	From:	$65	24100	Do-it-yourself	$320 to $400	4.9	22.0%	26.0%
	To:	$80	29700	Contractor	$350 to $465	5.7	19.0%	23.4%
Install Storm Doors on all Doors	From:	$ 9	3100	Storm Door(s) would save energy but would not be economically justifiable at the present time				
	To:	$11	3900					
Daytime winter thermostat setting is currently at or below the recommended level.								
Set winter thermostat at 60 degrees night	From:	$30	10400	Thermostat adjustment is a recommended, no cost action.				
	To:	$35	12900					
Set winter thermostat at 55 degrees night	From:	$50	17900	Thermostat adjustment is a recommended, no cost action.				
	To:	$60	22100					

Source: Illinois Institute of National Resources

The above chart is an example of the kind of energy audit your local utility can do for you. It shows something like the average savings a small homeowner might expect. The recommendations are for a one-story 1,400-sq. ft. home in the Chicago area, an area that approximates the national average climate.

Table 7

DOLLAR SAVINGS PER $100 OF ANNUAL FUEL COST ACHIEVED BY IMPROVING EFFICIENCY OF AN OIL-FIRED FURNACE						
From Original Efficiency of				To an Increased Efficiency of		
	55%	60%	65%	70%	75%	80%
50%	$9.10	$16.70	$23.10	$28.60	$33.00	$37.50
55%		8.30	15.40	21.50	26.70	31.20
60%			7.70	14.30	20.00	25.00
65%				7.10	13.30	18.80
70%					6.70	12.50
75%						6.30

Source: U.S. Department of Energy

Table 8

Energy-Saving Checklist for Home Builders, Buyers, and Owners

Building Shell	Yes	No	NA
1. Are storm windows and storm doors installed?			
2. Are window panes and frames properly caulked? Do windows open for natural ventilation?			
3. Are exterior doors weatherstripped? Are door frames caulked?			
4. Are ceilings and walls insulated to the highest level recommended for your geographic location?			
5. Does the home have a vapor barrier in the walls to prevent water vapor from passing through and condensing into the insulation?			
6. Are floors insulated over unheated basements, crawl spaces and garages?			

	Yes	No	NA
7. Do basement walls contain 2″ × 2″ furring with R-7 insulation?			
8. Have you considered 6″ walls with studs on 24″ centers to allow maximum space for insulation?			
9. Has a clock thermostat been installed to reduce, automatically, evening temperatures?			
10. In colder climates, is window space on the north side of the house at a minimum?			
11. Is the home efficiently shaped to limit heat loss, avoiding L-, T- and H-shaped configurations?			
12. Does the house have an overhang for the south wall that will protect it from summer sun but allow exposure to winter sun?			
13. Does the fireplace have a heat exchanger to collect unused heat?			
14. Is the fireplace a high-efficiency type with a tight damper?			
15. Is fluorescent rather than incandescent lighting used in the kitchen and bathroom?			
16. Are outdoor gas lamps essential for safety or merely decorative?			
17. Does the landscaping shade the house in summer and let in winter sun?			
Appliances	**Yes**	**No**	**NA**
1. Do appliances have the highest Energy Efficiency Rating?			
2. Is the hot water heater well insulated? Is the water temperature at a reasonably low level?			

Heating, Ventilating, and Air Conditioning	Yes	No	NA
1. Are hot water pipes or hot air ducts insulated in unheated passages?			
2. Are air leaks in ductwork sealed?			
3. Are exposed hot water pipes and hot water storage tank insulated to reduce heat loss?			
4. Have you considered a heat-recovery pipe that preheats outside air with exhaust air from the ventilation system?			
5. Are window or whole-house ventilating fans adequate for comfort?			
6. If home has air-conditioning units or a central compressor, are they shaded from the sun to increase efficiency and reduce energy use?			
7. Does cooling equipment have the highest Energy Efficiency Rating?			
8. Is cooling equipment the smallest size possible to do the job adequately?			
9. Is the heating system the most efficient? Is it the appropriate size? Oversized systems waste a great deal of energy. Is the oil furnace serviced regularly?			
10. Do heating and cooling systems provide for continuous fan operation, which often provides comfort without using the full system capacity?			
11. Does the attic have 1 square foot of ventilation for each 300 square feet of ceiling? This reduces the air-conditioning load, and should be done even with insulation having a vapor barrier in the ceiling.			

	Yes	No	NA
12. Have fuel costs and supplies been evaluated to select equipment and fuel on a lifetime cost efficiency basis?			

Source: U.S. Department of Energy

your life." The drawbacks are three: first of all, to take advantage of a reverse mortgage, you must usually sell your home at a price lower than current market value. Second, you have no further income nor equity if you should outlive the time it takes to pay off the agreed purchase price. Finally, you are liquidating a steadily-appreciating asset you might otherwise have left to your heirs. At least one company is trying to overcome the second drawback by coupling a reversed mortgage agreement with a guaranteed lifetime annuity, but the high cost of doing so makes it possible only for men over 65 or women over 70. In general, the reverse mortgage is a good idea only for those who must increase their immediate monthly income or for people who, having no heirs, want to "make hay while the sun shines."

As of this writing, a reverse mortgage can be obtained by people living in California and Ohio. But interest in it has been growing, and soon it may be available in your state. Look into it.

SOURCES FOR FURTHER INFORMATION

Your Present Property

Tax Information on Selling Your Home, IRS Publication #523.

For information about what selling your present home will mean to your tax situation, obtain the above publication from any IRS office. Check your tele-

Table 9

Average Annual Energy Consumption and Cost Estimates for Major Appliances
Unit efficiency

Appliance	High		Low	
Electric (at 5 cents/kWh)	kWh	Cost, $	kWh	Cost, $
Air conditioner				
Room, 10,000 Btu/hr, 750 hr	645	32	1,400	70
Central, 30,000 Btu/hr, 1,000 hr	3,000	149	5,769	287
Clothes dryer, 416 cycles	880	44	960	48
Clothes washer, electric water heater, 416 cycles	1,250	62	1,440	71
Dehumidifier, 20 pints/ day, 1,300 hr	485	31	618	24
Dishwasher, electric water heater, 416 cycles	1,240	69	1,780	87
Freezer, 16 cu ft				
Chest-type, manual defrost	807	40	955	48
Upright, manual				
Manual defrost	919	46	—	—
Automatic defrost	—	—	1,643	82
Furnace, 50,000 Btu/hr, 2,080 hr	23,360	1,152	23,360	1,152
Heater				
Space, 1,000 watt, 1,600 hr	1,600	—	1,600	—
Water, 64.3 gals./day	6,020	300	7,400	368
Heat pump, 50,000 Btu/ hr, 2,080 hr (efficiency varies with climate and dwelling design)	9,395	467	14,655	728

Average Annual Energy Consumption and Cost Estimates for Major Appliances
Unit efficiency

Appliance	High		Low	
Electric (at 5 cents/kWh)	**kWh**	**Cost, $**	**kWh**	**Cost, $**
Lighting	900	45	1,100	55
Oven, microwave, 600 watts	80	4	140	7
Range, conventional, 30-in. oven	675	34	825	41
Refrigerator-freezer, 17 cu ft, automatic defrost	1,008	50	1,908	95
Television				
Black & white, 19 in., 2,200 hr	107	5	150	7
Color, 19 in., 2,200 hr	170	8	366	18
Gas (at 37 cents/therm)	**Therms**	**Cost, $**	**Therms**	**Cost, $**
Clothes dryer, 416 cycles	45	16	65	24
Furnace, 50,000 Btu/hr, 2,080 hr	1,003	390	1,360	488
Heater, water, 64.3 gals./day	345	126	460	168
Range, conventional, 30-in. oven	60	23	130	53

Source: U.S. Department of Energy

Use the table above to estimate how much you may be spending each year to operate your large household appliances. If you have to replace a major appliance, to save energy and money over years of use, check the energy-use label on different models of the appliance and compare efficiency. In operation, different models of the same appliance may use widely differing amounts of energy.

phone directory under "United States Government" to see if there is an office near you. If not, write to the national office at the address below:

Internal Revenue Service
1111 Constitution Avenue NW
Washington, D.C.

COST OF LIVING AND YOUR HOME

For valuable information on this subject, write to the following organizations for their pamphlets:

U.S. Department of Housing and Urban Development
451 7th St., S.W.
Washington, D.C. 20410

American Association of Retired Persons (AARP)
1909 K St., N.W.
Washington, D.C. 20049

Write to the organization whose address is listed below and ask for its publication *Your Home and Your Retirement.*

Retirement Living
150 E. 58th St.
New York, N.Y. 10022

Canadian Sources

A good summary of all available statistics on the elderly—where they live, what kind of homes they own, how they cope financially etc.—is *Canada's Elderly*, published by Statistics Canada, Catalogue Number 98-800E, March 1979. It is available from:

Publications Distribution
Statistics Canada
Ottawa K1A 0T6

For information on federal assistance for housing, such as the Neighborhood Improvement Programs or the Residential Rehabilitation Assistance Program, write:

Canada Mortgage and Housing Corporation
Canadian Housing Information
373 Sussex Drive
Ottawa, Ontario K1A 0P7

DO YOU WANT TO MOVE OR RELOCATE?

Despite all the information on what older Americans are doing and where they are doing it, the statistics show that most of us, 83 percent according to the U.S. Bureau of the Census figures for 1979, spend the years after 65 in the home we lived in before reaching that age. Another 9.6 percent did move, but only to someplace else in the same neighborhood. Only 7.4 percent of the people 65 and over actually moved out of state. Nor were the next youngest group (ages 55–64) much more inclined to wander. Only about 20 percent of them moved. It would seem, then, that most of us are more comfortable in areas where we know people and are known and in a house or apartment that has memories for us.

However, if you are intent on moving or relocating, consider whether you want to rent or buy; your college-age children, if any; the type of housing you want and whether you'd like to relocate to one of the Sunbelt states or abroad. The following sections discuss these points.

Other considerations that you may want to think about before moving or relocating to a different state are climate, living costs, medical care, population concentrations by age groups and crime. You'll find state by state statistics on climate and living costs in the tables provided in this section.

SHOULD YOU RENT OR BUY?

Would you rather be downtown or down home? A playgoer or a gardener? A world traveler or a local political activist? Assuming you can afford to move and want to, these are the kinds of choices you face in deciding whether to rent or buy. In spite of soaring mortgage costs, it is probably still as cheap in the long run to buy as it is to rent, but when you buy, you face the prospect of tying up substantial amounts of cash that you won't get back until you sell. Upfront costs are quite high for buyers: downpayments usually run from 10 to 30 percent of total purchase price, and settlement costs, including real estate taxes, mortgage discounts and title search, can run as high as another 10 percent of the purchase price. Owners' continuing costs include monthly mortgage payments and maintenance expenses. When you rent, on the other hand, you generally pay only rent and monthly utilities. Though owners get a tax break for mortgage interest costs, the total investment value of their property may not surpass that of the spare capital a renter has available for investment in a high-interest savings account.

In other words, the buyer will usually give up something in cash flow in return for the pleasure and security of ownership. Buyers have a stake in their home and a sense of community. They may spend pleasurable hours tending the garden, improving the house or working with local homeowner's groups. The renter has more liquid capital and, consequently, may find it easier to raise funds for travel or frequent cultural enjoyments. In addition, renters may have more flexibility when it comes to living in urban areas. Only the rich can afford to buy a city townhouse, but people of more moderate means can often rent in the same areas.

Another increasingly popular urban option is cooperative ownership, an arrangement halfway between renting and buying. Under this scheme you buy shares in a cooperative, which is usually a consortium of residents in an apartment building. Your "shares" give you the right to occupy your apartment, and you pay a monthly maintenance charge, mutually agreed upon by members of the "co-op," to cover the expenses of maintaining the apartment. You get equity and tax advantages without having to put down as much as you would for outright ownership and without having to arrange your own maintenance. (For further information on co-ops, see "Apartments: Condominiums and Cooperatives.")

The younger you are, the more likely you will be to want to build up equity by buying your own home; the older you are, the more you'll want to keep your assets liquid, perhaps by renting or entering into some cooperative arrangement. Such a general rule, however, shouldn't be applied indiscriminately, especially in a high-inflation era. Evaluate your own situation carefully, considering the following factors: prevailing mortgage rates, any special rates you may be eligible for, rate of appreciation of home values in the area where you might buy and rent levels in that same area. A helpful government publication, *Rent or Buy?*, shows how to compare the financial advantages of the two options for any situation (see *Sources for Further Information*).

YOUR COLLEGE-AGE CHILDREN

I don't know why, but there seems to be an automatic assumption that people of retirement age just don't have children, that is, younger or teenage children. But, of course, this isn't so and will probably be less so in the future because many women today are putting off having children until they're in their late thirties.

Because costs become so important during retirement years, if you want your children to go to college, this may very well affect where you decide to live. The fees levied by our better private universities these days are calculated to drive to despair even younger parents with healthy incomes and years of productive work ahead of them. For older parents schools like Harvard, Stanford and MIT are really out of the question. And even scholarships may not help the older parents' plight. For example, if you are close to retirement and your income is still quite large but will soon shrink, you'll need savings in some form or other to send your child or children to college. You may not be able, at your age, to borrow on the open market for your child's education without putting a serious dent in your retirement income.

Certain changes in the eligibility rules for government-sponsored grants and loans may make it easier for older parents to send their kids to college. Anyone can get a Guaranteed Student Loan (GSL) at a low nine percent interest rate, and the government pays all the interest until the student finishes school. Under the 1980 amendments to the Higher Education Act of 1965, parents will be able to take out additional loans for their children and pay the same nine percent interest rate. But mom and dad must start paying the loan back within 60 days; if they should die before it's all paid back, the government will pay the outstanding amount.

The federal government also administers outright grants called Basic Educational Opportunity Grants (BEOGs) or Pell grants, named for Sen. Claiborne Pell of Rhode Island, who first proposed them. Eligibility is determined according to a complex formula that takes into account a family's total assets, discretionary income, number of dependents and number of children in college. You can get the appropriate forms for finding out if you're eligible from a college admissions office, or you can write to Basic Grants, P. O. Box T, Iowa City, Iowa 52243. In general, it's worth applying if you have a four-person family with one child in college and have a gross income under $25,000. If you qualify, your child could receive as much as $1,900 or 50 percent of his or her college costs, for the year 1981–82. Maximum scheduled amounts and percentages are slated to rise each year thereafter. Beginning in the 1982–83 academic year, the formula will change, to make it easier for middle-income families to qualify. Starting with applications for that year, families will not have to list the equity in their house as part of their assets. This change should be particularly helpful to older people with college-age children since such parents may have a comparatively small income and a lot of equity built up in their house.

Other grants and loans are administered by the states or by the universities themselves. For information on the Supplementary Educational Opportunity Grants (SEOG), the National Direct Student Loan (NDSL) and the College Work-Study (CWS) programs, consult the college's financial aid department. State Student Incentive Grants, funded by the federal and state governments, are available from state financial aid departments. To find the appropriate agency in your state, send for the U.S. Department of Education's *Student Consumer's Guide* (see *Sources for Further Information*).

You might also consider state and city university systems. In states like California and New York, there are truly excellent schools within the state's own educational system and the fees are far more affordable.

Some cities, too, have colleges and universities of their own.

Tuition charges will differ from one state to another, so look into them before you move. Also, check how long you have to be a resident of a city or state before your child can be admitted to college at in-city or in-state tuition rates. I know one family, well into middle age and with a flock of children approaching college age, who moved to New York quite simply because the state university system is both good and within their financial grasp.

And don't feel that you will be denying your budding genius the best opportunity in life by choosing a state school system. The days when you almost had to be an Ivy League graduate to make it big in business or one of the professions are, fortunately, long gone.

WHAT TYPE OF HOUSING DO YOU WANT?

Living in your own house has advantages—privacy and pride in your home, among them—but as you grow older, the advantages, both financial and social, often diminish. Friends and neighbors move away or die, and the expense, in money and time, of maintaining a large home may grow onerous. For those who can no longer afford the old homestead or who feel they're rattling around in it, we'll examine in this section an array of communal living arrangements and lower-cost home options.

Retirement villages vary greatly in price and services, but these generally offer a more manageable living space, congenial social environment and cultural and recreational activities. Congregate homes are often cheaper to live in than detached houses and can offer the convenience and comfort of a few close neighbors without the sense of isolation a retirement community may foster. Cooperative apartments, condominiums and hotels, also run the gamut of prices and services, at best offering cheaper accommodations, worry-free maintenance and desirable urban locations. For those who want a rural or at least suburban lifestyle but who don't like communal arrangements, a mobile home or prefabricated house can offer a comfortable and affordable alternative.

RETIREMENT VILLAGES

When I first became involved in the program that has the same name as this book, I thought the idea of people moving into a retirement village or any other setting where there were no young people and certainly no children was a terrible notion, just as I thought retirement itself was a surrender and therefore intolerable. But having looked at some retirement villages and talked to people who prefer living in them, I've come to a more tolerant conclusion—who am I, or any of us, to tell others how to live? And since we live in a youth-dominated world which, for the most part, has decided that the experience and knowledge we have acquired at such expense over the years has little meaning or value, then why not separate ourselves? Why not spend our time talking to people who care about what we have to say? The argument is made that all the generations need one another. We will be happy to recognize that need when the younger ones acknowledge it. Does living with the young keep us young? Maybe. But at one retirement village, I met a lot of older people zipping around tennis courts, whacking the heck out of golf balls, painting, woodworking, gardening and Lord knows what else— and they didn't seem to need rejuvenation.

Are retirement villages a good thing? It depends; it depends on what you want, how much you have to spend and a whole host of other things, which I'll now discuss in more detail.

Retirement communities are like snowflakes: no two are alike. They may be rural or suburban; have staff doctors, a complete hospital or nothing but a first-aid station; offer individual, condominium or cooperative ownership or even simple rental; consist of apartments or semi-attached or independent houses; provide a social hall, dining room, swimming pool, tennis courts, golf course, private lake, private theater, shuffleboard, lawn bowling, mineral baths and/or heated walkways. What all of the reputable ones offer are a stable community of older people (usually age 45 and up) and a security system designed with elders in mind. If you have more than $20,000 to invest in housing, want to live entirely among your peers-in-age and appreciate the kind of security that runs each of your visitors through a checkpoint, then a retirement community may be for you.

Costs depend largely on the services offered and the size of the dwelling you choose. Life-care communities offer the most thorough medical care and are often, therefore, among the most expensive. They provide a guaranteed lifetime residence and medical services, usually in return for a hefty entrance fee plus monthly payments. The once-popular life-care plan under which an elder would surrender *all* of his or her assets in return for guaranteed services for life is no longer widely practiced. The type of dwelling in life-care communities varies from hotel rooms and apartments to clusters of separate cottages. Medical services vary widely, and you should be absolutely sure *which* services are guaranteed by your monthly fee before you sign up. Be aware that most communities exclude pre-existing health problems from the plan's coverage. Entrance fees for a single man age 65 who is planning to occupy a studio apartment range from around $10,000 to $35,000, and even higher for luxury accommodations. These fees are usually figured on the basis of your life expectancy, so the fee may vary according to your age on entering and your sex. Monthly fees show an equally wide range. A high-quality life-care community in Pennsylvania, for example, charges $640 per month for a studio apartment; for your money you get maintenance, house cleaning, all meals, transportation, unlimited nursing and doctor's visits by a staff physician. Life-care housing offers relative independence coupled with ready health care. Many are also well equipped with recreational and cultural facilities. You are buying only the use of the facilities, however, so you have no equity in the property. Your union or church may have information about life-care communities it sponsors, and a directory listing 100 such communities nationwide is available from Kendall-Crossland (see *Sources for Further Information*).

Older retirees tend to opt for life-care communities; younger and more active people may choose a retirement village where gracious living, culture and/or recreation are the strong points. Costs at such places vary even more widely. Condominium ownership is the commonest form of arrangement, though cooperative ownership and outright ownership are sometimes used. Regardless, the resident still pays a monthly fee for use of the community's facilities. The cost of housing averages between $20,000 and $70,000, though luxury accommodations start at about $45,000 and go as high as $400,000. Monthly fees go from as little as $4 to more than the fees of an average country club (over $100). Often, homes with lower purchase prices require higher monthly fees. So when you compare costs, be sure to take monthly fees into account.

Since entering a retirement community involves such a significant investment, it's best to go in with your eyes wide open. Make a personal visit to the villages you contemplate joining, compare the facilities and costs and talk to the residents of each. While you're there, check to see if any residents are planning to sell their living quarters. If a spouse dies or a couple tires of the homogeneity of village living, the owner or owners may be willing to sell the dwelling for a price lower than that for units bought direct from the developers.

Whether you buy from a resident or the company, make sure you know exactly what you've bought. Under the commonest condominium arrangement, you own the space you live in, and you pay a monthly fee for the use of the community's facilities plus property taxes. The term "condominium," however, is often used loosely, so have a lawyer look over your contract and explain to you the exact extent of your ownership and rights. If the village is still under construction, you should exercise even greater care. Find out if your down payment will be held in escrow until satisfactory completion of your dwelling. Also, ask whether the developer or the resident's association will hold title to the community facilities. If the developer intends to turn over operation of the village to the residents' association, make sure there are plans for an orderly transition. Finally, have your lawyer learn whether or not the developer has secured loans to build the community by offering residents' homes and properties as collateral. Occasionally an unscrupulous developer may go bankrupt, leaving the residents to pay his outstanding debts.

Two other matters to look into are transportation and community rules. If the development is spread out over many acres, make sure there are regular buses connecting your home with community and recreational centers. Also, find out about transportation to the nearest shopping areas and cities. All retirement villages have some ground rules, ranging from prohibition of children in swimming pools to controls on the color you paint your house and the way you plant your garden. Since some of these may be distasteful to you, be sure to find out about them before you buy.

A *PRIME* LOCATION

One of the largest concentrations of older people in the country is to be found in and near Ocean County, N.J. Out of a population of approximately 300,000 people, over 82,000 are in the senior citizen category. Why this particular place? Phil Rubenstein, an outgoing, frank type who put in long years with the federal government, heads the extensive county program for elders. He speculates that this area is attractive to many people because, to begin with, it is near the ocean. People, particularly city people, associate the seacoast with good, clean air and therefore good health. Equally important, it is still close enough to New York and Philadelphia so that many of the residents do not feel divorced from their urban roots. They can visit when they like. What's more, the chances are good that living in Ocean County will make it possible to see quite a bit of children and grandchildren. This wouldn't be possible if they simply cut loose and moved to the Sunbelt.

Cost was an important factor, too. Land here was comparatively inexpensive, and there has been a tendency to cluster. One retirement village built here in the 1960s attracted others. Their existence was responsible for new programs so that there are now 110 senior clubs in the county. There are five Outreach programs and nine nutrition centers where, under the Older Americans Act, those wishing it can get a hot meal every day.

Most of the elderly in Ocean County need no help; only six percent fall into the indigent category. Some live in Holiday City, whose neat cottages are side by side on small plots now costing about $40,000 or more. Or in one of the three Leisure Villages, where the cost of buying a home currently runs to something over $60,000.

There are class distinctions here, no doubt about it. Places like Leisure Knolls have attractive one-floor homes set among trees,with guard houses and medical personnel on site. Constant patrolling protects the privacy of the residents and unannounced and unsponsored visitors are not welcome. Publicity is equally unwelcome. And one can see why. Here there are such amenities as tennis courts and a small lake—just for the residents. Their clubhouse provides excellent dining facilities for those wanting to get away from home cooking, but not too far away. The clubhouse bulletin board lists meetings of clubs, lessons, trips to points of interest. Places like this are a social ghetto from one point of view. From another, they are retreats for those who think they have had enough of the outside world's blows and who now are quite content to enjoy the leisurely, comfortable company of people like themselves.

Not very far away are two other substantial retirement communities: Rossmoor, where homes can range, according to the advertisements, from $52,900 to $117,000; and Clearbrook, a bit younger but built along side with the same price range. Rossmoor presents a colonial approach, reflected in the design of both the main buildings and the homes, some of which are individual, some in two-story buildings. Clearbrook tends toward contemporary. Rossmoor's population is WASPish, Clearbrook has mostly Jewish residents.

Not everyone in Ocean County's retirement villages is elderly or even retired. There is a nationwide tendency for such villages to spread their wings over a somewhat more diverse population whose principle point in common is that while children are welcome as visitors, they are not permitted as residents. So on any given day, there are people getting up to take the bus to work in a nearby town or even in New York. These tend to be somewhere in the area of the lowest acceptable age category, which is 48 at Rossmoor. And there are other residents heading off to the golf course, which is the core of this community or at least so it seems to a visitor.

PRIME-OF-YOUR-LIFERS

Walter and Frances Weiner

Walter Weiner used to work in public relations, and he still goes into the city to do some consulting work. Frances Weiner was a school teacher. Walter was 72 and Frances a bit younger when I talked to them. They are two of 2,700 residents of Rossmoor retirement village in New Jersey. The setting is comfortable and gracious. So are they. The Weiners complement one another. They tend to finish each other's sentences without even being aware that they are doing so. That's how comfortable they are together. And, apparently, they are just as comfortable with the life they have made here:

JM: Why live here?
WW: You have a certain psychological security from these outside destructive forces like in the suburbs where we used to live. We

had hotrod kids going through and kids
coming in having picnics on your lawn at
odd hours of the day and night . . . and we
don't have that here. Most of the people go
to bed early, which we do, and get up at
regular hours, and it seems to work out
well.

JM: But why live in this particular place? This
locality? Does it have to do with family?

WW: We still go to Westchester to see our former
friends who stayed there. And we have a
daughter and son-in-law and three grandchildren who live fairly close, and we see
them. I would say a good half of the people
who come to Rossmoor have lived in this
general area.

Walter works part time partially to keep
himself busy but also because of the sear-
ing effects of inflation; the money his part-
time consulting work brings in has now become important. A lesson here. When you
get older, even fairly generous pensions
and annuities start to look uncomfortably
small as inflation gnaws away. A double-
hip operation stopped Frances' tutoring at
the local schools. But she's active. She's
taken up golf. She plays bridge and sees
her friends. She's second vice-president of
the Garden Club.

JM: But what do your friends in the community
do to keep themselves busy?

WW: They play golf. They play bridge. They
play billiards. They play. . . .

JM: They play?

WW: They play. And that's all they want to do.

JM: Are they happy playing?

WW: I know they don't want any responsibilities
at all. I spoke to a very good friend of ours.

Mentioned some situation where something needed to be done. And he said, "Oh,
I don't have anything to do with those
things anymore. I worked very hard for 54
years"—he was a very successful business
man—"and I don't want any more troubles.
I don't want any more anxieties," he said,
"I've had it. I've done my share in life, and
this is it. I don't want to be bothered." And
it's a perfectly legitimate attitude on his
part.

JM: Does this mean there are people who stop
reading the papers, watching the news,
who just withdraw?

WW: This is one of the symptoms of old age that
you have to watch out for, really, the withdrawal from the world. And this is one of
the things you have to catch yourself on because sometimes it's very easy to crawl into
a shell and stay there and just say to hell
with it. But that's very common, and I know
that many, many people outside Rossmoor
stay in their house and don't go out.

APARTMENTS: CONDOMINIUMS AND COOPERATIVES

Buying an apartment is attractive to elders who
want the cultural advantages of city living but who
balk at pouring large amounts of money down the
drain in rent. Both are cheaper than buying a house,
besides those who sell homes to move into a condominium or cooperative apartment may be able to pay
the cost easily. People who need to take out a mortgage, however, will be in trouble, as long as rates remain at their historical peak. Federal Housing Admin-
istration- (FHA-) backed mortgages, which had

offered rates as low as four percent for qualifying elderly people, were cancelled as of October 1980, and
as yet no program has replaced them. Straight FHA-
insured mortgages are still being offered—at 13½ percent in December 1980—but you must have all the
qualifications for an ordinary mortgage in order to get
them and it is still up to the lending bank whether or
not to offer them. A new kind of mortgage, the Shared
Appreciation Mortgage (SAM), may provide a break
on mortgage notes, but in return you'll have to pay the
lender part of the profit when the place is sold. Note,
too, that buyers of cooperatives, since they're purchasing shares in a corporation rather than the dwelling
itself, can't get a mortgage at all! They must instead try
to get a personal loan, usuallly at a couple of points
above the current mortgage rate.

Cooperatives have other disadvantages vis-a-vis
condominiums. Co-op owners buy the number of
"shares" allocated to their apartment. Condominium
owners buy the apartment itself. Taxes and maintenance costs are shared proportionately in a co-op,indi-
vidually in a condominium. If one tenant should fail to
pay his or her share in a cooperative, the charge to the
other tenants must be increased to make up the deficit. Moreover, there are usually more "strings" attached to co-op ownership. You may have to get co-op
approval before you sell, rent or bequeath your apartment, and there may be limits placed on the kind of
internal modifications you can make.

Whether you buy a condominium or cooperative
apartment, exercise the same care in making your
choice as you would in moving into a retirement village. Make sure that your down payment is protected until the premises are completed to your
satisfaction. Ask for the bylaws, prospectus and sales
contract; make sure there are no rules offensive to
you, and have your lawyer do the same. Finally, try to
find out what major construction or renovation pro-

jects may be planned for the near future. These could cause your monthly fees to skyrocket.

For many of you, buying a condominium will provide an ideal combination of security and convenience of lifestyle. Owning a condominium is less responsibility than owning most other forms of property and the unit forms a good investment, comparatively secure from the ravages of inflation. Also, real estate taxes and any mortgage interest payments are deductible from your tax returns.

In addition to this growing equity, living in a condominium gives you the advantages of special security provisions and recreation and social facilities. Only the upkeep of the unit is your responsibility; the maintenance of the building and grounds is covered by a regular charge made to unit owners, and in some cases the allocation of this fund is directed by the residents themselves. (If you want to investigate buying a condominium in greater detail, see *Sources for Further Information.*)

CONGREGATE HOMES

Congregate homes are becoming more attractive, particularly for people who are not secure enough to cope by themselves. Whether they consist of entire apartment buildings, small apartment groups or clusters of detached houses, they aim to provide low-cost rental housing plus essential services for people who need minimal day-to-day help. Some religious and fraternal organizations have become interested in sponsoring such homes as an alternative to nursing homes. In one type, people have their own rooms and cooking facilities, taking one meal, usually dinner, together and taking turns with the cooking. There is usually a resident with nursing skills to provide help if needed. Other congregate homes may offer housekeeping, personal hygiene and transportation services as well.

To be eligible to enter a congregate home, you must have an income no greater than 90 percent of the median income for your area. An individual in New York City, for example, needs an income less than $10,755 to qualify. Rural limits are usually more stringent, since costs are usually lower. A single resident of rural Orange County, N. Y. must have an income less than $9,630 to be eligible. To find the specific requirements for your area and the location of local congregate homes, call your local area office of the U.S. Department of Housing and Urban Development.

Congregate housing is an excellent alternative to nursing homes, permitting relative independence for those who may be forgetful or occasionally incontinent but not actually ill. The problem with such housing—and the reason there are still relatively few congregate homes—is cost. Federal programs can subsidize rent, but food service, housekeeping and other care must be paid for out of state and local funds. Legislators are still looking for a way to finance more congregate homes. Consequently, those that exist may have long waiting lists.

MOBILE STRUCTURES

I've grouped the following alternatives together because they are variations on the same theme. They are for people who have wanderlust, who want to travel from one place to another, who don't need a lot of room and who are prepared to emulate the turtle and take their house right along with them.

Should you decide there is a lot of gypsy in your soul and this is the style of living that suits you, then you will be faced with decisions about acceptable degrees of comfort and, naturally, luxury.

MOTOR HOMES

One nice thing about motor homes is that everyone is together all the time because the driver sits at the front of a big movable room. Everything is neatly and compactly fitted in: dining area, partially or wholly convertible to sleeping space; stove; small refrigerator; leak-proof shower compartment; bathroom and a tank of water. They are quite something to examine and the newer models are handsome. Picking up and moving on is simplicity itself with a motor home.

TRAILERS

Trailers are not terribly different from motor homes. They are pulled, either by your car or by a small truck, depending on the size which, like the interior accommodations, varies quite a bit, as does the price. The hauling aspect can be an advantage if you want to separate and get some privacy once in a while on the road and like the idea of simply parking the trailer on occasion and taking off.

CAMPERS

Campers can either fit onto a small truck or be a unit that attaches to it. Such arrangements are smaller and cheaper but have fewer amenities. Having examined a number, I would hesitate to recommend them as living quarters. They may do well for vacations, when the savings compensate for the lack of luxury. And even then, you'd better be prepared for a lot of togetherness.

MANUFACTURED STRUCTURES

Mobile Homes

Mobile homes, of course, are only mobile in the sense that they can be moved from one site to another. The chances are that such a home will be moved once, maybe twice. These are real homes. It is my conviction, reached with some reluctance, that such housing represents the future of inexpensive and much moderate housing.

The advantages of mobile homes are cost (about half the price of what the mobile home industry calls "site homes," see Table 10 on p. 171) and convenience. The industry's figures show that a mobile home with more than 1,000 square feet of space, fully furnished but without land will cost about $16,500. Rental space in mobile home parks costs from $50 to $200 per month, and there are about 12,500 such parks around the country now. Although it used to be quite difficult to get a loan for such housing, financing is now substantially easier to obtain because of the increased acceptability of such housing—the industry expects to sell 300,000 manufactured homes in 1980. (See Table 11 on p. 172 for financing requirements through the Veterans Administration and the Federal Housing Administration.) In recent years resale values have also risen.

Originally, mobile homes were small, rather dinky arrangements. They have come a long way, and today they are by far the largest category of low-cost housing sold. New ones range for as little as $7,000 to about $30,000 for a home that is actually made up of two or more units. They can, of course, be much more expensive than that—$100,000 or more.

Arguments against mobile homes, some of which are still valid, focused on such things as safety, but that is no longer a problem. Since 1977 all mobile homes have had to pass a rigid test devised by the U.S. Department of Housing and Urban Development (HUD). They must, for example, have such features as two exterior doors, separated from one another; in every bedroom a window that pops out; smoke detectors; a proper electrical system; anchoring devices; and materials in the construction to retard fires that might be caused by a furnace or a hotwater heater.

If the idea of mobile home living interests you, make sure that what you buy is large enough. As you get older, the chances are that you will spend more time in your home. Be certain it is a home in which you will be comfortable. Sizes are so varied that this should certainly not be a problem.

Anchoring the house to the land will be new to you. Whether you buy the house for property of your own (in which case find out if the zoning laws permit it— often they don't) or rent space in a park, be sure your home is properly anchored. Manufacturers include instructions for proper anchoring with each new home. Be sure existing anchorage meets the manufacturers' specifications. This should be checked every six months.

When you buy, look for the HUD safety seal. It is supposed to be there. If you rent park space, be sure, as with all such matters, to go over the contract carefully. Also, walk around the place carefully. What does it have to offer in terms of recreation possibilities? Places to walk and sit? Enough space between homes? How much noise will there be? If you really want to know, check the place out about dinner time. As to the contract, be sure there are no hidden charges, that you know exactly how much you are going to pay and what you are going to get for it. And you'd be smart to check out the place with the local

Table 10

Cost and Size Comparisons of Mobile Homes and Site-Built Homes Sold°

Mobile Homes	1974	1975	1976	1977[1]	1978	1979
Average Sale Price (all lengths & widths)	$ 9,760°	$11,440°	$12,750°	$14,200°	$15,925°	$17,600°
Cost per Square Foot	$10.63°	$11.98°	$13.09°	$14.20°	$15.77	$16.76
Average Square Footage	910 sq. ft.	952 sq. ft.	966 sq. ft.	1,000 sq. ft.	1,010 sq. ft.	1,050 sq. ft.
Site-Built Homes Sold	1974	1975	1976	1977	1978	1979
Average Sales Price	$38,900†	$42,600†	$48,000†	$54,200†	$62,400†	$71,800†
Cost per Square Foot	$19.00‡	$21.10‡	$22.70‡	$25.35‡	$28.50‡	$32.00‡
Average Square Footage (living space)	1,670 sq. ft.	1,660 sq. ft.	1,710 sq. ft.	1,720 sq. ft.	1,750 sq. ft.	1,700 sq. ft.

°Includes furniture, draperies, carpeting and appliances but excludes land as well as costs of steps, skirting, anchoring and any other applicable set-up charges (approximately 15% of home cost).
†Excludes all furnishings; includes land.
‡Excludes furnishings, appliances and land.
[1]Restated from prior *Quick Facts* to be consistent with data series provided by the U.S. Department of Commerce.

Source: Manufactured Housing Institute

Table 11

FINANCING A MOBILE HOME THROUGH THE VETERANS ADMINISTRATION AND FEDERAL HOUSING ADMINISTRATION		
New Mobile Homes	**VA**	**FHA**
● Single-Section Term	No Maximum 15 years	$18,000 15 years
● Multi-Section Term	No Maximum 20 years	$27,000 20 years
● Maximum Guarantee	$17,500 or 50% of loan amount whichever is less.	See maximum loan amounts above.
● Furniture	Included	Included
● Rate Ceilings	14.5%	15%
● Down Payment	None required	5% of first $3,000. 10% over $3,000.
Used Mobile Homes		
● Single-Section and ● Multi-Section	Same as new mobile homes subject to VA's determination of reasonable value and estimated remaining physical life.	90% of appraised value of a used mobile home if the home was previously financed using FHA loan insurance.
Mobile Home Plus Improved Land		
● Single-Section Term	None 20 years	$23,500 20 years
● Multi-Section Term	None 20 years	$31,500 20 years
● Rate Ceilings	14% on home 14% on lot	14.5%
● Down Payment	None required	5% of first $10,00 10% over $10,000
Mobile Home Lots		
● Developed term	None 15 years	$7,500 10 years

Source: Manufactured Housing Institute

better business bureau.

Formerly, only mobile home parks, frequently oper-
ated by sharp dealers quite capable of inserting some
interesting zingers in rental contracts, would accept
mobile homes. And a customary demand was that if
one wanted to live in a park, the mobile home had to
be purchased from the park operator. The industry has
been trying to eliminate these shady characters and
claims substantial success. It is also true, especially in
new developments, that areas which formerly kept
manufactured homes out are starting to accept them.

FACTORY-BUILT HOMES

Prefabricated homes are much like mobile homes,
but they offer greater design flexibility. Most states
limit the width of an object that can be driven along its
highways to 12 feet. Even a "modular" mobile home
(having two or more parts), therefore, can't be more
than 24 feet wide. Because it comes in flat units, prefabricated housing escapes these load limits. You can
order prefabricated homes in virtually any dimensions
you choose.

You have a choice between two types of panelized
systems when ordering your home. An open-wall system offers pre-framed walls, but without outside wiring and insulation; a closed-wall system provides
complete walls, including all siding, insulation and
wiring. The latter costs about 15 percent more per
square foot, but unless you're a dedicated do-it-yourselfer, you're probably better off paying the added
cost.

A closed-wall system costs anywhere from $17,000
to $75,000 depending on the size of the home and the
materials chosen. Dealers usually include installation
as part of the purchase price. In comparing prices,
however, be sure to ask the dealer whether the price
includes the home's "mechanical core," that is, the

plumbing, appliances and heaters. Some closed-wall systems include this core; others do not. Also, the price of the home's foundation is seldom included. If you're buying a small home, count on an extra $2,500 to $7,000 for the cost of the foundation.

A useful introductory to factory-built homes is the *Guide to Manufactured Homes,* published by the National Association of Home Manufacturers. It includes sample floor plans and a directory of dealers and suppliers. You can get it for $4 from the National Association of Home Manufacturers, 6521 Arlington Blvd., Falls Church, Va. 22042.

THE SUNBELT STATES

The so-called Sunbelt states—the tier of warm-weather states anchored on the west by California and on the east by North Carolina—are (with important exceptions, such as fewer cultural amenities) basically cheaper, warmer and more healthful to live in than other areas of the United States. If the warmth of the Sunbelt calls you, be sure to check out the things of importance to you. A small house next to a sunny beach sounds great, but how about supermarkets? If you like theaters, libraries, music, you'd better check out what's available before making your move. Or if you are a city person with dreams of the peace and quiet of rural America, remember, it isn't always that easy to adjust to an absence of all the things you have grown accustomed to over a lifetime—yes, even the noise and bustle of the big city may have become a part of you.

There are books available that examine specific costs and you should know about them (see *Sources for Further Information*). But remember, costs are beginning to level out across the country, and while the Snowbelt may not be getting any cheaper, the Sunbelt is certainly getting more expensive as the population shifts in that direction.

When you think about relocating, ask yourself every question you can think of. If you are moving nearer to your children, would you really like to live where you can see them almost every day? Be frank with yourself. Would they really want you that close anymore? I hope the answer in both cases is yes. But it isn't always so.

If you're a Northerner, the social attitudes in most parts of all the Sunbelt states might require some adjustment on your part. For example, these states remain, by and large, quite conservative politically. This may not bother you at all. You may even find yourself in complete accord, but if you are to adjust successfully, it is important that you know what to expect.

Give some thought to the area's future. Our new oil laws favor states that are producers, and while California is not likely to become one of the cheaper places to live, oil money is likely to keep taxes down in Texas and Louisiana for a long time to come.

And also remember that the Sunbelt states, on the whole, have long recognized that older citizens and retirees are good citizens—they don't start crime waves and they are not a drain on local taxes because they don't have children to send to school anymore. A brief description of each Sunbelt state follows.

CALIFORNIA

What can anyone tell you about California that you haven't heard before? When you speak of climate, it offers almost everything from subtropical in the south to quite moderate temperatures in the northern part of the state. There is spectacular coastline, lush farmland and towering mountains, where the nights are chilly

Table 12

CLIMATIC DATA FOR SELECTED U.S. CITIES

City	(Ft.) Eleva-tion	Temperature °F				Precipitation		% Relative Humidity	Sunshine Hours	Wind Speed
		Winter	Summer	Highest	Lowest	(in.) Rain	(in.) Snow			m.p.h. Average
Albuquerque, N.M.	5,130	36.4	74.4	104	−16	8.06	7.0	50	3,408	8.0
Amarillo, Tex.	3,590	34.9	74.0	107	−16	20.99	20.1	—	3,495	12.5
Atlanta, Ga.	1,054	44.0	77.9	103	−8	49.75	2.3	72	2,776	9.9
Asheville, N.C.	2,192	39.2	71.6	99	−6	38.02	10.5	75	2,519	7.8
Bismarck, N.D.	1,670	12.0	67.3	114	−45	16.39	34.3	70	2,658	9.7
Boise, Idaho	2,842	32.5	69.8	109	−13	12.66	15.0	61	2,768	9.6
Boston, Mass.	15	29.7	69.4	104	−18	40.14	43.1	72	2,561	11.5
Brownsville, Tex.	16	61.2	83.3	104	12	31.05	—	81	2,723	10.6
Buffalo, N.Y.	693	25.5	67.8	97	−20	36.00	74.9	77	2,346	14.5
Burlington, Vt.	331	20.2	67.4	101	−29	32.30	65.6	72	2,144	10.2
Charleston, S.C.	9	51.3	80.4	104	7	45.22	.3	79	2,945	10.4
Cheyenne, Wyo.	6,144	27.1	64.2	100	−38	14.99	56.7	58	2,926	11.3
Chicago, Ill.	594	27.0	70.9	105	−23	32.81	33.4	73	2,645	11.0
Cincinnati, Ohio	761	33.6	75.1	108	−17	38.40	18.2	76	2,670	7.2
Cleveland, Ohio	787	26.7	69.9	103	−17	33.82	41.4	72	2,344	13.1
Denver, Colo.	5,221	32.1	70.2	105	−29	13.98	55.1	52	2,966	7.4
Des Moines, Iowa	800	24.0	73.6	110	−30	31.74	32.3	72	2,766	9.7
Detroit, Mich.	619	26.4	70.4	105	−24	31.47	39.7	74	2,367	11.0
El Paso, Tex.	3,920	46.6	80.9	106	−5	8.86	2.3	41	3,546	9.2
Fort Worth, Tex.	688	47.5	83.0	112	−8	32.16	0.2	67	3,610	10.3
Galveston, Tex.	6	55.6	82.6	101	8	46.55	0.2	80	2,850	10.7
Helena, Mont.	3,893	23.1	64.6	103	−42	12.69	54.4	60	2,666	8.0
Huron, S.D.	1,282	16.0	70.3	111	−43	19.51	28.2	—	2,856	10.9
Jacksonville, Fla.	18	56.6	81.2	104	10	49.74	—	81	2,802	8.8
Jackson, Miss.	316	49.5	80.8	107	−5	51.46	1.3	—	—	—
Kansas City, Mo.	741	31.9	77.1	113	−22	36.32	21.4	68	2,880	10.1
Knoxville, Tenn.	974	40.5	76.1	104	−16	48.10	9.4	73	2,603	6.6
Little Rock, Ark.	265	43.6	79.8	110	−12	47.61	4.8	71	2,831	7.5
Los Angeles, Calif.	312	56.4	69.5	109	28	15.40	T	68	3,217	6.1
Memphis, Tenn.	271	43.0	79.6	106	−9	47.66	5.2	71	2,808	8.5
Miami, Fla.	11	68.2	81.4	96	27	58.83	0.0	76	2,931	9.8
Minneapolis, Minn.	830	16.7	70.4	108	−34	27.19	41.1	72	2,614	11.2

*Less than one

T Trace

Elevation. The ground elevation at the Weather Bureau Office.

Temperature:

   Winter. The average of the daily maximum and minimum temperatures for December, January and February.

   Summer. The average of the daily maximum and minimum temperatures for June, July and August.

   Highest. The hottest temperature on record.

   Lowest. The coldest temperature on record.

Precipitation. Average annual.

   Rain. Includes actual rain plus the water equivalent of solid forms (hail, sleet and snow).

   Snow. Average depth of unmelted snowfall.

Relative Humidity. An average based on the 7:30 a.m. and p.m. records for all months.

Sunshine. Average annual hours.

CLIMATIC DATA FOR SELECTED U.S. CITIES

City	Wind Speed m.p.h. Highest	Clear	Pt. Cldy.	Cloudy	Rain	Snow	Thunder-storms	Fog	90° or Higher	32° or Lower	0° or Lower
Albuquerque, N.M.	68	197	114	54	50	5	43	4	49	126	1
Amarillo, Tex.	70	198	109	58	75	14	39	6	52	102	2
Atlanta, Ga.	52	129	108	128	122	2	49	20	57	43	0
Asheville, N.C.	40	122	131	112	134	25	55	31	4	82	—
Bismarck, N.D.	61	146	114	105	94	70	30	5	18	183	48
Boise, Idaho	56	124	95	146	93	14	17	17	40	120	1
Boston, Mass.	73	118	118	129	125	42	18	14	9	106	3
Brownsville, Tex.	80	112	146	107	75	—	26	14	104	3	0
Buffalo, N.Y.	73	74	130	161	165	98	30	12	1	128	3
Burlington, Vt.	54	73	111	181	148	48	29	9	4	148	19
Charleston, S.C.	81	130	134	101	111	*	56	14	27	9	0
Cheyenne, Wyo.	65	124	152	89	96	69	45	14	7	175	12
Chicago, Ill.	65	117	120	128	124	59	38	10	11	109	8
Cincinnati, Ohio	43	112	118	135	131	19	46	10	26	89	1
Cleveland, Ohio	61	90	121	154	154	45	35	5	4	114	3
Denver, Colo.	53	146	152	67	84	49	44	2	22	136	8
Des Moines, Iowa	50	124	118	123	104	50	46	6	24	128	16
Detroit, Mich.	—	97	124	144	134	38	29	11	9	124	4
El Paso, Tex.	63	216	112	37	50	2	29	1	88	44	*
Fort Worth, Tex.	55	158	115	92	76	4	49	6	90	29	6
Galveston, Tex.	71	148	123	94	99	*	49	18	13	4	0
Helena, Mont.	56	101	125	139	98	42	29	2	9	153	22
Huron, S.D.	63	136	132	97	94	—	38	8	24	169	35
Jacksonville, Fla.	58	125	142	98	121	0	77	11	59	6	0
Jackson, Miss.	—	—	—	—	100	—	—	—	—	—	—
Kansas City, Mo.	63	148	112	105	106	34	56	9	39	96	4
Knoxville, Tenn.	62	124	122	119	134	17	47	18	30	63	*
Little Rock, Ark.	49	141	107	117	107	7	58	9	51	40	*
Los Angeles, Calif.	48	179	128	58	39	*	5	24	14	*	0
Memphis, Tenn.	58	142	107	116	111	3	50	5	45	40	*
Miami, Fla.	123	101	151	113	134	0	69	2	6	*	0
Minneapolis, Minn.	65	104	114	147	107	71	39	8	14	147	30

Wind Speed:
   Average. Based on the records for all hours of the day and all months of the year.
   Highest. Maximum velocity for a five-minute period.
Days with Annual averages.
   Clear. Number of days that the average cloudiness does not exceed 3/10 of the sky.
   Partly Cloudy. Number of days that the average cloudiness is 4/10 to 7/10.
   Cloudy. Number of days that the average cloudiness is 8/10 or more.
   Rain. Number of days with 0.01 inch or more of rain.
   Snow. Number of days with 0.1 inch or more of snow.
   Thunderstorms. Number of days on which thunder is heard.
   Fog. Number of days with fog.
   90° or higher. Number of days with maximum temperature 90° or higher.
   32° or lower. Number of days with minimum temperature 32° or lower.
   0° or lower. Number of days with minimum temperature 0° or lower.
Source: U.S. Department of Commerce, Weather Bureau

CLIMATIC DATA FOR SELECTED U.S. CITIES

City	(Ft.) Eleva- tion	Temperature °F Winter	Temperature °F Summer	Temperature °F Highest	Temperature °F Lowest	Precipitation (in.) Rain	Precipitation (in.) Snow	% Relative Humidity	Sunshine Hours	Wind Speed m.p.h. Average
Montgomery, Ala.	201	50.0	80.8	107	−5	51.50	0.7	72	2,866	6.9
New Orleans, La.	8	56.0	82.1	102	7	60.27	0.2	78	2,642	7.8
New York, N.Y.	10	32.4	71.9	102	−14	42.99	30.9	70	2,685	14.8
Norfolk, Va.	11	42.5	76.9	105	2	42.25	9.1	76	2,735	11.4
Oklahoma City, Okla.	1,254	39.2	79.8	113	−17	31.65	7.6	68	2,999	11.1
Omaha, Neb.	978	25.3	74.9	114	−32	27.83	27.7	—	2,817	9.3
Pensacola, Fla.	11	54.2	80.4	103	7	58.60	0.1	78	2,914	10.4
Philadelphia, Pa.	26	34.3	74.1	106	−11	40.41	22.4	70	2,627	10.4
Phoenix, Ariz.	1,107	53.4	88.1	118	16	7.81	—	42	3,752	5.8
Pittsburgh, Pa.	1,248	32.0	72.4	103	−20	35.95	34.2	71	2,303	10.4
Portland, Me.	61	24.7	65.7	103	−21	42.16	70.6	72	2,586	9.9
Portland, Ore.	30	40.9	65.3	107	−2	41.62	12.9	73	2,155	6.9
Raleigh, N.C.	400	42.9	77.3	104	−2	46.56	7.6	75	2,724	7.3
Reno, Nev.	4,397	34.1	67.5	106	−19	7.16	28.6	53	3,370	6.9
Roseburg, Ore.	508	42.6	65.6	109	−6	32.28	5.9	74	2,293	4.3
St. Louis, Mo.	465	34.1	77.5	110	−22	39.23	17.5	68	2,693	11.0
Salt Lake City, Utah	4,260	29.8	72.7	106	−30	13.72	46.2	58	3,064	9.1
San Antonio, Tex.	782	54.1	82.9	107	4	27.09	0.5	68	2,721	8.3
San Diego, Calif.	19	55.7	67.0	110	25	10.03	0.0	71	3,015	6.7
San Francisco, Calif.	52	51.4	59.0	101	27	22.08	0.2	78	2,935	9.1
Sault Ste. Marie, Mich.	724	14.1	60.3	98	−37	29.94	79.3	80	2,125	8.5
Seattle, Wash.	14	41.8	62.9	100	3	33.33	11.2	75	2,049	8.8
Spokane, Wash.	1,954	30.0	67.3	108	−30	15.78	35.8	64	2,583	6.5
Tampa, Fla.	6	61.9	81.4	98	19	48.91	T	79	3,019	8.4
Washington, D.C.	72	35.6	75.0	106	−15	41.85	20.5	70	2,583	7.0
Wichita, Kan.	1,372	34.2	78.1	114	−22	30.13	13.7	67	2,827	12.6

*Less than one
T Trace
Elevation. The ground elevation at the Weather Bureau Office.
Temperature:
  Winter. The average of the daily maximum and minimum temperatures for December, January and February.
  Summer. The average of the daily maximum and minimum temperatures for June, July and August.
  Highest. The hottest temperature on record.
  Lowest. The coldest temperature on record.
Precipitation. Average annual.
  Rain. Includes actual rain plus the water equivalent of solid forms (hail, sleet and snow).
  Snow. Average depth of unmelted snowfall.
Relative Humidity. An average based on the 7:30 a.m. and p.m. records for all months.
Sunshine. Average annual hours.

CLIMATIC DATA FOR SELECTED U.S. CITIES

City	Wind Speed m.p.h. Highest	Clear	Pt. Cldy.	Cloudy	Rain	Snow	Thunder- storms	Fog	90° or Higher	32° or Lower	0° or Lower
Montgomery, Ala.	41	133	119	113	113	2	55	5	67	19	0
New Orleans, La.	66	119	139	107	119	—	74	15	53	4	0
New York, N.Y.	81	106	133	126	125	35	31	21	7	92	*
Norfolk, Va.	63	133	115	117	125	6	37	15	25	41	0
Oklahoma City, Okla.	57	163	109	93	83	6	44	8	64	70	*
Omaha, Neb.	73	132	120	113	97	22	41	8	30	120	14
Pensacola, Fla.	91	135	125	105	112	*	71	14	16	7	0
Philadelphia, Pa.	68	114	121	130	124	29	27	10	13	79	*
Phoenix, Ariz.	41	228	90	47	39	—	—	—	152	10	0
Pittsburgh, Pa.	56	85	129	151	149	64	40	24	16	102	2
Portland, Me.	48	130	109	126	237	37	15	28	3	135	6
Portland, Ore.	43	93	100	172	153	14	4	9	6	27	0
Raleigh, N.C.	56	133	114	118	120	4	41	12	37	50	*
Reno, Nev.	59	195	100	70	49	39	14	3	32	154	2
Roseburg, Ore.	38	110	121	134	134	5	2	47	15	33	*
St. Louis, Mo.	62	138	118	109	111	31	48	10	36	79	2
Salt Lake City, Utah	60	136	113	116	85	59	34	9	49	132	5
San Antonio, Tex.	63	133	132	100	83	—	35	16	104	12	0
San Diego, Calif.	44	180	109	76	46	0	3	21	1	0	0
San Francisco, Calif.	50	157	115	93	67	*	2	15	1	*	0
Sault Ste. Marie, Mich.	56	85	101	179	155	73	21	18	1	158	29
Seattle, Wash.	60	77	107	181	150	14	5	27	1	21	0
Spokane, Wash.	42	97	107	161	111	54	10	17	19	112	4
Tampa, Fla.	75	122	159	84	114	*	84	16	62	1	0
Washington, D.C.	53	126	120	119	124	12	32	11	26	83	*
Wichita, Kan.	68	161	113	91	86	12	53	10	52	93	3

Wind Speed:
  Average. Based on the records for all hours of the day and all months of the year.
  Highest. Maximum velocity for a five-minute period.
Days with Annual averages.
  Clear. Number of days that the average cloudiness does not exceed 3/10 of the sky.
  Partly Cloudy. Number of days that the average cloudiness is 4/10 to 7/10.
  Cloudy. Number of days that the average cloudiness is 8/10 or more.
  Rain. Number of days with 0.01 inch or more of rain.
  Snow. Number of days with 0.1 inch or more of snow.
  Thunderstorms. Number of days on which thunder is heard.
  Fog. Number of days with fog.
  90° or higher. Number of days with maximum temperature 90° or higher.
  32° or lower. Number of days with minimum temperature 32° or lower.
  0° or lower. Number of days with minimum temperature 0° or lower.
Source: U.S. Department of Commerce, Weather Bureau

and where, in season, snow can block passes and bring down avalanches. It is beautiful beaches and stark desert, culture and hoopla. California is everything you ever dreamed of, good and bad alike.

The state of California is a great place to live, as almost any resident will tell you with no pressure whatsoever. And it is ridiculous to make generalizations about the state, except one—you do not decide to live in California because it is inexpensive. As far as anything else, you can pick your own lifestyle and find it there, whether it be devoting your days to getting the ultimate tan in southern California or soaking yourself in the culture of San Francisco. But remember that warning—it's not cheap.

ARIZONA

Arizona isn't cheap either. But it also presents a variety of scenery. Except for sweeping ocean vistas, you can pretty well have your choice. Many people think of it as flat and dry. Much of it is. But there are lakes and forests as well as deserts. Almost everything you have in mind in the way of outdoor living is within easy traveling distance. However, there are major differences in climate within the state that you should investigate (see *Sources for Further Information*.)

If a heavy diet of culture is what you want, the Southwest, including Arizona, isn't going to match up to the big cities in the East or West, but that's not what most people go there for. It is not gentle countryside and this can frighten off Easterners used to less-obtrusive scenery and a greater concentration of people. But it certainly is spectacular. And it's friendly, too.

Getting back to costs. When you say Arizona isn't cheap, the comparison is with some of the other Sunbelt states. Compared to the Northeast, almost everything from housing costs to taxes are substantially lower.

NEW MEXICO

In New Mexico taxes and housing are lower than in Arizona. You can live quite inexpensively in this vast state. And if you like mountain country(and your doctor thinks such country is for you—it isn't for everybody), then you may be quite content in New Mexico. Distances are vast, however, and towns are few and usually quite small. As is true in any part of the country, if you want city life, you're going to have to pay for it. It costs more to live in cities because they have to provide services small towns do without.

According to Peter A. Dickinson in *Sunbelt Retirement,* New Mexico has not come as far as a retirement state as some of the others. With a smaller population, it has not attracted the same kind of medical care some retirees might need.

TEXAS

People transplant rather readily from California to Texas and vice-versa. It's easy to understand. The two states have a lot in common other than sheer size, particularly the "everything-is-possible" attitude that permeates the atmosphere.

Like California, generalizations are dangerous in discussing a state with as much variety as Texas. You can have a subtropical climate and Gulf breezes near Harlingen, way in the south. You can enjoy a dash of Hispanic culture and color if you chose the El Paso area, while remaining safely in this most American of states (ask anyone!). You can become part of the business hustle of the oil empire whose capital is Texas.

Or you can stand and look out on endless prairie horizons in the Great Plains area north of Midland and west of Wichita Falls.

The climate and scenery is quite different in the east bordering on Louisiana and in the west near New Mexico. It can be very hot a good part of the year in one portion, and there are parts of the state where blizzards are not unknown.

Much of Texas is not very impressed by culture. On the other hand, it has an important value in a place like Dallas, which, sad to say, is not one of the less-expensive areas in the state. Then too, much of Texas pursues a culture, in the true sense of the word, no less authentic for not being shared by Boston, New York and Chicago.

Taxes are low and will probably stay lower than in most states for a long time, mainly because Texas has so many money-bearing resources. Housing is comparatively inexpensive, too. There are good medical facilities in many of the state's cities and many organizations dealing with matters of interest to senior citizens, who have found Texas as hospitable as Texans like to think themselves to be. It is one of the major retirement states in the country.

ARKANSAS

This is a state with charms of its own, perhaps insufficiently appreciated. The climate is not as mild as in some of the other Sunbelt states, but much of the scenery is lovely, and the people are friendly. It is inexpensive here—taxes are low, and housing is comparatively cheap (nothing is truly "inexpensive" anyplace in these United States today). As is usual, amenities are more readily available in the larger cities, such as Little Rock. And as is also usual, it is more expensive to live in or near such places. Again, even with this caveat, metropolitan Arkansas is still quite a bit cheaper than most other places to the north.

Although it has no seacoast on which you can bask, there are beautiful lakes in the Ozarks, and a lot more people are coming to appreciate them. Arkansas lacks the warmth of the coastal Sunbelt states, but by and large, its climate is probably more moderate than that of most other states.

Are you a friendly, undemanding person who simply wishes to live in modest comfort with little need for theaters and a variety of good restaurants? Then Arkansas may well be just the right place for you.

LOUISIANA

You'll find no shortage of theaters and good restaurants if you choose to make the New Orleans area your home. Compared to the more Western regions of the nation, this is not a very large state, but the contrasts between the French-influenced southern part of Louisiana and the northern portion, which is more typical of the rest of the South, are startling.

Louisiana has much to offer retirees, including quite low costs for almost everything. This includes housing and food. You can choose the rural life, or you can opt for New Orleans or somewhere near it and still be spending relatively little compared to other parts of the country. New Orleans has considerable cultural life in any area that may interest you. It has a fine orchestra, and it has excellent jazz. Artists feel at home here, and perhaps you will too. Certainly the cost of things should please you, and in most portions of the state, so will the climate. Medical facilities and other services that are important to elderly people are not found in uniform excellence, and you cannot expect the food in Shreveport to match what you can dine on in New Orleans. But Louisiana welcomes older Amer-

icans and, with its variety of lifestyles, should have
something to offer almost anyone, except, I suppose,
snow skiers.

MISSISSIPPI

There is no city in Mississippi that can claim the
unique charm and culture of New Orleans, but that's
probably an unfair statement since there aren't many
places in this or any other country which can. The
coastal areas of Mississippi are attractive, the northern
part of the state probably less so. If you are not one of
those who can make your own entertainment, the state
will not have much to offer in the way of making it for
you.

The climate is largely good, though, and costs, as
compared to other states, are still quite low. It is uncertain whether they will remain as comparatively
low as they have been, however. In some of the Sunbelt states, oil and the tax structure surrounding it are
providing new revenue to keep taxation low. Mississippi is trying to raise its standard of living and is ear-
nestly making an effort to attract new industry, which
it hopes will be drawn by cheaper labor costs. However, industrialization inevitably brings higher costs
along with the hoped-for increased prosperity, and
this is bound to affect elders who come to the state. At
any rate, at this time Mississippi is a bargain and in
many areas a beautiful one at that.

ALABAMA

This state already has some of the industry that Mississippi is striving to get. The most popular areas for
retirees are on the Gulf of Mexico coastal portions.
Not surprisingly, these are also the more expensive

Table 13

HOW LIVING COSTS VARY AMONG SELECTED
U.S. CITIES
(U.S. Urban Average = 100)

Indexes of comparative costs based on a higher-level
budget for a retired couple
FAMILY CONSUMPTION

Area	Trans-porta-tion	Clothing	Personal Care	Medical Care	Other Family Con-sump-tion
URBAN UNITED STATES	100	100	100	100	100
Metropolitan areas...............	102	101	99	101	108
Nonmetropolitan areas	93	98	102	97	75
NORTHEAST:					
Boston, Mass.	98	101	96	99	113
Buffalo, N.Y.....................	108	100	99	96	110
Hartford, Conn..................	115	103	118	99	118
Lancaster, Pa....................	98	100	89	100	105
New York-Northeastern N.J........	99	99	101	102	115
Philadelphia, Pa.-N.J.	92	95	94	98	111
Pittsburgh, Pa.	102	99	98	97	111
Portland, Me.	103	101	89	96	109
Nonmetropolitan areas	99	96	103	98	79
NORTH CENTRAL:					
Cedar Rapids, Iowa	103	111	99	99	106
Champaign-Urbana, Ill.	98	117	100	100	103
Chicago, Ill.-Northwestern Ind.	95	109	100	100	109
Cincinnati, Ohio-Ky.-Ind..........	101	100	90	97	105
Cleveland, Ohio.................	103	104	109	96	111
Dayton, Ohio	99	96	92	98	109
Detroit, Mich....................	98	107	104	99	110
Green Bay, Wis..................	99	114	93	101	102
Indianapolis, Ind................	101	99	97	100	105
Kansas City, Mo.-Kans.	109	107	109	103	107
Milwaukee, Wis.................	99	104	94	97	105
Minneapolis-St. Paul, Minn.	102	108	102	97	109
St. Louis, Mo.-Ill.	115	100	89	97	102
Wichita, Kan....................	99	100	92	98	102
Nonmetropolitan areas	91	107	109	96	75

HOW LIVING COSTS VARY AMONG SELECTED U.S. CITIES
(U.S. Urban Average = 100)

Indexes of comparative costs based on a higher-level
budget for a retired couple
FAMILY CONSUMPTION

Area	Trans-porta-tion	Clothing	Personal Care	Medical Care	Other Family Con-sump-tion
SOUTH:					
Atlanta, Ga.	101	96	98	100	108
Austin, Tex.	101	95	89	100	106
Baltimore, Md.	103	97	106	102	108
Baton Rouge, La.	104	89	92	97	106
Dallas, Tex.	104	92	99	105	108
Durham, N.C.	101	94	94	104	105
Houston, Tex.	103	92	99	103	105
Nashville, Tenn.	101	111	89	100	104
Orlando, Fla.	98	89	89	100	105
Washington, D.C.-Md.-Va.	110	93	109	103	107
Nonmetropolitan areas	93	89	95	96	73
WEST:					
Bakersfield, Calif.	106	90	97	105	100
Denver, Colo.	100	106	99	99	102
Los Angeles-Long Beach, Calif.	113	97	99	107	102
San Diego, Calif.	104	94	93	105	102
San Francisco-Oakland, Calif.	118	104	115	108	108
Seattle-Everett, Wash.	103	99	100	102	108
Honolulu, Hawaii.	118	93	107	101	114
Nonmetropolitan areas	91	117	118	99	74
ALASKA:					
Anchorage	116	143	168	121	83

Source: Bureau of Labor Statistics

areas in which to live. On the other hand, they are still comparatively cheap. The winter weather is excellent, and the summer heat is alleviated by breezes from the sea.

Increased industrialization has given Alabama some of the employment problems experienced by the states to the north. By and large, though, it presents a Southern way of life, if that is something you think you would enjoy. Cultural opportunities are not extensive, although they are growing. Birmingham's medical facilities are world famous, and according to reports, their services in the areas most important to retirees are competent. Overall, Alabama has much in common with Mississippi, its next-door neighbor.

FLORIDA

Without a doubt, the most popular retirement state in the nation. What brings people to Florida is climate, a climate that is glowingly painted in real estate and airline commercials all over the country, except in California of course.

Florida almost exists for summer-style vacation and retirement, though the area around Miami is becoming increasingly important both in commerce and industry. Since Florida's main sources of income, other than its potent agriculture, are vacationers and retirees, every effort is made to keep these golden geese happy. Medical facilities are excellent. So are all kinds of warm-weather recreation. There are orchestras and good universities. Special attention is paid to elders, with retirement communities everywhere and good roads connecting them.

With all this, Florida remains substantially cheaper than most of the country if, of course, you avoid the play spots of the wealthy. Food, housing and clothing all cost less here, as they do in such places as the

southern part of Texas. On the other hand, if you have
a lot of money to spend, you can really do it in style.

There is no point in saying what part of Florida is a
particular retirement Valhalla. These days retirees
flock to all parts of the state. One word of caution,
though: people of similar backgrounds and, yes, reli-
gions usually do stick together here. The panhandle
portion of Florida is very much like Alabama, with the
same climate and the same social mores. It is definitely Southern, quite different from the other parts of
Florida, particularly the large urban centers to the
south like Miami, which has a much greater ethnic
and religious mix.

Florida won't offer you startling geography. It has
just what it advertises—clear, sunny skies and warmth.

GEORGIA

Georgia is a state of contrasts. Its capital, Atlanta, is
bustling, growing and ambitious for a lot more growth.
This region sees itself on its way to new and unprece-
dented progress. In cities like Augusta, however, the
graciousness of the Old South still prevails. And some
of the coastal cities are both historical and relatively
sophisticated. Farther to the west and up into the
mountains of rural Georgia, change has been slow.

Scenically, the state is often very beautiful. It is also
comparatively inexpensive and has become a haven
for many retirees from other portions of the country,
though it is not as popular as Florida. Climate and cost
are the attractions, but do not expect quite the every-
thing-for-the-tourist attitude that Florida maintains.

SOUTH CAROLINA

We are moving up the East Coast of the country
now, so naturally there is some change in climate.
Still, South Carolina and Georgia are much alike in

the same sense that Mississippi and Alabama resemble one another. The coastal climate is warmer, and the coastal areas are more accustomed to people of diverse backgrounds and travelers and hence somewhat more comfortable with strangers from the North.

South Carolina welcomes retirees, but it has been doing things in its own way for a long time now, and change does not come too readily. One important benefit of this attitude, however, is the state's deep involvement with its history, which has led to a conviction that beautiful old things should be cherished. So, in smaller towns as well as in the better-known large cities, particularly Charleston, there are historic districts and buildings lovingly preserved and a pleasure to live with on neighborly terms.

Costs remain low, unless you choose to live in one of the swank resort areas, such as Hilton Head, that have been developed in recent years along the seacoast.

You cannot swim every day of the year, not even on the coast, even though the Gulf Stream does pass close by. But you can do lots of other outdoor things just about all year-round. If you love country music, then your radio will be a source of delight. Otherwise, bring records. South Carolina still prides itself on being as Southern as a state can be, but it has been making earnest—and rather successful—efforts to attract Northern industry. Good medical facilities are not universal here, though Charleston is one of the leading medical centers in the country.

NORTH CAROLINA

North Carolina is the most Northern of the Sunbelt states, both in atmosphere and climate as well as geography. It is a beautiful state, with the majestic Appalachian Highlands in the west and the historic port cities on the coast.

In many ways, North Carolina is the most attractive of the retirement states. It has several important universities and cities that seem to be just the right size for both convenience and facilities. Medical care available to everyone, not just the elderly, is good in most places, excellent in some. The climate offers four seasons, though winter is almost invariably quite mild, certainly compared to the Northeast and the Middle West. Although it may not be as cheap a place to live as, say, Mississippi, it certainly offers more in the way of contrast. If you like things to do and some, but not too abrupt, changes in seasons, you would do well to examine North Carolina.

LIVING ABROAD

Do you have fond memories of trips to Europe? And vague remembrances about that delightful village you passed though in southern Italy? Along the Rhone of France? Or that marvelously scenic place in Andalusia, where the people were so friendly, and everything was so cheap?

Hold onto that last thought for a moment, and remember how long ago it was that you made that visit. It isn't so cheap now—especially if you are dealing in American dollars. Most of Europe, even the formerly inexpensive parts, such as Spain, southern Italy and Greece, cost, overall, just about what it costs to live in your own country.

Let us assume that cost is not all that important. You are looking for a different, somewhat exotic kind of existence, maybe in a quiet pocket of southern Europe. These places are charming, partially because they are so different, but perhaps more to our eyes than to those of local people who migrate in droves to the big European cities. If it's a small town you choose, I hope you have at least a smattering of the language. There are always enough English speakers to rescue you from the dangers of communication blackout in the big places. It isn't always so in the small ones.

Also, in a foreign country your notions of everything from what constitutes good manners to how food is cooked are likely to be different from the people into whose company you have entered. And remember, it is their country.

Take nothing for granted should you choose to live abroad. Your standards for medical care will be different and probably a lot higher. You are used to a country where, regardless of its cost, the standard medical care is as high as can be found anywhere in the world. Rural hospitals in many parts of Europe, however, are likely to prove quite a shock to you should you require medical care.

LIVING ABROAD—A PERSONAL EXPERIENCE

My bosses at NBC once sent me to head a news bureau in Rome. We—my family and I—decided to look for a house, a villa of modest dimensions rather than an elaborately modern apartment in town. We found just what we had dreamed of: a converted farm house a few miles outside of the city and only a few hundred yards off the Appian Antica, the old Roman road. In places, the paving stones that once rang to the clangor of war chariots were exposed. The catacombs ran beneath the route, and there was also a medieval tower whose walls practically oozed history. The drive into work each day would be a feast! And the house seemed just right, with a small fireplace,

an adequate kitchen and a charming dining room
with a long, solid refectory table. In a few words,
just what we wanted with the bonus of several
citrus trees, just outside our French windows, in
a cobbled courtyard, where the trickle of a Ren-
aissance fountain would give a feeling of cool-
ness on hot summer days. It was perfect! Perfect!

Well, perhaps not so perfect when we received
the rental contract and along with it the begin-
nings of our education. There were, it seems, two
contracts, one stating the amount of rent on which
we had agreed, the other the amount of rent the
owner of this development thought he'd like to
divulge to the authorities. Needless to say, the
amounts on the two contracts differed—substantially. I had to sign them both. Three months in a
foreign country and I was already a party to
breaking the law! When I feebly muttered something about wondering whether it was, you know,
alright, the agent, the lawyer, everyone including, I think, the agent's cat raised a collective
eyebrow at this painful breach of good manners.
When in Rome, I thought—and signed. It was
only the beginning.

Things, I am trying to say, are done differently
in different parts of the world. In Italy you do not
pay your own taxes in the way we do in this country; you certainly do not get the necessary documents and the scores of signatures needed on
them by yourself. These things are done by people who have made not only a science, but a living by knowing how to skirt, penetrate, bypass
and, if necessary, corruptly wheedle the pon-
derous bureaucracy that overlays everything. I
became convinced that if the system were simpli-
fied, half the nation would be on the unemployment roles. It is the way things are done.

Many other things are done differently. Order

something made and you will be told, with a magnificent sweeping Latin gesture, that it will be ready when you wish. Friday? "But of course," is the reply. Only it will not be ready on Friday, but telling you so would be rude. Maybe it will be ready Monday. Maybe the Friday after. You suddenly notice that there is no hot water in your charming new apartment. In this country, hot water is a separate item. Heating will probably be billed on a separate basis. Did you discover there are no closets? There rarely are. One buys them separately in Italy. And getting back to the matter of heat, in our charming home it was provided, when needed, by a coal furnace, the kind I personally filled and emptied as a boy. But this furnace was somewhat small for the size of the house, which meant that if not properly attended, it would give out around, say, 4:30 on brisk winter mornings. Have you ever built a fire in a coal furnace in a dank basement at 4:30 on a winter morning?

Mind you, these are not complaints. In time, we discovered how life is lived and adjusted to it. For my family it became a delightful experience, cut far too short, sad to say, by transfer elsewhere.

My experience is that settling into a foreign country, even one you have good feelings about, can be divided into three possible stages. You arrive, live initially in a hotel, are charmed; you move into your own home, are shocked, possibly horrified, because nothing works the way it is supposed to work, the people don't do things the way you are used to having them done (deep down inside you think they don't do them right and are probably stupid and certainly stubbornly mired some place about three and a half centuries back, but you don't want to look like a bigot so you

don't say so) and everything is a mess. This is the cru-
cial time. If you can survive it, shrug and concentrate
on all those things you like while slowly acclimating
to what may be perhaps a sensible adjustment to existing conditions, rather than stupidity, then you can
move into stage three and have that great experience
you anticipated.

SOURCES FOR FURTHER INFORMATION

Moving or Relocating in General

There are many sources of information to go to if
you're interested in moving or relocating.

Have you thought about a small town or rural area as a
retirement alternative? There are special provisions
and some helpful breaks for people who choose such a
lifestyle. You can find out what this alternative can offer you by writing: Farmers Home Administration,
U.S. Department of Agriculture, Washington, D.C.
20250. If there is an office of the Department of Agriculture near you, write to it.

Every state has an office of aging, and they will be
happy to send you information about living in other
states.

If you have a specific area in mind, write to the local
chamber of commerce. Remember, though that such
agencies are boosters by nature.

Don't neglect your own local sources. They include:
your church or any other group, social or fraternal, to
which you may belong. They have access to lots of

materials you may find useful. Your local senior center or office on aging. The savings and loan association in your own town about the value of your own home and/or the market in the area in which you live.

Some books on the subject in general, many of which can be found in your local library, are:

Buckley, Joseph C. *The Retirement Handbook*. 6th ed., revised by Henry Schmidt. New York: Harper & Row, 1977.

Dickinson, Peter A. *The Complete Retirement Planning Book: Your Guide to Happiness, Health, and Financial Security*. New York: E. P. Dutton, 1976.

Renting or Buying

A useful government pamphlet on the advantages and disadvantages of renting or buying is *Rent or Buy? Evaluating the Alternatives in the Shelter Market*. You can obtain it by writing to:

Superintendent of Documents
Washington, D.C. 20402

The Type of Housing You Want

RETIREMENT VILLAGES

The titles of the following books explain how they can help you in deciding on the most suitable retirement village:

Heintz, Katherine McMillan. *Retirement Communities—For Adults Only*. New Brunswick, N.J.: Rutgers University Center for Urban Policy Research, 1976.

Musson, Noverre. *National Directory of Retirement Residences: Best Places to Live When You Retire.* New York: Frederick Fell, 1975. (A revised edition is due in 1982.)

1981 Sunbelt Retirement Handbook. Highland Park, Ill.: Woodhall Publishing, 1980.

CONDOMINIUMS

Both of the following publications will answer many of your questions about buying a condominium. Obtain them by writing to the addresses given.

Questions About Condominiums
U.S. Department of Housing and Urban Development
Publications Division
Washington, D.C. 20410

Condominium Buyer's Guide
National Association of Homebuilders
15th and M Sts., N.W.
Washington, D.C. 20005

For yet more information and a complete listing of condominiums located throughout the United States, write to:

National Association of Condominiums
1121 Daywood Avenue
Washington, D.C.

To get an idea of the cost of buying a condominium and the facilities available, see the two complexes in Florida listed below. The prices given are, of course, subject to change depending on inflation and current real estate market trends. Contact the listed manager for up-to-date prices.

Alconbury Villas
1686 New View
Palm Beach, Fla. 37143
Manager: Ted Croot
Complex of 151 one-bedroom apartments ($13,500) and 200 two-bedroom apartments ($17,800–25,000). Laundry, shops, swimming pool, clubhouse and bowling alley. Ground care managed by residents.

Cambridge Condominium
601 Lennon Road
Largo, Fla. 33247
Manager: P. Nugent
Apartment building with 176 one-bedroom apartments ($23,990–27,000) and 80 two-bedroom apartments ($30,000–34,000). Ocean frontage, air-conditioned, kitchen appliances provided. Ground care organized by residents. Swimming pool, boating lake, clubhouse, and poolroom. Shops one mile away.

MOTOR HOMES, TRAILERS AND CAMPERS

Two associations offer services, including group insurance, trip routing and mail forwarding to their members. They also publish magazines. Membership dues run from $15 to $35 per year.

Family Motor Coach Association
8291 Clough Pike
Cincinnati, Ohio 45244

National Association of Trailer Owners
Box 1418
Sarasota, Fla. 33578

A reputable guide to the assortment of recreational vehicles on the market is the *Buyer's Guide to Recreational Vehicles*, available for $5.95 from your local bookstore or direct from Woodall Publishing, 500 Hyacinth Place, Highland Park, Ill. 60035. If you order by mail, add $1 postage.

MOBILE HOMES

For detailed information on mobile home living, the following organization is a good place to write or phone. It's a comparatively new organization and a very enthusiastic one. Lots of information is available.

Manufactured Housing Institute
1745 Jefferson Davis Highway
Arlington, Va. 22202
Telephone: (703) 979-6620

FACTORY-BUILT HOMES

For a free directory of manufacturers or a $4 booklet explaining prefabricated homes, write to:

National Association of Home Manufacturers
6521 Arlington Blvd.
Falls Church, VA 22042

Sunbelt States

If you are interested in a state-by-state breakdown (even community by community), from almost every point of view, I recommend this book:

Dickinson, Peter A. *Sunbelt Retirement: The Complete State-by-State Guide to Retiring in the South and West of the United States.* New York: E. P. Dutton, 1980.

Living Abroad

Smith, Martha Ligon. *Foreign Retirement Edens.* Austin: the Naylor Company, 1967.

PLANNING YOUR LIVING SPACE

Strangely enough, we tend not to give very much thought to our physical environment. Often we leave our homes just as they've always been or look at new quarters with the same eyes, searching for the same conditions that were appropriate when we were 30.

Don't. That deep chair may have gone through the years with you, but if you can't get out of it without struggling now, it can be a curse. Soft, dark lighting may be romantic at 25, but at 75 you can miss seeing things and get hurt bouncing off a sharp object you can't see. You need more light.

Light is increasingly important for us. This means that you should have good-sized windows in all rooms as well as proper fixtures. This is important so that you can see better not only inside your home, but outside as well. I don't know how people in high-rise apartments can solve this kind of isolation—but windows are for visual communication as well as light, even if it amounts to nothing more than looking out and watching other people go about their daily tasks. Do you like having indoor plants to lighten the winter days? Then make sure that there are broad spaces in front of those windows. And don't forget the importance of security. Is there a peephole that allows you to look out without having to open the door, or to let whoever is outside see you?

Look for the small but important conveniences. You may want to substitute door handles that have edges for round ones that may become harder to turn. Think of your living space as a machine for comfortable living. Stretching, bending, kneeling, even groping didn't bother you much when you were young. Had you been interested in convenience, you probably would have planned things more intelligently even then, but exertion is not important to young people.

They also do not have to worry as much about hurting themselves. HUD has sponsored a competition on comfortable and convenient living spaces for elders and has come up with some thoughts worth keeping in mind if you are remodelling your own quarters or seeking new ones. Here are some suggestions from the report.

If you are moving into smaller quarters and have a lot of furniture you hate to part with, look for rooms that have good wall areas and corners to give the maximum amount of space into which the furniture can be put. Make sure that access from one important area to another is direct and open—you don't want to be in danger of stumbling because you have to walk around too many things. Incidentally, rugs on polished floors are a rotten idea. Slipping and falling is far too easy. Wall-to-wall carpeting may never have appealed to you before, but think of it now, particularly between bathroom and bedroom. It's a blessing when you want to use the bathroom on a cold night and don't care to go around searching for slippers.

Remember to put things where they are convenient. I particularly have the television set in mind. A lot of the people who write about matters of interest to the elderly hate television and don't like even to mention it. I admit to a professional bias, but most of us know what a blessing the infamous tube is to elders, so be sure it is in a convenient place where the maximum number of people in the room can see it.

The kitchen becomes increasingly important. You may find yourself using it for snacking or small meals. You may want to do most of your eating in it. Under any circumstances, here as in everything in this living machine of yours, remember convenience. Be sure everything in the kitchen is easily reachable. This means good working space, next to the sink, stove, and refrigerator if at all possible. Can you sit while you work? You should be able to. Shelf space deserves a chapter of its own, but if you use your own good sense, you know that shelves way up or way back are a bad idea. You want them easily visible and within reach. Don't put shelves over the stove, for example.

DINING AREA

Your dining area will please you more if you can put it right next to the kitchen, or with an opening between the kitchen and dining area for easy passage of food. Also for companionship—people find all living spaces pleasanter in their older years if they can see others and be in contact with them.

BATHROOM

Bathrooms require special attention. Hot and cold water should flow through a single tap—it's harder to burn yourself with scalding water that way. Handholds in the bath and next to the toilet will be helpful as will a nonskid surface, that is, a ribbed one, in the bathtub.

OTHER AREAS

How about the areas just inside and outside your front door? Do you have a table or shelf inside? It's convenient to have some place where you can put things down and organize them, or reorganize them. Is there a closet? And a space convenient enough so that people can take off raincoats and boots without tracking up the whole place?

And, finally, how about the outer space? If you are going to be living in some kind of group development, make sure that there are places to walk and to sit.

Make sure that some kind of public transportation is convenient. And—security again—that you can see what is going on around you, where your neighbors live, and that they can see if anything is amiss around your place, too.

SOURCES FOR FURTHER INFORMATION

The National Safety Council publishes *Home Safety Briefs*, a set of three pamphlets, which explains how to avoid falls, fires and electrical hazards. The publication is free and can be obtained by writing to:

National Safety Council
444 North Michigan Avenue
Chicago, Ill. 60611

A useful personal manual entitled *Safety Guide* is available from the American Association of Retired Persons. For members, it is free; for nonmembers, it costs 25¢. It can be obtained by writing to:

American Association of Retired Persons
1909 K. St., N.W.
Washington, D.C. 20049

COOKING AND BUYING FOOD

COOKING

Our society is still sexist enough so that the very word "cooking" conjures up a vision of a woman in a kitchen. And it is true that even in families where both husband and wife work, it is the woman who still does most of the cooking. And that is not fair. Now, don't get me wrong. When I say unfair, I mean that obviously it is unfair to the woman unless the husband does some of the other household chores. But it is also unfair to the man because he is depriving himself of something that can be pleasant and which gives a sense of accomplishment. I speak from recent experience.

As a child I wasn't about to eat anything whose taste wasn't disguised by large quantities of applesauce. It must have been a grisly sight. Potato covered with applesauce. Vegetable smothered with applesauce. But, of course, as time went by, I discovered taste buds I never knew I possessed. And as more time went by, I realized that the only way I was really going to please those taste buds and their growing interest in new and piquant dishes was by cooking for myself. My wife is a fine cook but it bores her, so she doesn't waste much time on the new and different.

So this led to discovery number one, almost unbelievable! Take all the things the recipe says, put them together in the way they tell you to, and it works! Lesson number two: in addition to giving the fledgling cook a feeling of new-found power, it is fun. It's fun, that is, if you cook when you want to cook. I think that's the reason men are so often better cooks than women. Women have spent their entire lives cooking meals on this-is-my-job-so-let's-get-this-one-over-before-it-runs-into-the-next-meal basis. That feeling doesn't make for superb cooking. It does not bring joy. It makes for a what-can-we-get-from-the-freezer-meal-department attitude, and you can't blame the women.

When I started to cook it was interesting because it was new. And then it became fun to see what new concoctions I could come up with. The big thing, of course, is to start. How do you start? In my case, I began by looking at recipes in the newspapers, which are swamped with cooking recipes these days. Once I

learned the abbreviations, it was no big deal. I could
do it. Why not? I know how to read. However, let me
pass on a few tips that I've learned by trial and error:

1. Select a simple recipe to begin with—one that
   instructs you a step at a time rather than one
   that calls for three different things to be happening at the same time.
2. Get out every ingredient and utensil the recipe
   calls for beforehand. If you don't do a little advance organization, you might find yourself
   skidding around the kitchen like a pig on ice,
   picking things up and putting them down because they are not what you want, and just generally making a mess.
3. Believe your recipe, and don't attempt to im-
   provise while you're still a novice. These recipes really work, men.

Do all this, and once you've done it successfully, I
promise you'll be hooked. And in no time at all, you'll
be as big a bore as those guys at the club who tell you
just how they placed the ball on that dogleg to the left
of the 16th hole, describing your cooking triumphs
as though you were Escoffier himself.

PRIME-OF-YOUR-LIFER

Henry Creel

The author of *Cooking for One*, Henry Creel,
learned to cook in much the way I did. While

working for Shell Oil, he began to collect recipes
and make notes about the ones he liked, even—
unlike me—what he thought could be done to
improve them. (Don't you do that at first. I mean
it. You can create disasters by doing some of that
ad lib stuff when you're beginning. Believe me, I
know.)

Anyway, Mr. Creel kept on piling up recipes
and changing them until, voila, he had his own
book. He not only lives alone and cooks for himself, but he enjoys it:

HC: Well, if you have a nice little kitchen. And
     if you have a television. And if you have,
     maybe, a cocktail. And if you fix up some-
     thing good because, maybe, your stomach
     needs something by that time, it's very
     healthy. It gives you home life. I call it
     hearth, which to me, means home life.

     I live alone and have for a long time. And
     I enjoy my apartment, which is a very
     pretty little apartment, and the idea of fix-
     ing something, working a little bit, creating
     something in the kitchen and then having it
     for dinner and not having to go out but be-
     ing able to stay there, look at the television,
     something you want to see, turning it off
     and reading what you want after dinner, it's
     home life. I enjoy it.

     I don't particularly like getting up and
     going out and searching for this, that and
     the other. I'm the shy type. I don't even
     talk on the telephone very much as far as
     that's concerned. But to me, it's home life.
     It really is. It's economical. And it's
     healthy, the three H's, I call it.

JM: Which are?

HC: Hearth, which is home. Health. And Help.

JM: But, you hear people say, "What's the plea-
      sure in eating alone? I'd rather go out, even
      if it's only for a hamburger and a cup of cof-
      fee."

HC: Those people simply need education. First
      of all, if you like to eat, you can think of
      something and then make it. It isn't that
      difficult. The great satisfaction is to think of
      something good and then not just imagine
      it, but go into the kitchen and make it and
      then eat it.

      And, for me, he's right.

My colleague, Lew Davis, who goes around the
country demonstrating and lecturing about cooking
and food for the Ethan Allan furniture people (when
he's not doing our television show), thinks that meals
should be in the same category as entertainment. I'm
inclined to agree. When you read books about nutrition and diet, it tends to get pretty depressing. You are
given lists of things you absolutely have to swallow, as
though life would come to an end in one hour and
fifty-eight minutes if you didn't have your two glasses
of milk or their dairy equivalent before sundown. And
after I've attended a lecture on nutrition, I leave feeling convinced that one of the least enjoyable expendi-
tures of time in the world is eating and feeling absolutely certain that if I take one piece of pie my teeth
will immediately fall out and my brain will melt.

Lew's emphasis is a happier one. He quotes the famous French chef, Brillat-Savarin, who said happily that the last thing to go with us humans is our taste for food. Eating is a kind of ritual. A meal should be looked on as a civilized occasion for enjoying both food and, if you are in the mood, company. I like that approach better.

Thought of in terms of civilization, dinner should be the most important meal. Alas, nutritionally it is the reverse. Davis says (and the nutritionists agree) that breakfast is the most important meal, lunch next and dinner the least important. He likes to think of breakfast as king, lunch as prince and dinner as pauper. Nevertheless, meals as social events make sense. If you live alone, you might be discouraged at the very notion of cooking for yourself. But who says you have to? Why not get together with a few other people and each take turns cooking for the group? Cooking for five isn't really more difficult than cooking for one. And look at the dividends. You cook a full meal once in five days. You get to eat a number of dishes you might not otherwise meet up with, and you have companionship, all for the price of that one cooking session.

Cooking in larger quantities, even when you are only doing it for one or two, can also make sense. It is, after all, cheaper, and it becomes practical if you take what is not eaten at the end of the meal, divide it up into several portions, each sufficient for a meal by itself, and freeze it. Practically everyone has at least a small freezer these days. Make the most of it.

A lot is made of what you can save by eating less expensive foods. Considered by itself, eating cheaply is a depressing notion. But eating cheaply and well is another story.

BUYING FOOD

Food prices have not soared as much as housing or health care, but they certainly have risen dramatically, and it pays to be careful. But when one talks about saving, the association should be more with the process of shopping rather than with which meat or vegetable costs a few pennies more or less than the other. Shopping is where you can really save money, partly by what you buy, but largely by what you don't buy. Every time you go into a supermarket, you are engaging in a duel of wits with expert psychologists (the marketing professionals behind the supermarket concept) who want you to buy more, not less, and who want you to buy things you never even dreamed you wanted, not just things you need. Most supermarkets are laid out with this ongoing battle in mind. We want you to win, so here are some strategies.

MAKE LISTS

You need three lists. One of them is really an ongoing inventory—a list of what you have, both in the refrigerator and on the shelves. How many times have you returned home with, oh, a box of raisins, only to discover that there are three boxes already there? Or a head of lettuce, which can now snuggle down in the refrigerator with the two already there? Most of us don't go rooting around in the fridge. We just try to remember what we have and don't have, and we do it too late, which means after we're already in the enemy's own territory. Another strategem: when you put leftovers into a container, label it. Keep a roll of tape around the kitchen, and when you put something away, pull off a bit of tape, put it on the container and write "green beans" or whatever on it. Not hard, and a big saver. You know you can spend weeks without looking inside one of those containers.

List number two takes the most discipline. Keep an ongoing account of what things cost. Right at this minute you, like most of us, don't know what a can of green beans costs on the average. But if you start keeping this information in a notebook, you will soon reach the point where you know what things should cost you, which means you will then be that rare person who can go into a store, look at something, and say to yourself that it's too expensive. You can wait until you see it for less.

List number three contains the things you really need to buy, or that you intend to buy, which is not necessarily the same thing. Lists complete, you are now off to do battle.

OUTSMART THE SUPERMARKET

The first question here should be, what type of food store will you shop at? Not your local supermarket if you can possibly avoid it and if you want to reduce your food costs considerably. Rather, shop at food discount stores and/or food coops. Food discount stores are no-frill places, which means that they don't provide the customer services that regular supermarkets do. For example, there are no elaborate exhibits. Food is usually displayed in the packing case in which it arrived, the case being cut open and simply stuck onto a shelf. When your purchases are checked out, you will have to do your own packaging and carrying. By eliminating such customer services, the store reduces its operating expenses and can therefore discount prices. And this makes it possible for you to save also—from 10 to 30 percent on most purchases. Some of the items for sale may be brands with which you are familiar. Some will have unfamiliar names and plain labels that give little more than the size of the container and the identity of the contents. Don't let this frighten you. Wise consumers have discovered that the quality of such merchandise, while it may not be as fancy as some of the brand name items, is still good. There are lots of reasons for being glad you live in America. This is one of them.

Food coops can save you even more than discount markets, though you may be called upon to do a few hours work per month. Retail markets are in business to make a profit, so they take a mark-up over and above the costs of the goods they sell. Under the coop arrangement, the buyers go directly to wholesale outlets, purchase goods, and sell them to coop members at cost. Savings average 10 to 30 percent over an ordinary market. For maximum savings many coops have their own members volunteer to do all the shopping, manage the store and keep records. Others may hire people to perform these functions. Doing so adds to costs, but the savings are still significant.

If you have to do your shopping at a regular supermarket, here is where the battle between temptation and need begins. But armed with some advice and a strong will, you can not only win the battle but also save on your food bills.

The first thing to do on entering the store is to pick up your supermarket's store-coupon sheet, which advertises the weekly specials. If these are listed in your paper, then bring that along. Although the coupons may be part of the store's strategy to get you into the supermarket, the point is that there are special values here; you can't expect to have it all your own way. Forget the store's motives. Use the coupons.

RESIST IMPULSE BUYING

After you've picked up the store-coupon sheet, walk as firmly past the non-food items as ever Ulysses did when faced with the temptations of Scylla and Charybdis, by which I mean that unless you have already decided you want to buy plants, glasses or whatever other goodies are on display in this section, walk straight through to where the food is, looking neither to the right nor to the left. Remember, temptation is the enemy's secret weapon. And when you've made your way safely to the food section, you'll be faced with yet other temptations: enticing ready-prepared foods from soup to meat—nice, easy and time-saving, without question, but more expensive; chickens already cut up for you—anything somebody else cuts up involves paying somebody to do the cutting, and you'll be the one to pay the final bill. According to Lew Davis, cutting up chickens isn't hard. Your fingers will tell you by feel, where the outlines of breast, thigh and leg are. With a sharp knife and perhaps some shears, all you have to do is spend a few minutes cutting and you will get a lot back in savings.

Temptation will be all around you in many guises. Enticingly packaged breads, proclaiming their natural health. We make far too much of bread, at least as far as health is concerned. If you like those high-priced loaves because of the taste, that's one thing, but the most ordinary of white breads, soft or not, is packed with vitamins these days. The difference between this and the one with nothing but "natural" ingredients? Almost infinitesimal, according to *Consumer Reports*.

COMPARE UNIT PRICES

Because of advertising, you'll see products in the store that you know and that you'll be tempted to buy. But resist and examine. Look, for example, at the unit-price label (usually attached to the product shelf), that will tell you the actual unit cost of a product, and compare that unit cost with the unit cost of other products of the same type. For example, if an eight-ounce box of cereal is 64 cents with a unit cost of eight cents and a 12-ounce box of the same type of cereal is 72 cents with a unit cost of six cents, it's clear that the 72-cent box of cereal is the better buy because you're paying less per ounce or unit. Of course, with a little arithmetic, you can figure this out yourself without the unit-price labels. But to save time, shop at supermarkets that provide this customer service. In some states supermarkets are legally required to do this. (To find out whether supermarkets are required to do this in your state, call your local consumer affairs office.)

UNDERSTAND FOOD GRADES

Are you a snob about ratings on things like meat and eggs? You don't have to be, and you will save money if you're not. Government food grading systems were originally created to help wholesalers sort their goods. The grades refer to sensory characteristics like taste, texture, and color rather than to nutritional value. What's more, grading is entirely voluntary, and may actually add to the cost of the product, since the government charges private companies for the use of its grading inspectors and labels. A high grade assures you the product will be nice-looking and tasty, but a lower grade or no grade at all doesn't mean the product is in any way nutritionally inferior. Though many fresh foods are graded at the wholesale level, the only retail items on which they frequently appear are beef, butter, eggs and turkey. Only the last of these is cheap enough to make buying the top grade economical.

What you buy when you get meat rated USDA

Choice, the usual—forgive me—choice of most people, is meat which has more fat on it than meat rated only as "Good" which will be both leaner, and therefore better for you, and cheaper. Lower ratings do not mean less wholesomeness. Or that meat is older, or from an inferior part of the animal. It concerns only tenderness and flavor.

You can buy butter in three different grades (though your doctor may have suggested you switch to a low-cholesterol margarine). The main differences between grades AA, A and B are in their texture and sweetness. Grade B butter may have a slightly acid taste and has a less smooth texture than Grade A or Grade AA. It's cheaper than either of the higher grades, however, and just as nutritious.

With eggs, too, AA doesn't mean the egg is better than an egg that is Grade A or Grade B. If you are making an omelet, or scrambling your eggs, or using them for cooking, the lower ratings will save you money and do you fine—just as well, in fact. The higher grades are eggs with a more uniform appearance, but in cooking, what difference does that make?

UNDERSTAND LABEL INFORMATION

All processed foods—frozen, canned, ground, dried or whatever—must include a complete list of ingredients on the label. You'll always be able to tell just what—besides the "eight great tomatoes"—are in "that itty-bitty can." Such simple information can be quite useful, especially when the use of additives like sugar and MSG is becoming more and more common. Sugar may be all natural, but it's not all that good for you; so if you don't want extra sugar in your canned peaches, check the ingredients. MSG is a flavor enhancer that unfortunately gives some people a strange, prickly feeling on their necks when they eat foods treated with it. If you're such a person, the ingredients list will tell you what to avoid.

Any processed food claiming to be, say "Zippo! Wow! Extra energy! Full of vitamins!" must prove it by providing a breakdown of the product's nutritional contents right on the label. The government has developed a set of "Recommended Daily Allowances" (usually called U.S. RDAs) for the essential proteins, vitamins and minerals. Any food claiming nutritional advantages must list the U.S. RDAs of each nutrient by the percentage in each serving. This list of nutrients looks pretty foreboding on a label, but if you pay close attention to the relative percentages of protein, carbohydrates and fats, you should get a good idea of how accurate the product's nutritional claims are. For products not claiming special food value, the listing of U.S. RDAs is voluntary, but many manufacturers— particularly those with something to brag about, like milk and yogurt producers—voluntarily include the listing.

One piece of label information that is *less* informative than it looks is a stamp saying "inspected by the federal government." Companies sometimes use variations on this stamp as a marketing tool, implying that their bread is government-approved whereas the competitor's is not. In fact, all production of processed foods is subject to sanitation and wholesomeness laws enforced by the Food and Drug Administration, the U.S. Department of Agriculture and the U.S. Department of Commerce. The "government-inspected" stamp is a frill. The company pays to have a federal inspector grade the product, but the company simply reports that the product was "inspected." They don't even say what the results of the inspection were! The presence of this stamp is certainly no reason to reject a product; nor is it a reason to buy a product priced significantly above competition.

SOURCES FOR FURTHER INFORMATION

Cooking

Creel, Henry Lewis. *Cooking for One Is Fun.* New York: Quadrangle/The New York Times Book Co., 1980.

Buying Food

The organization listed below has excellent pamphlets on shopping and nutrition:

American Association of Retired Persons (AARP)
1909 K St., N.W.
Washington, D.C. 20049.
Check your local phone book. They may have a branch near you.

Information about consumer food cooperatives and how to start them is available from the following organization. Be sure to ask for material on Food Coops.

Cooperative League of the USA
1828 L St. N.W.
Suite 1100
Washington, D.C. 20036

Canadian Sources

For any information relating to consumer education, write:

Consumer & Corporate Affairs
Consumer Services
Place du Portage
Ottawa-Hull K1A 009

or

Consumers' Association of Canada
Head Office
200 First Avenue
Ottawa K1S 5J3

Many provincial governments also publish a newsletter that often contains a "Senior Citizens' Issue" column. Contact your local government offices to be put on their free mailing list.

GETTING FINANCIAL HELP

There are a number of programs available if you have severe financial problems. These are Medicaid, which I discuss in Chapter Five; food stamps; supplemental security income; welfare; and disability. The last four are dealt with in the following sections.

FOOD STAMP PROGRAM

The U.S. Department of Agriculture is responsible for the food stamp program; it is administered by state welfare agencies and actually run by the counties. Eligibility is determined annually, on a national basis, by calculating the average incomes needed for families of different sizes to purchase a cheap but adequate supply of food. Net income limits are fixed for families of each area: those above the limits receive no food stamps; those below the limits receive the coupons in proportion to how far below it their income falls. The 1981 limits are as follows:

1-person family	$316/mo.
2-person family	$418/mo.
3-person family	$520/mo.
4-person family	$621/mo.

Don't give up yet, even if your gross income is above this figure. Everyone is allowed a standard deduction of $85 from gross income plus a deduction of 20 percent of earned income. You can't deduct social security and pension income, but if you're over 60, you do get two special deductions. You can deduct all medical expenses above $35, and you have no limit placed on the shelter expenses you can deduct.

The formula for deducting shelter expenses works like this: first, subtract the standard $85 deduction and the deduction for earned income (if any) from your gross income. Divide the remainder by two. Any shelter expenses *above* that amount are deductible from gross income. Take an example: together, you and your spouse gross $500 each month, all from social security and pensions. First, take the $85 standard deduction. (Because you have no earned income, you can't take the 20% deduction.) Your adjusted income is then $415 per month. Dividing this figure by two, you get about $208. Say your shelter expenses (whether rent, mortgage payments, and/or utilities costs) amount to $350 monthly. Subtracting the $208 from $350, you find that you'll be allowed a shelter deduction of about $142! (Persons under 60 years old can only take up to $115 for this deduction.) Now let's figure your net income for determining eligibility. Even assuming you had no medical deductions, your net income is $500 *minus* $85 *minus* $142, that is, only

$273. If you're a family of two, that's well below the 1981 limit, so you're eligible for food stamps after all!

Just how much you'll get in food-stamp coupons depends upon how much below the limit you fall. If you were a two-person family making $400 *net* income per month, you'd get less than $10 monthly during 1981. The same family with *no* net income would get $128 per month. Our example family, with its $273 net income, would get about $46 each month. If you think you may be eligible, contact your county's social services or public welfare department. They'll assign a caseworker to help you fill out the necessary forms. The above figures should be valid for 1981 throughout the contiguous United States, but *not* in Alaska or Hawaii.

The Food Stamp Program is currently helping over 22 million people. It is significant that a recent study of over 500 elderly Americans indicated that only 12 percent of them received food stamps, although many more are eligible, with inflation sending the figures ever higher. In fact, although nobody has any firm figures, it is estimated that another six or seven million people have the right to get food stamps. The use of the word "right" is intentional because it is a right. The program was not started as a charity, but as a recognition that a large number of hard-working people don't make enough money to eat decently. This even includes some members of the armed forces.

It would, of course, be better if all Americans had enough money to eat decently and to live decently; since we have not yet achieved that state, however, food stamps make sense.

SUPPLEMENTAL SECURITY INCOME

For many of you, the amount of social security the government pays you is too little to live on. It was for precisely this reason that Congress created the Supplemental Security Income (SSI) program, which is administered by social security and which began operating in 1974. It covers people over 65 as well as the blind and disabled in all of the 50 states. Check with your local social security office to see if you qualify.

What happens is that if an individual has an income of less than $238 a month or a couple has less than $357, SSI will make up the difference. Many states supplement this support. In California, for example, state supplements mean that an individual over age 65 who makes less than $402 per month can qualify. Couples who qualify can get supplements up to $746 monthly. Be careful when finding out about state supplements, however. A few states demand a lien on the recipient's property before they'll pay the supplement. This can mean the state will take your property when you die! This allows the state to collect what they have paid you after your death. This is a rotten thing to do. We all want the feeling of passing on something to those dear to us and this certainly applies to that most important of all possessions, the home. But there it is.

WELFARE

Welfare general assistance programs should not be left out of our listing. These are mandated by the state government and run by the state or county. If you are desperately in need, and this can happen to anyone of us, then this is help to which you are entitled. There is a state or county welfare office near you. It is not unknown for Americans to go hungry, even desperately so, but the laws are made to prevent that from happening and when it does, something is wrong.

DISABILITY PROGRAMS

Disability may be of importance to you if you are still at work. Five states have temporary disability programs. They are California, Hawaii, New Jersey, New York and Rhode Island. Puerto Rico has it, too. Such programs providing quick help can be invaluable, since the federal disability program keeps you waiting for five months.

SOURCES FOR FURTHER INFORMATION

Food Stamps

Write or call your local social security or welfare office for information about food stamps.

For theoretical information on food stamps, the following book is useful:

Ball, Robert. *Social Security, Today and Tomorrow.* New York: Columbia University Press, 1978.

SSI

Your local social security office, the senior center in your area or your local office on aging can advise you on what you need to do to qualify for SSI.

DEALING WITH CRIME

Some cities are quite active in devising new programs for crime prevention (Seattle; New York City; Mansfield, Ohio—just to mention a few), while others offer little more than lip service. Maybe nothing more.

Programs have been sponsored with help from the Law Enforcement Assistance Administration in Washington, D.C., an agency that is under sustained attack in these money-conscious days. Still, there have been a number of interesting and fruitful approaches. A few are mentioned below. But to find out what programs are available in your area and for general information on the subject, see *Sources for Further Information* at the end of this chapter.

SELF-HELP PROGRAMS

The police, it is recognized, can't cover everything, even less so now that most of them patrol in cars rather than on foot, and police departments in many cities have been cut, ironically, at a time of rising crime rates. Still, you can do quite a bit for yourself. One approach that is increasingly popular calls for variations of the block-watcher theme. People watch out for one another. They usually go through a policy-administered orientation program on what to look for that might constitute suspicious behavior. In all such programs, they are asked to call a certain telephone number if they see anybody strange in the neighborhood acting in an unusual way. Some obvious things to watch for would be a stranger prowling around someone's backyard, using some device to get into a car that you know belongs to someone else or leaving a house loaded down with suitcases or household goods which people don't ordinarily carry around the streets. If you're interested in starting a neighborhood watch, you should check first with your neighborhood or block association. The association can request a meeting with police specialists and help publicize a gathering of the whole neighborhood.

MARKING HOUSEHOLD POSSESSIONS

Another program involves marking important household goods that have cash value. Television sets are a prime example. The police station will provide etching tools to put your social security number indelibly on your property, thus, it is believed, drastically reducing its resale value for a thief.

CASH FUNDS

In some cities cash funds have been established so that, should an elder person be robbed, there is immediate emergency money available. This can be very reassuring. One of the worst fears is knowing that if you are robbed, you may have nothing and be unable to get essentials, such as food, to keep you going. The reassurance that quick help is available can be important.

POLICE HELP

Many cities have police officers who specialize in helping older people and understanding how to talk to those who have been robbed. Many of us are so shocked by such an incident that even ordinary communication becomes difficult. It helps to have someone to talk to who is both knowledgeable and sympathetic.

And there are classes in what to do to prevent yourself from being victimized. Lectures on what not to do: for example, don't carry a bag slung over your shoulder—it can easily be ripped away. Ladies and gentlemen both, don't travel in difficult areas alone. Preferably, go in groups when you shop or attend social events; safety in numbers, remember? Such police lectures may also warn you about misguided bravery. The macho image is probably still with us all, regardless of the passage of years and of muscle. Most of the time, the temptation to get tough with someone half your age should be firmly resisted. A few dollars are not as precious as your life.

Still another important preventive program is a safety audit of your home or apartment. Local police officers in many cities can be made available to spend an hour or two going over your apartment and pointing out what can be done to make it more secure.

Fears of being victimized by crime are higher among elders for obvious reasons—their diminishing capacity to resist violence being first among them—but here is a fact that may offer you some reassurance: according to evidence presented to the House Select Committee on Aging, the crime rate against senior citizens is actually six or seven times lower than for persons aged 20 to 34. One possible explanation: older people don't wander around as much.

SOURCES FOR FURTHER INFORMATION

The reading list given below is mostly from materials commissioned or collected by the Law Enforcement Assistance Administration (LEAA), U.S. Department of Justice, Washington, D.C. 20531. You can write for free copies of these publications at the addresses given.

The Community Anti-Crime Program: A Preliminary Assessment of the Concept. Contact W. Victor Rouse, Principal Investigator, American Institutes for Research, 1055 Thomas Jefferson St., N.W., Washington, D.C. 20007. Tel: (202) 342-5000.

"Grandma Helps Fight Crime: Senior Power, Pow!" *The Police Chief*, vol. 44, number 2. Write to International Assn. of Chiefs of Police, Inc., Gaithersburg, Md. 20760

Katz, Ruth; Crowe, Timothy D.; Cotter, Catherine; and White, Suzanne. *Comprehensive Crime Prevention Program Guide*. Write to Comprehensive Crime Prevention Programs Division, Office of Community Anti-Crime Programs, LEAA (address as listed above).

National Institute of Law Enforcement and Criminal Justice. *Community Crime Prevention*. This program has been labeled an exemplary project. If you wish to know more than the pamphlet discusses, contact Edward Good, Project Director, Community Crime Prevention Program, City of Seattle, Law and Justice Planning Office, 607 Alaska Building, Seattle, Wash. 98104. Tel: (206) 625-4724.

We Can Prevent Crime. Write to LEAA (address as listed above).

Each of the organizations listed below have specific crime prevention programs for senior citizens. One or more of them is certain to be within a reasonable distance of you.

ARIZONA

Maricopa County Sheriff's Department
Bureau of Crime Resistance
120 S. First Avenue
Phoenix, Ariz. 85003

CALIFORNIA

Fresno County Probation
Victim Services
P.O. Box 453
Fresno, Calif. 93709

Los Angeles County Department of Senior Citizens
Affairs
Interagency Task Force on Crime Against the Elderly
601 South Kingsley Drive
Los Angeles, Calif. 90005

Office of the Attorney General
Prevention—Crimes Against the Elderly
3580 Wilshire Boulevard, Suite 938
Los Angeles, Calif. 90010

Sacramento Police Department
Crime Prevention Program
625 H St.
Sacramento, Calif. 95814

DELAWARE

Wilmington Crime Resistance Task Force
Wilmington Crime Resistance Program
P.O. Box 1872
Wilmington, Del. 19899

DISTRICT OF COLUMBIA

Chief Postal Inspector
Fraud Prevention Program
475 L'Enfant Plaza, S.W.
Washington, D.C. 20260

Special Concerns Staff-Office of Housing Management, HUD
Security Planning for HUD-Assisted Housing
Room N 9108, 451 7th St., S.W.
Washington, D.C. 20410

FLORIDA

Crime Prevention Unit
Office of the Mayor
1245 E. Adams
Jacksonville, Fla. 32202

Jacksonville Sheriff's Office
Sheriff's Jacksonville Community Posse
1041 South McDuff Avenue
Jacksonville, Fla. 32205

Pinellas County Sheriff's Department
Pinellas County Junior Deputy League
250 W. Ulmerton Road
Largo, Fla. 33540

Miami Beach Police Department
Community Services
120 Meridian Avenue
Miami Beach, Fla. 33139

City of St. Petersburg/Junior League of St. Petersburg, Inc.
Project: Concern
1510 First Avenue North
St. Petersburg, Fla. 33705

Office of Crime Prevention
Locks for the Elderly
1510 First Avenue North
St. Petersburg, Fla. 33705

Sarasota City Police Department
Crimes Against the Elderly
P.O. Box 3528
Sarasota, Fla. 33578

GEORGIA

Lithonia Police Department
Senior Citizen/Invalid Contact Service
6980 Main St.
Lithonia, Ga. 30058

ILLINOIS

Chicago Police Department
Crime Prevention Program
1121 South State St.
Chicago, Ill. 60605

INDIANA

Evansville Police Department
Symposium on Safety
15 N.W. 7th St.
Evansville, Ind. 47708

South Bend Police
Senior Citizen Lock Project
701 West Sample St.
South Bend, Ind. 46601

KENTUCKY

Louisville Division of Police
Crime Prevention for Senior Citizens
633 West Jefferson St.
Louisville, Ky. 40202

MARYLAND

Mayor's Coordinating Council on Criminal Justice
Crime Prevention Program for the Elderly
Room 1101, 26 South Calvert St.
Baltimore, Md. 21202

International Association of Chiefs of Police
Crime, Safety and the Senior Citizen
11 Firstfield Road
Gaithersburg, Md. 20760

MICHIGAN

Detroit Police Department
Cass Corridor Safety for Seniors Project
3150 Second
Detroit, Mich. 48226

MINNESOTA

Minneapolis Police Department
Crime Cautions for Seniors
Room 130, City Hall
Minneapolis, Minn. 55415

MISSOURI

Mid-America Regional Council
Aid to Elderly Victims of Crime
20 West 9th St.
Kansas City, Mo. 64105

Aid to Victims of Crime, Inc.
607 North Grand, Room 705
St. Louis, Mo. 63103

Mayor's Office for Senior Citizens
Senior Home Security
560 Delmar Boulevard
St. Louis, Mo. 63101

NEBRASKA

Omaha Police Division
Crime Prevention Education for Senior Citizens
505 South 15th St.
Omaha, Neb. 68102

NEW JERSEY

Jersey City Police Department
Crime Prevention Unit
282 Central Avenue
Jersey City, N.J. 07307

NEW YORK

Bronx Foundation for Senior Citizens
Crime Victims Service Program
153 E. 170th St.
New York, N.Y. 10452

Jamaica Service Program for Older Adults
Safety Committee for the JSPOA Senior Citizens Advisory Council
92-47 165th St.
New York, N.Y. 11433

New York City Department of the Aging
Victimization of Elderly
250 Broadway
New York, N.Y. 10007

New York City Police Department
Bronx Area Senior Citizens Robbery Unit
450 Cross Bronx Expressway
New York, N.Y. 10457

New York City Police Department
101 Precinct
Community Service Volunteer Program
16-12 Mott Avenue
New York, N.Y. 11691

Syracuse Police Department
Senior Citizens Crime Prevention Program
511 South State St.
Syracuse, N.Y. 13202

OHIO

Cuyahoga County Commissioners
Senior Safety and Security Program
1276 West 3rd St.
Cleveland, Ohio 44113

Mansfield Police Department
Crime Prevention for the Elderly
27 West 2nd St.
Mansfield, Ohio 44902

OKLAHOMA

Eastern Oklahoma Development District
Law Enforcement for the Aged
P.O. Box 1361, 800 West Okmulgee
Muskogee, Okla. 74401

OREGON

Cottage Grove Police Department
Senior Citizens Crime Prevention Program
28 South 6th St.
Cottage Grove, Ore. 97424

Multnomah County Division of Public Safety
Older Americans' Crime Prevention Research
10525 S. E. Cherry Blossom Drive
Portland, Ore. 97216

PENNSYLVANIA

CLASP (Citizens Local Alliance for Safer Philadelphia)
Senior Safety Program
1710 Spruce St.
Philadelphia, Pa. 19103

TEXAS

Center for Studies in Aging, North Texas State Uni-
versity
Improving the Reporting of Crimes
Denton, Tex. 76203

UTAH

Brigham City Police Department
Senior Citizens Law Enforcement Involvement
20 North Main St.
Brigham, Utah 84302

WEST VIRGINIA

Charleston Police Department
Operation Good Morning
P.O. Box 2749
Charleston, W. Va. 25330

Huntington Police Department
Operation Lifeline
Huntington, W. Va. 25717

WISCONSIN

Milwaukee County
Neighborhood Security Aide Program
901 North 9th St.
Milwaukee, Wis. 53233

Individual communities have started numerous projects that have produced results for them. If you wish to know what they have already done or wish to see new project reports on dealing with crime as they come out, write to: National Institute of Law Enforcement and Criminal Justice, Law Enforcement Assistance Administration, U.S. Dept. of Justice, Washington, D.C. 20531.

Organizations that have information and programs on a number of aspects of crime control are provided in the list that follows.

COLORADO

National Information Center on Volunteerism, Inc.
P.O. Box 4179
Boulder, Colo. 80302

DISTRICT OF COLUMBIA

The Center for Community Change
Community Crime Prevention Services Project
1000 Wisconsin Avenue, N.W.
Washington, D.C. 20007
(202) 333-5700

Handgun Control Project
U.S. Conference of Mayors
1620 I St., N.W.
Washington, D.C. 20006

National Alliance of Businessmen
1730 K St., N.W.
Washington, D.C. 20006

National Association of Counties
Criminal Justice Programs
1735 New York Avenue, N.W.
Washington, D.C. 20006
(202) 785-9577

National Association of Criminal Justice Planners
1012 14th St., N.W.
Washington, D.C. 20005

National Association of Police Community Relations
Officers
36 8th St., N.E.
Washington, D.C. 20002
(202) 544-6900

National Burglar & Fire Alarm Association, Inc.
17 Pennsylvania Avenue, N.W.
Washington, D.C. 20006
(202) 785-0500

National Criminal Justice Association
444 North Capitol St., N.W.
Washington, D.C. 20001

National Neighborhood Watch
(Burglary Prevention)
National Sheriffs' Association
1250 Connecticut Avenue, N.W.
Washington, D.C. 20036

National Retired Teachers Association
American Association of Retired Persons
Crime Prevention Program
1909 K St., N.W.
Washington, D.C. 20006

Police Foundation
1909 K St., N.W.
Washington, D.C. 20006
(202) 833-1460

Volunteer: The National Center for Citizen Involvement
Crime Prevention Project
1214 16th St., N.W.
Washington, D.C. 20036
(202) 467-5560

GEORGIA

National Association of Citizens Crime Commission
52 Fairlie St., N.W.
Atlanta, Ga. 30303

ILLINOIS

National Center for Youth Outreach Workers
826 South Wabash
Chicago, Ill. 60605

KENTUCKY

National Crime Prevention Institute
2100 Gardiner Lane
Louisville, Ky. 40205

MARYLAND

National Organization of Black Law Enforcement Executives
Coppin State College
2500 West North Avenue
Baltimore, Md. 21216

National Criminal Justice Reference Service
Law Enforcement Assistance Administration
Box 6000
Rockville, Md. 20850

NEW JERSEY

National Council on Crime and Delinquency (NCCD)
Continental Plaza
Information Center
411 Hackensack Avenue
Hackensack, N.J. 07601

NEW YORK

National Alliance for Safer Cities
165 East 56th St.
New York, N.Y. 10022
(212) 751-4000

National Urban League
Administration of Justice Division
500 East 62nd St.
New York, N.Y. 10021
(212) 664-6500

Vera Institute of Justice
30 East 39th St.
New York, N.Y.
(212) 986-6910

TEXAS

National Center for Community Crime Prevention
Institute for Criminal Justice Studies
Southwest Texas State University
San Marcos, Tex. 78666

CHAPTER
4

GETTING THINGS DONE

Politically, it has become very dangerous to try to take something from the elderly by legislative action. Attempts to delete some of the provisions of the Social Security Act in the 1979 and 1980 sessions of Congress were a total failure. There were members of Congress who felt that some of the proposed changes made sense but admitted that there was no way they could vote such a conviction. To older Americans, any change in social security that spells less in any area means danger. Discussion is not possible. The elderly may not be united in all things, but they stand firmly together when it comes to their financial security. And politicians realize that their chances for reelection or political advancement can only be hurt by taking away what the elderly have gained.

So the battle for an old age that can be lived in dignity and at least with a modicum of decent comfort has not yet been won—not by a very long shot, as I'm sure you well know. Yes, seniors are better off now than they were 10 or 15 years ago. Indexing social security has helped, but the proportion of older people who are at or below the poverty level is frighteningly high.

It is not right that people who have worked hard all their lives should be forced to live their last years in fear of inflation, which undermines their fixed incomes the way termites destroy what looks like a solid house. It is not right that people who still want to work don't have the opportunity to do so even though they are still capable. It is certainly a tremendous wrong that women, pushed by society's rules into dependent positions, should find themselves totally unable to cope financially when that person on whom they have been dependent is removed from their lives. And it is heinous that the grip of discrimination on minorities is tightened when they become old.

Nor are all of the attempts to alleviate the distress of hard-pressed older people aimed in the right direction. It is nice of municipalities and states to lower taxes for those of us who are poor and to provide some financial assistance for insulating homes and for meeting the ever higher cost of fuel. Things like discounts for seniors on certain days at supermarkets and shops, reduced fares on public transportation during off-peak hours, cut rates at movies during times when nobody else wants to see them and lower prices for newspapers (all of which require proof that you are, indeed, satisfactorily aged) are of course well-meaning, but they ultimately wind up being insulting.

The fight—and fight it will be—must be directed toward the goal of assuring an adequate income for all elderly Americans who have contributed a lifetime of work to society, an income that will enable them to pay the same prices as everyone else pays. To achieve this goal, private pensions must be made available to almost all workers and they will have to be portable, pensions that workers can take with them as they go from one job to another. There are many problems involved in bringing this about (the financial condition of small companies and the restlessness of the average American worker, for example), but since social security can never be raised to the point where it represents an adequate income, reform and expansion of the private pension system is probably the ultimate economic victory the elderly must win. Meanwhile, there are plenty of smaller fights directly ahead. But large or small, you must do the major part of the fighting for your rights. How can you go about it? By forming your own group, by organizing a group within an already existing club or organization or by simply joining and keeping abreast of the activities of any of the numerous organizations that represent the concerns of the elderly.

Strategies will vary enormously with the scope of the problem in question and the extent and tenor of public preconceptions about it. The county school board may informally agree to your group's petition for use of a school bus to take elders marketing each week, but if it's nursing home reform you're after, you'll need a dedicated staff and well-planned legislative and media campaigns. An actual guide to political organizing is beyond the scope of this book, but you'll find several of the most up-to-date books on the subject listed under *Sources for Further Information.* What follows is an example of how a group advocating local regulation of nursing homes might organize itself to work with legislators and the media.

FORMING YOUR OWN GROUP

By forming your own group, I do not necessarily mean creating a new organization. Sometimes it is easier to use one already in existence. Senior clubs and centers abound these days. If you have a particular concern that seems important to you, the best initial step might well be to create a committee in an existing center or club dealing with that concern. Say, for example, that your concern is reform of the laws regulating nursing homes. Here is how you might proceed in organizing a group to bring about such reform.

But first, it might give you confidence to remember this: in politics (and almost everything these days is politics) there are two things that count, and only two. The first is money, which you and your friends probably don't have. The second is numbers, and that you and your friends certainly do have. While it is true that the variations in interests among all of you are vast, it is also true that you have more in common than any other group. And the single thing that binds you most closely together is the need for various kinds of security—security against the threat of poverty, security against the threat of violence and security against the threat of illness. This common need means that politics and party are probably less important to you than to others, and this in turn means that you can more easily unite in demanding what you wish from politicians. And the politicians must listen. They have no choice because 65 percent of us vote, and in some quite large constituencies, we represent as much as 20 or 25 percent of the total vote. Those are the kinds of numbers that win the respect Rodney Dangerfield always complains about not getting!

So, you form your committee on nursing home regulation. And you form it with people who are prepared to participate actively. Each should have a task. The most important immediate task is research. Exactly what are the existing laws regarding nursing homes in your community and state? What are the laws in other states and how do they work? How have other communities dealt with similar issues? What is the record of your own national and state legislators in this area?

The better your information on these subjects, the more convincingly you can build a case for reform. Media liaison workers, public speakers, writers of petitions and door-to-door canvassers will all benefit from a well-organized battery of supporting data.

Sources of information will vary with the project you embark on, but in almost all cases, your state legislator's or congressman's office should be able to point you in the direction of the laws relevant to your cause. They'll also tell you about your representative's position on an issue and how he or she has voted on relevant laws. You can often double-check the status of the law—and find out how others around the country are dealing with it—by finding a national association interested in the problem. The Gale Research Company's *Encyclopedia of Associations*, available in most libraries, indexes thousands of such associations by the "key word," or subject, they are concerned with. Entries provide a brief description of each association, together with address and phone number. Always check to see who runs the organization before you call it. A nursing home association run for the benefit of nursing home operators will have a far different point of view from that of an organization run for the benefit of nursing home residents. These two basic sources will usually give you the toehold you need to begin learning about a subject.

Meanwhile, your committee should pick someone who organizes events well and assign him or her to invite your legislator, or legislators, to speak on the issue to the whole club and perhaps to others in the community who may be interested in the subject. Believe me, it will be a rare legislator who will refuse such an invitation. He may even be prepared, once you make your wants known, to introduce legislation of the kind you feel is needed. If not, then you have another matter to deal with, a politician who needs to be replaced.

Once your needs are stated, the case must be made. Your committee will then have to turn to politics and public relations. Someone with a flair for writing, possibly a retired media person, should be assigned to convert your mass of facts into convincing arguments. Such a person should remain "on-call" for the purpose of composing press releases and position papers. A sample media release is provided to show what information should be included and how it should be presented.

MEDIA RELEASE FORMAT
Letterhead or Name of Organization

MEDIA RELEASE
    Date
    Name of Publicity Contact
    Telephone

EVENT:
    Give title or simple description, with few adjectives or descriptive phrases. For example: "Press conference to announce nursing home court victory." Do not try to write journalistically, simply convey basic information.

PLACE:
    Give name of senior center, hall or other location and exact address, plus the main cross street. Include city. Directions should appear if clearly helpful: "165 Grove St. (across from City Hall)."

TIME:
    Give exact date and time: "Saturday, June 20, 1981, 2:30 p.m."

ADMISSION:
    For a fund-raising event, list the ticket price or suggested donation; explain when tickets may be obtained, and whether they will be sold at the door. Or write "Free," if no charge is to be made.

SPECIAL INFORMATION:
    Present concisely the most interesting current facts about your activity, what makes it unique or new: "Senior Center leaders and local transit officials will announce the county's first five-cent fare for people over 65. Transit

	will also extend the bus line three blocks to stop at the Senior Center."
BACKGROUND, MORE DETAILS:	Elaborate briefly, giving background or other pertinent information. If the press finds an event newsworthy, reporters may want information about key individuals, such as guest speakers, or about the organization (perhaps a brief statement of aims and purposes). If more than a few lines of information are included, prepare separate sheet of material.
PHONE:	Make a phone number available. "For further information the public may call: (area code) number."

Another member, one who is good at explaining things and gets on well with people, should be assigned the job of contacting the media. What it takes is a comparatively simple strategy. You must find out the names of reporters on newspapers, radio or TV stations who cover news concerning the elderly. You must then start cultivating these people. When you are planning to have an event—hold a meeting, stage a rally, picket an unfriendly politician, send a bus of elders to the state capital—your media contact should be informed within plenty of time. You must learn how the media works. What are the deadlines for various newspapers? Stories for radio are good at any time, but for TV anything you schedule should be done fairly early in the day. If it takes place at five in the afternoon, you can forget about getting it on the six o'clock news. Press conferences sound impressive, but avoid them whenever possible. Reporters and, more especially, editors have no great love for a news story that is going to appear in exactly the same way on every other station and in every other paper—which is why you must learn to cultivate relationships with journalists. Know what kinds of stories the different reporters like best or their organizations are most likely to use. You can learn this by studying the paper or station. Then try to feed the story to a reporter who is likely to get it aired. Remember, it must be a *news* story, with information that is new or an angle that is different. A local angle is almost always appreciated. For example, if a national study which has just been released shows that large numbers of nursing homes are understaffed, try to find a startling example of such understaffing in your own community and link the study with the example.

You may think the reporter should simply do what you want because it's for a good cause, but news editors don't see it that way. Have plenty of facts available. Reporters often cover a number of stories a day. It is unlikely that they will have the time to dig up all the pertinent data. You do. Have it for them. And always tell them the truth. This does not mean you should fall all over yourself bringing out some item that may be harmful to your cause. But when you say something is so, it must be so. When you say something is going to happen, be sure, as best you can, that it will happen. Most good reporters will allow themselves to be misinformed by someone just once.

These points I have been bringing up are not the product of theorizing but of experience. And they need not be employed only for a single effort. Tell your local paper how many of the elderly there are in your community and how much they buy. The editor may be persuaded that a column on senior matters is a useful idea. Many already have started these columns.

Or you may be able to convince the local radio station that a regular program on senior matters would be of interest. If it's a radio station specializing in short feature-like presentations, tell them that you are prepared to provide a regular schedule of spots on matters of interest and importance to people over 45. It isn't all that hard. In Ohio, for instance, the state now presents three-minute announcements on a wide spectrum of events—it could be Medicare matters, sex, whatever. A retired insurance executive and his wife, Ed and Irene Martin, both in their sixties, do these spots. Incidentally, neither had any previous broadcasting experience. And what Ohio is doing must be reasonably popular: "New Age Radio," as it's known, is now being played on 120 stations in the state.

Think also in terms of TV. The potential here is great. Remind the station manager that there are 45 million Americans over 45, and that they control over 50 percent of the disposable income in the country. Not all the elderly are poor, and not all the people who buy things are women between 19 and 49. If the station can't see its way to doing a regular program, you might point out that I've been cohosting a successful program dealing with elderly interests for over three years in New York City. Also a program on the elderly would count as very valuable public affairs time, winning brownie points with the Federal Communications Commission, and would put the station in good with the fastest growing group of people in the country.

ADVOCATES FOR THE ELDERLY

Organizations that advocate on behalf of the elderly first came into national prominence during the 1971 White House Conference on the Aging. Such organizations include the American Association of Retired Persons (AARP), the National Council of Senior Citizens (NCSC) and the National Council on Aging (NCOA). And because of their increased advocacy and militancy during the preparation period before the conference (when it seemed as though the interests of the elderly poor were in danger of getting short shrift)

and the major role some of them played in determining the conference's conclusions, they now have some
degree of power. These organizations have grown in
strength, as have other organizations concerned with
specific though sometimes overlapping elderly concerns, and they have been joined by new organizations, some national, some local. Let's take a look at a
sampling of them in terms of how they represent the
elderly in getting things done and how, in some cases,
you can become a member, either to get involved in
their programs or simply to keep abreast of their activities. (See *Sources for Further Information* for addresses of each of the following organizations).

AARP AND NRTA

The American Association of Retired Persons is the
offshoot of the National Retired Teachers Association
(NRTA). A retired high school principal, a remarkable
woman named Ethel Percy Andrus, founded NRTA in
California in 1947 after discovering what a miserably
mistreated lot retired teachers usually were. Her particular concern at that time was that so many teachers
found themselves with little or no pension protection
during their retired years. Popular demand by people
outside the teaching profession led her to found the
AARP in 1958. The AARP offers virtually the same
benefits as its sister organization, but anyone over age
55 may join. The concern of the NRTA/AARP for the
welfare of retired teachers and, later, retired persons
in general led into many different areas. In its cam-
paign to establish minimum income levels, promote
the passage of Medicare and Medicaid, lower the cost
of drugs, win tax breaks for the elderly and so on, the
NRTA/AARP naturally latched onto new programs,
such as furnishing cheaper drugs to its members by
mail order, organizing inexpensive vacations and lob-

bying in Congress and state legislatures for other measures—national health insurance is the best example.

This judicious combination of providing programs and support continues to grow. The NRTA/AARP's AIM division supplies corporations with carefully planned pre-retirement programs. AIM membership is also available on an individual basis, at a cost of $5 per year, to people 50 and over who are planning to retire. AIM publishes its own magazine and offers its members a series of free retirement-planning guides. Such NRTA/AARP benefits as low-cost pharmacy and discount travel services are included in AIM membership as well. Its Institute of Lifetime Learning has been a major influence on educational institutions all over the country, both in getting such institutions to create programs of special interest to seniors and, by its example, in enrolling more elders into already existing programs for little or no cost at all.

The AARP is involved in promoting health and safety, in getting jobs and in both advising and influencing legislators and executives. It has been successful in making carefully planned financial investments and in attracting a large number of retirees to its ranks.

The combined NRTA/AARP represents a total of over 11 million people, at $4 a year per person. The membership fee, in addition to entitling members to take advantage of a large number of programs and benefits, also covers the cost of the organization's numerous publications, which are both useful and easy to read. Although its members are predominantly middle class, the NRTA/AARP has served as an effective advocate for those elderly people who are poor.

NCSC

The National Council of Senior Citizens (NCSC) was founded by a number of groups whose primary

goal back in 1961 was to get the government to pass a
medical care program based on the same principle as
social security, that is, medical care for the elderly as a
right. Principal leadership and support originally
came from the trade union movement. Although this
has been somewhat diluted in recent years, unions—
including the United Automobile Workers, Operating
Engineers and Machinists unions—are still extremely
important in the NCSC's activities.

After the AARP, the NCSC is the largest of the senior organizations, with about 3.5 million members in
3,800 senior clubs. Its political strength, which is not
to be ignored by any politician with a reasonably well-
developed sense of self-preservation, is notable. Recent political successes include a Buffalo, N.Y. volunteer lobbying effort to get local merchants and public
transportation to offer discounts for senior citizens.
The program succeeded so well that the county has
now funded a permanent office to help seniors get discounts. On the national level, NCSC encouraged Congress to give the largest funding possible to the Low-
Income Energy Assistance Project, a program
designed to help the elderly and the poor pay their
utility bills. Like the AARP, it is strong because it has
member clubs all over the country. The NCSC insists
that it is not a partisan organization except, of course,
in its advocacy on behalf of the elderly and their al-
lies. Through its publication and continual contacts,
the NCSC has followed the old labor adage of rewarding one's friends and punishing one's enemies.

Though neither organization would like to admit it
publicly, just as there is a resemblance between the
NCSC and the AARP, there is also some rivalry. This
is unavoidable since both provide many of the same
services to their members, such as low-cost travel arrangements and discounts, car rentals, health insurance and drug programs. The NCSC has now entered
into the field of pre-retirement programs for private

industry and other organizations, thus making the resemblance and the rivalry even stronger.

Membership is $5 a year if you join one of NCSC's local clubs, $6 a year for those who join independent of a local club.

NCOA

Although the National Council on Aging (NCOA) is made up mainly of professionals in the field of gerontology and organizations operating in the same area, its scope is so wide and its component and related organizations so all-embracing that it has always exerted a broad influence. It is an organization whose resources give it a significance larger than its numbers would indicate. Like those mentioned previously, this organization has made its weight felt when senior concerns have been at issue.

The NCOA is involved in a substantial number of projects for which it has set up various institutes. The 1974 study funded by its National Media Resource Center on Aging resulted in the first national survey of attitudes towards older people. This, like the 1979 study done for the House Select Committee on Aging, was the work of the Louis Harris organization.

NCOA projects include the National Institute of Work and Retirement; the National Institute of Senior Centers, which involves the NCOA indirectly with large numbers of the elderly through county-run senior centers nationwide; the Public Policy Center; and the Media Resource Center, which helps people like me keep informed. Each of these institutes produces documents of interest to professionals in the respective special fields, but they are also a useful source of information for seniors' political action groups.

GRAY PANTHERS

"What makes a Gray Panther?" This question is answered, in part, in the introduction to the Gray Panther Manual:

> We focus on societal issues (for example, health
> and inflation) that affect people of all ages, and
> view the particular problems of old people as aspects of the economic and social needs created by
> our wasteful, competitive, profit-centered society.
> We are building exciting coalitions of people of
> different ages, bringing together people whom
> our age-segregated society has separated. . . .
>
> We are working to develop new forms of political
> action based on broad public interest principles.
> We are convinced that older Americans must not
> become another self-serving what's-in-it-for-me
> lobby. Older Gray Panthers consider themselves
> the "elders of the tribe," concerned more about
> the tribe's survival than their own special needs.
>
> We join in coalitions and in public demonstrations with other groups with whom we are in
> agreement—such as those opposing assaults on
> the environment, those fighting budgetary "restraints" that mean cuts in social services while
> increasing military outlays, those seeking to eliminate all forms of racism, sexism, and ageism that
> still plague our society.

The manual then goes on to outline how you can organize yourselves and society, including the media, to fight these battles.

Whatever the Panthers may or may not be, no one can accuse them of being dull. Although their numbers are not great (they don't go in for counting, but it is estimated that they are less than 10,000 strong), activists love them for their very brashness. They pride themselves, rightly, on being well informed and they positively relish embarrassing the establishment when that seems necessary. The local group in Albuquerque, N.M. sent questionnaires to all Arizona political candidates, soliciting their views on a variety of issues. The group then published the results in time for the elections. Their very unexpectedness works in their favor. Maggie Kuhn, one of the founders and by far and away the best known of the Panthers, looks like the kind of sweet, gentle old lady one might expect to see presiding graciously over a church supper. The reality is something quite different. I remember an interview with Maggie on our program, "The Prime of Your Life," when she had just returned from China after the fall of the so-called Gang of Four. It had already become clear that the new government was sheering away from the radicalism of its predecessors, and Maggie made it clear that this was not at all to her liking.

It is, in my opinion, this tilt towards politically radical thinking that limits both the numbers and the effectiveness of the Gray Panthers. Older Americans are not, by and large, fire-eaters, and the Panthers are. Still, they do constitute a force, especially on the local level. The Seattle and Boston Panthers' organizations, for example, have started a "shared-living" project, finding compatible older people to share living costs by becoming roommates. The Boston group is also experimenting with a communal situation in which 15 people of all different ages share life together. In San Francisco the Panthers are pressing owners of the city's residential hotels to stop converting them from havens for older people into more lucrative luxury hotels. All over the country, the organization's local chapters provide courses in grassroots advocacy and lobbying.

If you send a $5 contribution to the Gray Panthers, they'll put you on their mailing list. Local groups sometimes have a membership charge, but the amount varies. Unlike some seniors' groups, the Panthers don't aim to provide services like low-cost drugs and travel, but they do promise stimulating work for the politically committed.

GERONTOLOGICAL SOCIETY

The Gerontological Society's membership is made up of people from the various professions that deal with problems of aging: doctors, biologists and social scientists. Its publications reflect a professional approach. These include two bimonthly publications, *The Journal of Gerontology* and the *Gerontologist*. This organization, too, has left its mark on legislation affecting older people, and it has been influential in forwarding the cause of seniors in other arenas. Its influence has come, at least in part, because of its prestige. It was instrumental in the creation of the National Institute on Aging, and it regularly advises the Administration on Aging regarding funding levels. Nevertheless, it is true that in the public's perception the Gerontological Society has lost ground, and in talks with some of its leaders, I had the distinct impression that the intention is to show a more progressive profile in the future.

NATIONAL SPECIAL INTEREST ORGANIZATIONS

NARFE

The National Association of Retired Federal Employees (NARFE) is the oldest (founded in 1921) of the various organizations representing retired people, and if you measure success by what an association does for its members in the material sense, you have to consider it the most successful. Although its numbers have never gone over 300,000, retired federal employees can boast a pension system with benefits that should make employees of private companies turn green with envy. Federal employee pensions are noncontributory, and they offer the option of retirement at full pension at age 55 with 30 years service, age 60 with 20 years service or age 62 with five years service. The pension benefits are also increased twice a year to meet the inroads of inflation, and the pensions provide generous sick and death benefits. Only the military pensions and those offered by some municipal governments are better. Finally, while the law now says that workers cannot be retired before age 70 in the world of private industry and business, the government worker can, according to another law, go on practically forever.

There are now NARFE pre-retirement programs for government workers and their families and local chapters that provide the same facilities and advantages offered by other senior centers. Over the years, the NARFE's role has been augmented by the powerful government unions (including the Postal Workers Union, the AFL-CIO's Public Employees Division and the National Federation of Federal Employees) from which it draws its membership and NARFE has often worked in tandem with the AARP and other groups representing seniors.

Many of the other special interest senior organizations that are strong on advocacy grew out of the trade union movement and remain closely associated with it. The United Automobile Workers (UAW), the United Steelworkers, the International Ladies Garment Workers Union (ILGWU), the American Federation of State, County and Municipal Workers, the Dis-

. tributive Workers and the Textile Workers have all given birth to affiliated elder groups that provide benefits, entertainment, social opportunities, lectures and the chance to continue participation in various causes and even, in some cases, union affairs. Among older ex-workers, whose union ties go back to the days of the Great Depression, the bonds to these unions are strong indeed.

Some of the major union-related organizations and others that serve special interests are discussed in the following sections.

UAW PROGRAM

Members of the United Automobile Workers (UAW) may retire from their work at a relatively early age, 59 or 60, but if they wish, they can remain active in union affairs for the rest of their lives.

The UAW Retired and Older Workers Departments have been in existence since 1966. Each local has an affiliated Older Workers Department that meets every month, and each department can vote for the administrative officers of the local and elect a member of the local's board. The union's locals are grouped into 18 regional councils, and at least one member of each regional council is elected from the Older Workers Departments. These departments have an 18-member advisory council that parallels the union's international council; this advisory council meets four times a year. The seniors also have a voice at the union's national convention. The departments are financed by $1-a-month dues payments from their membership, augmented by a 1¢-per-capita draw on general union dues. This financing pays for many different kinds of programs—some social, some connected with volunteer work in the community and a great deal having to do with reform of such things as laws covering nursing homes and other matters of direct interest to older people. To anyone familiar with the history of the UAW, it should not be surprising to hear that the Older Workers Departments are active in politics.

Since much of the membership has left the chill of Detroit, as well as the other Northern cities where cars have traditionally been built, for climatically friendlier parts of the country, there are now regional councils where previously there were no locals, in places like Florida, Arizona, Louisiana, Nevada and New Mexico. In these areas there are drop-in centers, which also hold monthly meetings. Instead of belonging to a chapter, each elder member in these areas belongs to the regional council.

ILGWU PROGRAM

Different union retirees have different needs. The International Ladies Garment Workers Union (IL-GWU) probably has more older retirees, proportionately, than most unions. Under an innovative program begun in 1967, the Friendly Visitors, retirees who range from 65 to 86 themselves, compile lists of those in need of visitation and make such visits on a regular basis. If more active help is needed—shopping assistance or transportation to medical appointments, for example—the program provides it. The Friendly Visitors are paid the minimum wage to start. In 1967 a federal grant provided the money to pay the Friendly Visitors; now the funds come from union dues.

Another program helpful to elders is the union's health service. Health center facilities are available for seniors, and they can get prescription drugs at the center for as low as $1.

It is the nature of the garment industry to divide up workers into specific skills, which are usually each represented by a "local." Many of these locals have

senior clubs that meet on a regular basis. But retired
workers are not forgotten on the national level either.
There is a regular senior column in the union's paper,
Justice.

OLDER WOMEN'S LEAGUE

There are two singularly impressive facts about
women over 65, and they both stand out starkly. The
first is that they are the fastest growing minority in this
country. The second is that they are the single poorest
group in the country. Four hundred of them met in
October 1980 at Des Moines, Iowa to form the Older
Women's League and to elect —absolutely nobody
was surprised—Tish Sommers, the dynamic activist
for women in general and older women in particular,
as their new president.

The need for organization is obvious because the
need for action is so clear. For example, the average
weekly income of women over 65 in this country is
$59, compared to $109 for men of the same age.
Among widows in this age bracket—there are hundreds of thousands of widowed women because
women live so much longer than men—one-third live
below the poverty level.

Legislation to protect divorced women and to reform the social security laws so that they provide
greater equity for both widows and divorced women
with no career of their own are among the reforms the
League intends to achieve. Tish Sommers told the October meeting, "We are not over the hill. We are
women with one-third of our lives left, and if we get
together, we can have a real impact on legislation."
Their intention is to establish state chapters in all 50
states. Next will come the obligatory headquarters at
the seat of power in Washington, D.C. The League
hopes to accomplish this by 1982.

NCCBA

There are four million blacks 55 years of age and over in the United States. Blacks still live a shorter life than whites on the average, but their life span has also been growing, and just as poverty is a grim problem for so many older white people, so it is, and to a substantially greater degree, for blacks.

The National Caucus was founded in 1971 to provide a strong voice for minorities at the White House Conference on Aging that year. And it did, out of all proportion to its small numbers. It was a struggle to survive in 1971. And it remains a bitter struggle.

Following the establishment of the National Caucus, the Center on the Black Aged was started, sort of as a working arm. In the fall of 1980 the two organizations merged to form the National Caucus and Center on the Black Aged (NCCBA). The goal is to provide advocacy and to train people to be advocates. Lack of knowledge on how to run a program, keep accounts, make application for grants, etc. has been a serious hindrance to black ambitions. To overcome this handicap the NCCBA trains and helps place black professionals in organizations for the aging, such as those involved in nutrition and social services. At the same time, the organization is trying to correct this problem while also serving as a direct advocate for programs that are of use to older blacks. The NCCBA sponsors a number of programs, such as the Elderly Escort Program in Springfield, Mass., where young people are employed to take some 2,000 elders in safety to doctors, to shopping centers—to wherever their needs might bring them. Those served are largely, but not exclusively, black.

Another project is the newly opened housing facility called the NCCBA Housing Estates in Washington, D.C. This is an $8 million 175-unit apartment building for elders where the dwellers, all 62 or over, pay no more than 25 percent of their income for comfortable housing designed to give them the opportunity to live independently. Ten percent of the residents must be handicapped, by regulation of the Department of Housing and Urban Development (HUD), whose money paid for part of the project. The NCCBA was instrumental in securing funds for the project and was in charge of screening potential tenants.

There are currently employment programs for the black elderly in six states and small volunteer chapters in 25 that, by design, are composed of both elders and young professionals. Current membership is about 3,000. Membership costs $4 yearly for seniors, $25 per year for other individuals and $10 per year for students. Members receive a newsletter, have access to the center's information bank and get help in finding professional or paraprofessional jobs. Development of the program to its full potential is extremely difficult. The present executive director, Dr. Dolores Davis-Wong, says that failure is almost a self-fulfilling prophecy, built into the project because it is totally dependent on the Administration on Aging for its funding, and the amount given by that agency, about a quarter of a million dollars yearly, is just about all that keeps Dr. Davis-Wong and a core staff of eight going. Still, when she speaks of the difficulty in functioning, she does so with a cheerfully optimistic air that belies her pessimism. Obviously, keeping the NCCBA alive and reasonably well has always been a difficult task. Six and even seven days a week in the Washington office was common, but there is no indication that anyone intends quitting.

Asian-Pacific, Indian and Hispanic Councils on Aging are being launched, but as with the NCCBA, financial dependency on the government is an inhibiting factor.

LOCAL ORGANIZATIONS

One very exciting development in the area of orga-
nizational activism is the burgeoning of local groups.
Here are a few examples that may inspire you or
others to consider creating a club, organization or institute that will be particularly active in meeting the
needs of the elderly in your community.

INSTITUTE FOR THE PUERTO RICAN/HISPANIC ELDERLY

The furniture in the headquarters of this two-year-
old New York City program is, in the words of one
staffer, "mostly recycled." The director's desk has a
broken leg, but it makes little difference since she is
rarely to be found behind it. That director is a young
dynamo named Suleika Cabrera Drinane. When I first
interviewed her on our TV show, there was a name
and a need for the program and that was about it.

The need was painfully clear. Nobody knows for
sure how many hundreds of thousands of poor elderly
Hispanics there are in New York City alone. Most do
not speak English. They have no idea of what they are
entitled to or how to go about getting assistance if they
need it. The problem is finding and informing them of
their rights. This is rather an awesome task that Ms.
Drinane has taken upon herself.

Today, her small office operates with a three-year
grant of $96,000 from the Federal Department of
Health and Human Services. With a core staff of two
paid workers and 13 CETA employees in senior centers around the city, the Institute for the Puerto Rican/
Hispanic Elderly is attempting both to train elderly
Hispanic people to advocate for their own needs at all
levels of government and to seek out others in need of
help. The Institute has a weekly radio show on a local

Spanish-language station that discusses issues important to seniors, like supplementary security income,
food stamps and utility subsidies. Volunteers man a
daily telephone "hot line," which offers advice (in
Spanish) on the rights of older people and helps put
callers in touch with Spanish-speaking contacts at appropriate government agencies. Older workers also
visit bodegas (the small Puerto Rican grocery stores)
and other places simply to find those elderly Hispanics needing assistance. The life experience of
these older people does not lend itself to automatic
trust of strangers claiming they want to help, but talking to them for a while on a one-to-one basis will usually allay any suspicion they may have. The Institute
also organizes local political action. It sends speakers,
for example, to public hearings on such issues as mass
transit subsidies for older people.

The same problems found in New York City exist in
other parts of the Northeast and the Institute hopes to
be opening offices in New Jersey and Connecticut
about the time this book goes to press. The staff will
be glad to offer advice to groups planning to start a
similar agency in their own communities.

NASSAU SENIOR FORUM

Conditions differ from place to place. Problems for
everyone and certainly for the elderly are quite different in an area where the population is spread out,
where most people live in private dwellings, rather
than apartments, and where the great majority still depends on the automobile for transportation. Older
people in such areas are more concerned about property taxes than are apartment dwellers in the cities.
They are also concerned about getting public transportation of any kind, whereas the city dwellers, to
whom it is readily available, are worried about the

cost. Of course there are problems in common, but it is the different local needs that inspire communities to create their own organizations.

The Nassau Senior Forum, now 11 years old, is an outspoken advocate for the elderly, a description that surprises no one who knows one of its founders, that feisty battler for senior rights, columnist Lou Cottin. Last year at its 10th anniversary party, there was some discussion of the improvements in the condition of elders since the Forum's founding, but speakers spent more time talking about strategies to deal with the problems that still exist—poor transportation, rising property taxes and increased rental fees, in particular.

Through a combination of letter-writing campaigns, orderly demonstrations and testimony at public hearings, the roughly 700-member organization has recently fought for such advances as reduced-fare taxi service for elders and extension of rent stabilization on a county wide basis. The organization also monitors the city and county budgets in the Nassau area, hoping to limit and gradually reduce property taxes for people with low or fixed incomes.

The Nassau Senior Forum will gladly share its expertise with individuals interested in starting similar groups in their own communities. The organization's president, George Krieger, also stresses the need for close communication among an area's senior groups. Unity is the key. Says Krieger, "Were all the senior citizens' groups in any county united as one, then that old joke about politicians starting to kiss senior citizens instead of babies wouldn't be a joke anymore."

PROMOTING RENEWED INDEPENDENCE FOR THE DEPRIVED ELDERLY (PRIDE)

The full name of this organization may be a bit unwieldy, but its purpose, to make it possible for frail older people to remain at home rather than be forced to spend the rest of their days in a nursing home, is, I am convinced, a noble idea.

PRIDE was founded by Dr. Philip Brickner in 1980 in the Greenwich Village section of New York City. Operating under the aegis of the Community Medicine Department of St. Vincent's Hospital, it has demonstrated that even very sick and afflicted old people, most well up into their eighties and with several chronic, often terribly disabling illnesses, can be maintained in their own homes. The organization's primary concern is to get the Medicare law amended to make home maintenance possible for anyone who does not absolutely require the continuing services of a hospital or an intensive care nursing home.

No one connected with PRIDE has any illusions that the nursing home industry will happily welcome such a reform, but this fact has not deterred the organization. Dr. Brickner is willing to answer questions from people interested in starting a similar program in their own community (see *Sources for Further Information*).

And so we come to the end, which, I hope, is also a beginning. There is much to be done. I know from experience that joining in on the doing is not only rewarding but fun. Elderly activism is the most exciting thing happening at this time. I hope you too will be a part of it.

SOURCES FOR FURTHER INFORMATION

Forming Your Own Group

The following publication is a versatile, basic workbook for seniors' political organizing and it contains a very helpful bibliography. It is available for $2 from the University of Southern California's Andrus Gerontology Center, Publications Office, University Park, Calif. 90007.

Hess, C.W., and Kerschner, P.A. *The Silver Lobby: A Guide to Advocacy for Older Persons.* Los Angeles: USC Andrus Gerontology Center, 1978.

Listed below is a more comprehensive book on senior activism; it is available at your local bookstore for $8.95 or at your library.

Cottin, Lou. *Elders in Rebellion: A Guide to Senior Activism.* Garden City: Doubleday, 1978.

A booklet describing the experiences of some elders' organizations and providing useful suggestions, especially about contacting the media, is the following publication, which is available at certain libraries.

Kleyman, Paul. *Senior Power: Growing Old Rebelliously.* San Francisco: New Glide, 1974.

A scholarly history of elders' political action is available for $5.95 at your bookstore. Look for:

Pratt, Henry J. *The Gray Lobby.* Chicago: University of Chicago, 1976.

Contacting Seniors' Organizations and Groups

The following list gives the addresses of organizations and special interest groups that lobby on behalf of the elderly.

AARP/NRTA
1909 K St.. N.W.
Washington, D.C. 20049

Gerontological Society
1835 K St., N.W.
Washington, D.C. 20005

Gray Panthers
3700 Chestnut St.
Philadelphia, Pa. 19104

ILGWU Program
201 West 52nd St.
New York, N.Y. 10019

Institute for the Puerto Rican/Hispanic Elderly
105 E. 22nd St.
New York, N.Y. 10010

NARFE
1533 New Hampshire Ave., N.W.
Washington, D.C. 20036

Nassau Senior Forum
129 Jackson St.
Hempstead, N.Y. 11550

NCCBA
1424 K St., N.W.
Washington, D.C. 20005

NCOA
1828 L St., N.W.
Washington, D.C. 20026

NCSC
1511 K St., N.W.
Washington, D.C. 20005

Older Women's League
388 Harrison St.
Oakland, Calif. 94611

PRIDE
St. Vincent's Hospital and Medical Center of New
York
153 W. 11th St.
New York, N.Y. 10011

UAW Program
8731 East Jefferson Ave.
Detroit, Mich. 48214

CHAPTER
5

HEALTH

Most people tend to think of the elderly as being either in bad health, though still functioning, or actually in a nursing home. Both pictures are false. In fact, most seniors think of their health as being anywhere from fair to excellent.

Ninety-five percent of older people live in the community, not in any kind of institution. And of those 95 percent, almost 90 percent, by their own account, consider their health anywhere from fair to good. The statistics come from the U.S. National Center for Health Statistics, Division of Health Interview Statistics, and the agency got them by going around and interviewing the people most concerned, the elderly themselves, in their own homes. There are variations within the elderly population, of course, some of which may surprise you. For instance, a lot more people in big cities (metropolitan areas, as the survey calls them) think of themselves as being in excellent health than do people in small towns (that is, nonmetropolitan areas). But to us the most interesting figure revealed by this survey is the fact that 87 percent of all elderly Americans think of themselves as being in fair to excellent health. So that disproves the old stereotype, that older people go around feeling miserable and sick.

But of course there's no denying that as we get older, we experience physical changes; we are more prone to get certain diseases; we may have to make some adjustments in our diet; we are more concerned about health insurance and hospitalization; and we might have to make a decision about choosing among different types of nursing care. In this chapter I'll discuss all these concerns.

THE AGING PROCESS

Until this century, life was a precarious affair of short duration. Our early ancestors had little more hope of living out their time than the animals that they hunted for food. Life expectancy didn't improve much until about the time of the American Revolution. For the next 125 years or so, it inched its way upwards. Then in this century, the upward surge became dramatic.

The change was not only in the number of years a person could expect to live but also in how early a person began to age physically. The Romans started to look old in their thirties. And during our own colonial days, reaching 60 was still an unusual achievement. Today, we might ask whether our ideas about when middle age ends and old age begins need to be revised. The answer seems to be "yes" when we look at Table 14 on page 267.

In the United States the fact that poverty and perhaps the strain of prejudice still handicap nonwhites of both sexes is a national disgrace. But it is important that we are living longer. Not only do we live longer, but we also stay vital and healthy longer. A famous gerontologist, Bernice Neugarten, thinks that today we should speak of the people between 55 and 75, the group that used to be considered middle-aged, as the "young-old" and of those over 75 as the "old-old." But however age is defined, it seems safe to say that we have

Table 14

LIFE EXPECTANCY
EXPECTATION OF LIFE AND EXPECTED DEATHS, BY RACE, AGE AND SEX: 1977

AGE IN 1977 (years)	EXPECTATION OF LIFE IN YEARS					EXPECTED DEATHS PER 1,000 ALIVE AT SPECIFIED AGE				
		White		Black and other			White		Black and other	
	Total	Male	Female	Male	Female	Total	Male	Female	Male	Female
At birth ...	73.2	70.0	77.7	64.6	73.1	14.21	13.98	10.75	23.91	19.73
1	73.2	70.0	77.6	65.2	73.6	.93	.97	.74	1.37	1.13
2	72.3	69.1	76.6	64.3	72.7	.73	.73	.58	1.12	.92
3	71.3	68.1	75.7	63.4	71.7	.58	.58	.47	.93	.74
4	70.4	67.2	74.7	62.4	70.8	.48	.49	.38	.78	.60
5	69.4	66.2	73.7	61.5	69.8	.42	.45	.32	.66	.48
6	68.4	65.2	72.8	60.5	68.9	.37	.42	.28	.57	.39
7	67.5	64.3	71.8	59.6	67.9	.34	.40	.25	.50	.33
8	66.5	63.3	70.8	58.6	66.9	.30	.36	.22	.45	.28
9	65.5	62.3	69.8	57.6	65.9	.27	.30	.20	.41	.24
10	64.5	61.3	68.8	56.6	65.0	.24	.26	.19	.39	.23
11	63.5	60.4	67.9	55.7	64.0	.24	.26	.20	.42	.23
12	62.6	59.4	66.9	54.7	63.0	.30	.33	.22	.49	.26
13	61.6	58.4	65.9	53.7	62.0	.41	.51	.28	.62	.31
14	60.6	57.4	64.9	52.8	61.0	.57	.77	.35	.80	.38
15	59.6	56.5	63.9	51.8	60.0	.75	1.05	.44	1.00	.46
16	58.7	55.5	62.9	50.8	59.1	.92	1.32	.52	1.21	.55
17	57.7	54.6	62.0	49.9	58.1	1.06	1.53	.58	1.45	.64
18	56.8	53.7	61.0	49.0	57.1	1.16	1.68	.61	1.70	.71
19	55.9	52.8	60.1	48.1	56.2	1.22	1.76	.60	1.97	.78
20	54.9	51.9	59.1	47.2	55.2	1.27	1.84	.60	2.25	.85
21	54.0	51.0	58.1	46.3	54.3	1.33	1.92	.60	2.53	.93
22	53.1	50.1	57.2	45.4	53.3	1.36	1.95	.60	2.80	1.00
23	52.1	49.1	56.2	44.5	52.4	1.37	1.93	.59	3.05	1.07
24	51.2	48.2	55.2	43.6	51.4	1.36	1.86	.59	3.27	1.13
25	50.3	47.3	54.3	42.8	50.5	1.34	1.79	.59	3.51	1.20
26	49.3	46.4	53.3	41.9	49.5	1.32	1.71	.59	3.74	1.27
27	48.4	45.5	52.3	41.1	48.6	1.31	1.65	.60	3.90	1.33
28	47.5	44.6	51.4	40.2	47.7	1.31	1.61	.62	3.97	1.38
29	46.5	43.6	50.4	39.4	46.7	1.31	1.59	.65	3.97	1.42
30	45.6	42.7	49.4	38.6	45.8	1.32	1.58	.69	3.95	1.47
31	44.7	41.8	48.5	37.7	44.9	1.35	1.59	.73	3.96	1.53
32	43.7	40.8	47.5	36.9	43.9	1.39	1.61	.78	4.05	1.62
33	42.8	39.9	46.5	36.0	43.0	1.45	1.67	.83	4.25	1.75
34	41.8	39.0	45.6	35.2	42.1	1.55	1.76	.89	4.54	1.92
35	40.9	38.0	44.6	34.3	41.2	1.66	1.88	.96	4.87	2.11
36	40.0	37.1	43.6	33.5	40.3	1.78	2.01	1.04	5.20	2.31
37	39.0	36.2	42.7	32.6	39.3	1.93	2.17	1.13	5.57	2.53
38	38.1	35.3	41.7	31.8	38.4	2.10	2.34	1.25	5.97	2.79
39	37.2	34.3	40.8	31.0	37.5	2.29	2.54	1.39	6.40	3.06

LIFE EXPECTANCY
EXPECTATION OF LIFE AND EXPECTED DEATHS, BY RACE, AGE AND SEX: 1977

AGE IN 1977 (years)	EXPECTATION OF LIFE IN YEARS					EXPECTED DEATHS PER 1,000 ALIVE AT SPECIFIED AGE				
		White		Black and other			White		Black and other	
	Total	Male	Female	Male	Female	Total	Male	Female	Male	Female
40	36.3	33.4	39.8	30.2	36.7	2.50	2.77	1.54	6.87	3.37
41	35.4	32.5	38.9	29.4	35.8	2.75	3.03	1.71	7.39	3.70
42	34.5	31.6	38.0	28.6	34.9	3.01	3.34	1.89	7.91	4.04
43	33.6	30.7	37.0	27.9	34.1	3.30	3.69	2.09	8.42	4.37
44	32.7	29.8	36.1	27.1	33.2	3.62	4.10	2.31	8.95	4.71
45	31.8	29.0	35.2	26.3	32.4	3.97	4.55	2.54	9.49	5.07
46	30.9	28.1	34.3	25.6	31.5	4.35	5.04	2.80	10.11	5.46
47	30.0	27.2	33.4	24.8	30.7	4.77	5.58	3.07	10.84	5.92
48	29.2	26.4	32.5	24.1	29.9	5.24	6.19	3.36	11.72	6.47
49	28.3	25.5	31.6	23.4	29.1	5.75	6.86	3.68	12.73	7.08
50	27.5	24.7	30.7	22.7	28.3	6.31	7.60	4.02	13.83	7.75
51	26.7	23.9	29.8	22.0	27.5	6.91	8.40	4.39	14.98	8.44
52	25.9	23.1	29.0	21.3	26.7	7.53	9.22	4.78	16.16	9.14
53	25.0	22.3	28.1	20.7	26.0	8.16	10.06	5.18	17.34	9.83
54	24.2	21.5	27.2	20.0	25.2	8.82	10.94	5.60	18.55	10.52
55	23.5	20.8	26.4	19.4	24.5	9.50	11.84	6.04	19.72	11.20
56	22.7	20.0	25.5	18.8	23.7	10.25	12.86	6.53	20.99	11.93
57	21.9	19.3	24.7	18.2	23.0	11.16	14.09	7.12	22.56	12.83
58	21.2	18.5	23.9	17.6	22.3	12.29	15.61	7.85	24.53	13.97
59	20.4	17.8	23.1	17.0	21.6	13.60	17.37	8.68	26.82	15.28
60	19.7	17.1	22.3	16.5	21.0	15.06	19.31	9.62	29.50	16.87
61	19.0	16.4	21.5	15.9	20.3	16.55	21.31	10.59	32.16	18.45
62	18.3	15.8	20.7	15.4	19.7	17.94	23.30	11.50	34.15	19.52
63	17.6	15.2	19.9	15.0	19.1	19.13	25.21	12.30	35.05	19.80
64	16.9	14.5	19.2	14.5	18.4	20.22	27.10	13.05	35.13	19.58
65	16.3	13.9	18.4	14.0	17.8	21.31	29.05	13.85	34.62	18.97
70	13.1	11.1	14.8	11.4	14.5	31.53	43.16	21.05	49.67	32.75
75	10.4	8.6	11.5	9.7	12.5	49.84	66.26	36.43	74.90	55.75
80	8.2	6.8	8.8	8.7	11.3	75.07	98.72	60.23	96.26	71.70
85 and over	6.4	5.3	6.8	7.3	9.6	1,000.00	1,000.00	1,000.00	1,000.00	1,000.00

Source: U.S. National Center for Health Statistics, *Vital Statistics of the United States,* annual

come close to making true the old cliche that you are, indeed, just about as young as you feel.

We know what we mean when we speak of getting old. There are the visible changes: graying, baldness in some men, sagging skin, loss of strength and endurance and so on, ending inevitably in death. These criteria, based on simple observation, are enough for most of us, but not for the scientists who want to know what the actual biological and chemical processes are and if these processes can be altered so that we can live still longer and be healthier. Arriving at a definition of aging, however, still escapes them. There are a number of more or less popular theories. According to one, we all have senescence, or aging, genes in our bodies. When we are growing up, these genes are useful. But when our reproductive stage is over, the genes supposedly turn on us and accelerate deterioration. If these genes are present, they have not been identified as yet, but some genetic component in aging is suggested by experience. People with healthy parents usually live longer than those with less healthy parents.

A second theory maintains that in the process of cell manufacturing, mistakes are inevitably made. These mistakes accumulate over the years, until the body is no longer able to function normally. Even more telling, identical twins (those formed from a single egg in the mother) have a strong tendency to die at about the same age, whereas fraternal twins (those formed from two eggs) show a much weaker correlation. The specific genetic coding present in both of the identical twins seems to "program" them to similar lifespans.

Yet another theory supposes that our bodily functions depend on the presence of traces of certain metals. It is believed that the amounts of these metals (nickel is an important one) change with the years. Some may even vanish. The lack of minerals adversely affects the operations of the cells resulting in deterioration and, finally, death.

A fourth aging theory suggests that metabolic by-products (so-called free radicals) which are policed by enzymes in the young body remain longer in the bodies of older people. Elders are known to have a lower level of enzymes than do younger people. The theory holds that the enzymes in the older person's body are unable to restrain the "free radicals" from linking up to make larger molecules in the body's tissues. This process is thought to cause such phenomena as wrinkling of the skin, and some argue it can cause damage to cell membranes and to the genes themselves.

Yet another theory claims what seems self-evident to most of us: our cells wear out. Some cells—those in the liver and the skin, for example—can reproduce themselves, but some very important cells, like those in the heart and nervous system, don't reproduce. With constant use they deteriorate.

Closer study of the aging process may lead to a longer life for future generations if, that is, those generations can learn to handle the interaction of people better than we have so far. For most of us now alive, all this will probably remain highly speculative. Our concern has to be with the things we already know—the physical and mental manifestations of change that take place as we grow older and how we can deal with them.

Careful observation has shown that longevity tends to run in families. If all of your grandparents lived to a ripe old age, the chances are that you will too. On the other hand, if members of your family have died of heart disease while comparatively young, your risk of heart problems is greater. You may take steps to control your diet and stress levels, however, and end up living as long or longer than those to whom heredity gives an apparent advantage. Every species known to man has an age beyond which it has never survived. The trick is to live a full life during that allotted time.

FITNESS

Back when I was in college, my sport was swimming. I was pretty good at it, varsity letters for three years; not too many people in the country could beat me at my distance then. Today I still swim, and I'm still pretty good at it. I can swim a mile or so for exercise and feel just fine. But as I swim along in my lane, younger men and women pull ahead of me with little effort. I used to swim well by any measurement, but now I'm only good when compared to people my own age. Still, the difference between my swimming now and four or five years ago is slight. If I keep it up, it will be that way for quite some years to come.

That's the way it is with almost everything. In fact, what you've just read is the worst of it because it is in the areas of bodily strength, endurance and skill that we deteriorate most noticeably. Athletes notice it most because their attainments have been the greatest. Even in the late twenties and at most by the early thirties, everyone slows down. The baseball pitcher must start using his brain, out-thinking batters instead of blowing a fast ball by them; a good golfer must learn to substitute precise strokes for those carefree, long-distance whistlers of earlier days. For the athlete the change can be traumatic. It means an end to top-flight, often highly lucrative competition.

For the rest of us, the adjustment is one we automatically begin to make as the changes take place. You don't weep because you can't run as fast as you could when you were 20. You adapt to it. That is important, that adaptation. What is equally important is to keep at it. If you don't go on exercising your faculties through the years, then you will have to face the kind of deterioration we all fear. If you do continue to exercise, then you can enjoy the delightful feeling of good conditioning and good health all the years of your life. Indeed, studies have shown that regular exercise can add years to your life. In one study the death rate among nonexercising men over age 45 was found to be almost five times that of men who kept physically fit! And in a 1968 experiment, Dr. H.A. De Vries showed that 70-year-old men who engaged in regular exercise were able to match the reflexes of the average 40-year-old!

Muscle deterioration is inevitable. At 75, you'll have only about 55 percent of the gripping power you had when you were 30. Your other organs face similar declines in efficiency, so that all in all you will be less able to stand sudden pulls, stretches and exertions than you could when you were young. This doesn't necessarily mean you should give up favorite sports like tennis, weight lifting and basketball—sports that require sudden, high levels of exertion—though you should certainly consult your doctor about the levels of exertion to aim for.

The activities most beneficial to your muscle tone, reflexes and flexibility are those that require steady levels of moderate exertion. They also improve the condition of that most important of all muscles, the heart. Many people have remarked on the alertness, good health and longevity of symphony conductors; researchers are inclined to think that these benefits are due at least in part to the steady, moderate movement of the upper body that conducting entails! For those of us who are not conductors, the best form of moderate exercise is probably swimming. It involves regular, rhythmic exertion, but it puts no strain on the joints. Bicycling is another recommended activity, as is jogging, though the latter can put considerable strain on hip and knee joints. The most convenient form of exercise is walking or hiking, and contrary to what you might expect, you'll get a good workout of the muscles of the torso and abdomen as well as those of the legs and feet. A few disciplines combine excellent exercise with the pleasure of learning a new skill. These include dance, yoga and Tai Chi Chuan, which resembles a cross between karate and dance, emphasizing rhythmic movement, balance and flexibility. They require a *skilled* teacher who knows your needs and limits. For all these activities, the basic advice is the same: consult your doctor about the best program for your needs. Start slow and work up to a moderate, steady pace. Follow a regular, disciplined routine. Don't just quit when you've finished your routine: gradually reduce your exertions so your body has a chance to "warm down." And don't stop to window shop or wool-gather along the way.

It takes at least six minutes of moderate exercise to begin to produce a beneficial effect on the body, but there's no reason to stop there. You can *gradually* expand your routine and increase its pace as your body's condition improves. Don't worry if your heart is beating strongly and your breath is coming fast just after you stop exercising. That's normal. But if your breath is still short and your heart rate fast several minutes after you've stopped, you're probably over-exerting yourself. Cut back to a slower and/or shorter routine. Serious overexertion—too strenuous a bike ride or too long a jog—may produce indigestion or nausea. These are sure signs that you should proceed with caution. Consult your doctor if they persist.

Light calisthenics, isometric exercises and weight lifting can also be beneficial to your health—especially to your strength and alertness—though the "stress-relax-stress" pattern of isometrics and weight lifting is not recommended for those with heart problems. Several efficient, graded exercise routines for people over 60 are available in book form (see *Sources for Further Information*).

SKIN

Until very recently it was thought that nothing could be done about aging of the skin. Older people accepted the fact that their skin would start to wrinkle and sag, turn dry and become flaky. Now, however, there are things that can be done, and since serious research on skin care is being conducted for the first time, the prospects are even better for the future.

Skin has two layers: the epidermis, the top layer, and the dermis, the bottom layer. The epidermis is composed of cells that form in the underlying dermis and get pushed up to the surface. In time they dry up and are shed. These cells, however, are constantly being renewed. But when we get older, the cells do not renew themselves as quickly. Their shapes become irregular, and under magnification, it can be seen that they are dried out. This process actually starts in the bottom layer of the skin, the dermis. Among the blood vessels, collagen and elastin found in this layer, cell production is initiated.

All that could be done before now to prevent dried-out skin was to use a moisturizer, which gave the skin a better appearance for a time by filling the cracks. But moisutrizers don't actually change the skin. Now laboratory experiments aimed at speeding up cell renewal, the vital step toward better skin, are meeting with success. Scientists are achieving this success with vitamin A acid. It is applied to the skin, and not only does it appear to speed up cell renewal, it also seems to restore the normal appearance of the cells. What it means in practical terms is younger-looking skin.

Vitamin A acid is still sold only as a prescription drug, and it is uncertain when and under what conditions it will be available as an across-the-counter item. But some companies are starting to market other products that they claim can help in speeding up renewal of skin cells. Whether these claims are valid is still uncertain. Check with your doctor before buying such products.

HAIR

There is nothing now known that will restore hair once it starts to fall out or to return it to its youthful color once it starts to go gray. Hair, of course, is produced by hair follicles. These do not disappear with age. But for some unknown reason, hair follicles on men's heads (and occasionally women's) sometimes become inactive. Why this should be so on the top of the head but often not on the sides, why the hair follicles on the face continue to produce the same amount of hair and why follicles in the ears suddenly become active in the elderly are mysteries awaiting answers. Lots of cures are advertised, but the only currently successful method for restoring hair is through the lengthy, painful and expensive method of hair transplant.

The graying of hair presents no mysteries. It comes about because the rate of pigmentation production in the follicle slows down.

VISION

If you are over 45 and do not need glasses for reading or other close-up work, consider yourself lucky. Most people begin to need corrective lenses for this kind of thing between the ages of 40 and 45. In most cases the ability of eyes to see keenly begins to diminish before 45, though we all know of exceptions. Once the process begins, we usually adjust more slowly to light changes because the pupils get smaller and don't react as quickly. There is a loss of peripheral vision, that is, the ability to see things far out on either side without turning the head. Finally, there is a loss of ability to see well when the light is dim. These problems are the result of damage to the transparent portions of the eye. At this time such damage can't be prevented or altered, but through the use of proper glasses, it can be minimized and made tolerable.

In addition to the regular checkup your doctor gives you, it is a good idea to have an opthalmologist check your eyes every other year. The examination an optometrist performs is not quite as thorough. Your checkup should definitely include a test for glaucoma, which is a disease of the eye marked by increased pressure inside the eyeball and gradual loss of vision. Glaucoma is, in fact, one of the leading causes of blindness. But it needn't be. If the disease is diagnosed and treated early, serious damage can be averted.

HEARING

Hearing is affected by age. It begins with a difficulty in hearing words properly. Another symptom is that the ability to hear highs and lows starts to diminish. When you pass 60, it's likely that you will not be able to hear frequencies over 4,000 cycles. It is also likely that you will not notice the decline in your hearing since it is gradual.

Nothing can be done about this gradual deterioration, but far too many people, upon discovering that they do not hear as well as they once did, put it down to age and simply try to live with it. Don't you do this. Hearing loss can come from something as simple as wax in the ear (which a doctor can remove) to the formation of deposits that inhibit the mechanical functioning of the ear and cause loss of hearing (which often can be corrected by surgery). There are many reasons for loss of hearing that are medical and not age-related. If you are starting to have trouble with your hearing, see your physician. If your physician can't help you, he or she should send you to a specialist—for example, an otologist or an audiologist—who will find out what kind of nonmedical therapy may be of assistance. It is quite possible that the best answer to the problem will be a hearing aid.

TEETH

More than half of the over-65 age group have false teeth, but it doesn't have to be that way. Regular visits to your dentist can prevent many dental problems.

With the years come changes all around the mouth, in the chemical content of the saliva, in the joints, in the bone around the teeth and in the teeth themselves. One of the most common problems after the age of 50 is periodontal disease, which, if not treated, eventually leads to the withdrawal of the bones that support the teeth, resulting in teeth loss. But something can be done about it, just as something can be done about repairing teeth or replacing them if nothing can be done to save them. Preventive periodontal care requires regular visits to the dentist, once a year at least, and twice a year to your dentist's hygienist. The hygienist uses dental instruments to remove plaque that gets under the gums where you can not get at it by self-treatment. However, with a combination of regular treatment at home, which your dentist will instruct you in, and yearly visits to the dentist, you will keep and enjoy your own teeth for many more years than was possible years ago.

If dentures are required, proper fit and proper care are absolutely essential. It is not necessary to keep them in expensive solutions overnight. Vinegar will do just as well. Just remember to brush your dentures before putting them back in your mouth.

Good teeth mean more pleasure from life because you can eat and even speak better and more comfortably. But they are also essential to good health and have not been given the attention they deserve.

SEX

Why do people have sex? Or to put it less clinically, why do people make love? Obviously because it feels good. It is a physically unique act, extraordinarily pleasurable. Most people never find any sensation they prefer to it. Is that all? No. While it is one of the most sensually enjoyable acts people can do together, it presents other dividends just as enjoyable and perhaps even more important. Making love is the most intimate contact two people can have. Barriers break down in this shared experience. That aloneness in which so much of ordinary life is spent is, for the duration of lovemaking, stripped away. We encounter, almost simultaneously, pleasure, peace and fulfillment.

Then why should older people want to discontinue such a desirable experience? Why should it be the exclusive property of the young or middle-aged? The question would seem to answer itself, but it isn't so. Researchers in this highly important field have discovered attitudes ranging from the view that it is somehow "wrong," even immoral, for older people simply to have sexual desires to a belief that sex after 50 or 60 is no longer enjoyable.

We are afflicted with stereotypes: a sexually active young man is a stud—admirable; a sexually active older man is an old goat—reprehensible. The idea that an older woman who enjoys sex and still wants to have it is somehow distasteful. If she is a widow, quite likely since women now live to be 75 or more while men die at about 70, and she is thinking of remarrying, it is somehow shameful. If she establishes a relationship with a man outside the bounds of matrimony, it is totally mortifying. Many grown children cannot abide the idea of even their own aging parents continuing to make love. Alex Comfort recently commented on this, saying that older people "have been hoodwinked out of continuing sexual activity by a society which disallows it for the old, as they have been hoodwinked out of so many other valuable activities of which they are fully capable. . . ."

The answers to the questions older people (and those interested in them) might wish to ask about continuing sexual activity are those common sense would seem to suggest. As we get older we cannot run as fast or throw as hard. With the passage of the years, we are weaker. We do not move quickly or with the same agility. So it is with our sexual functioning, though it is interesting to note that sexual decline is not as rapid nor does it go as far as physical decline. Few people are still hitting tennis balls in their old age, but one study shows that 15 percent of those over 78 were still sexually active. There is another valid comparison to activity in sports. Sex, like sports, remains thoroughly enjoyable—on its own level. As one might expect, however, it takes longer for some things to happen, and some reactions are no longer as strong.

In brief, it has been established that men take longer, starting at about 50, to achieve erection. When the orgasm comes, it is of shorter duration and is less forceful. Occasionally, the older male (and not infrequently the younger one, for that matter) will fail to achieve ejaculation. This often worries the individual involved. It does not worry the investigator of sexuality because it is not something to get anxious about. It does not mean the end of manhood. This supposed "failure" does not spell the end of sexual capacity. It can present an advantage because it then becomes possible soon after to achieve erection once again. It is the anxiety itself that is the real enemy, possibly leading to the conclusion of a self-fulfilling prophecy, that is, losing one's powers simply from becoming convinced that those powers are going or gone.

Aging presents men with another advantage. Having reached what is called a plateau in the act of making love, they can usually maintain this plateau longer than younger men.

Roughly the same qualifications hold true for women. There is, first of all, absolutely no truth to the stereotype that making love is no longer pleasurable after menopause. Enjoyment of sex comes primarily from stimulation focused on the clitoris. This response remains pretty much the same through life, and so sexual pleasure in the act of lovemaking should continue. It is true that after menopause, because of changes in the walls of the vagina, it takes longer for a woman to lubricate. This calls for more preliminary lovemaking. But since older men also take longer to reach the point where they are ready for the act of intercourse, no problem should be presented.

Most problems, in fact, are the result of social perceptions, such as the notion that the elderly do not need or should not indulge in sex. Actually, many people do need it, to the extent that today masturbation, once so frowned upon, is in many cases considered a sensible alternative.

Nor is it any more valid to believe that only young people look attractive, or "sexy," and therefore only they should have the privilege of making love. This is based on no sensible or firm foundation, and fortunately it is diminishing, perhaps because the number of older people and their percentage of the population are increasing.

Practice may not make perfect, but it does help. In a Duke University study done in 1968, Pfeiffer, Verwoerdt and Wang discovered that "if one's sex life has been full and one's sensuality not blocked by anxiety or convention, sexuality in old age becomes a different and quieter experience, but not less sexual than in youth." Other studies maintain that those who were sexually active when young will continue to enjoy it longer when old. The Franklin approach of saving for a rainy day does not apply to sexuality.

It is not, however, compulsory for everyone to enjoy sex after 60—many people lead what they consider to be a full and happy life without it. The choice to have or not to have sex is, properly, one's own. The point is that this does not change simply because people age.

There can be health problems preventing or inhibiting sex. Diabetes is one of them. If diagnosed and treated early enough, this disease need not interefere with having sex. However, 30 to 60 percent of men who get diabetes find themselves unable to achieve an erection or to maintain one long enough to have a sexual episode. There is also an assumption that a prostate operation leaves a man impotent. While this actually happens in only about 30 percent of all prostate cases, a number of others think they are impotent as a result of the operation and really need psychological counseling to deal with the problem.

PRIME-OF-YOUR-LIFER

Mary Steichen Calderone

Dr. Mary Steichen Calderone's success is not based on having been the daughter of Edward Steichen, one of America's most famous photographers. Dr. Calderone's achievements are her own, and the most important have been in the once forbidden area of sexuality.

In her youth—she is now 75—the study of sexuality and its importance and of the need for people to understand themselves sexually was scandalous. Mary Calderone was called everything from a pervert to a communist subverter in those pioneer days. But she clung to the conviction that understanding what sex means and what it does, for all people at all ages, is absolutely basic to a happy life.

Dr. Calderone considers the establishment of the Sex Information and Education Council of the United States (SIECUS) her principal achievement. It is a clearinghouse for information and is responsible for books and periodicals on sexuality and its significance in many fields. One of these concerns the elderly (see *Sources for Further Information*).

SIECUS, now 15 years old, is affiliated with New York University. As for Dr. Calderone, she too is as active as ever, great-grandmother or no. Since her father lived to a vigorous 94, she finds no reason to be surprised by her continued vitality.

MEMORY

As we get older, some of us do have a little more difficulty in retrieving quickly from memory a specific name or place. If it should happen to you, the answer is not to be troubled by it. The name will come. The problem may lie with all the information that you've stored up over the years. I remember talking to Averell Harriman, former governor of New York, ambassador to the Soviet Union, Secretary of Commerce, special State Department emissary and Lord knows what else, when he was well over 80. Mr. Harriman complained mildly that his memory was not what it had been, while giving a virtuoso performance of remembering everyone and everything pertinent to the entire history of our former entanglement in the affairs of Vietnam. We are not all Harrimans, but in our own way we can keep exercising our memories and our minds.

There is no particular trick to this. You do not have to undertake a special series of mental exercises to keep your mind sharp and to keep your ability to learn at a high level. But do discard the notion that there is no point in keeping abreast of new ideas because of some absurd idea that this is not for older people.

If you do decide that this is actually a good time to study, even if it's been some time since you actually set out to learn something new, you will be in very good company. A growing number of elders are going to universities and colleges, some studying solely for fun, but others competing against youngsters on even terms, no advantages requested or given, and doing it quite successfully, thank you!

SENILITY

One of our foremost researchers in the area of senility, Dr. Arthur Freese, writes in his book *The End of Senility* that there really isn't any such thing. What is called "senility" is sometimes the result of a virus infection, sometimes really nothing but depression (both of which are treatable) and sometimes the result of something called organic brain syndrome.

Organic brain syndrome can be brought on by a number of illnesses, such as pneumonia, heart conditions, arteriosclerosis and emphysema, and by the overuse of some drugs. Tranquilizers and "psychotropic" (mind-changing) drugs, like the phenothiazines often used to combat depression, have been known to produce organic brain syndrome. Popular brands of this drug family are Thorazine and Mellaril. Another family of drugs associated with organic brain problems are the steroids sometimes used to fight arthritis. If you feel any side effects from the medication you are on, notify your doctor immediately.

What happens in these cases is that the brain does not get the nourishment it must have, hence the so-called senile symptoms—disorientation, forgetfulness, cognitive lapses and facial paralysis. Never simply accept the onset of what seems like senility as inevitable. If diagnosed early, almost all experts in this field say it can be reversed or at least

controlled. Only where actual brain damage has occurred—
and this is a small minority of cases, perhaps 10 percent—is
there no possibility of improvement.

Being in constricted surroundings and having nothing to
do can lead to conditions that seem like what is called
senility. Lack of intellectual or emotional stimulation, a
depressing atmosphere or a feeling of being unable to cope
and having nobody to help can also cause an elderly individual to exhibit all the symptoms of being mentally incapable
of dealing with life when actually there is no loss of brain
function. Given the estimates that between 10 and 30
percent of older people are chronically depressed, imagine
how many people who are thought of as senile may really be
just sad.

CHRONIC ILLNESSES

About eight percent of our population will have one or
more chronic illnesses by the time they reach 65. Some of
these can become very severe: arthritis, diabetes, cancer and
heart disease. But although we are, after all, going to die of
something, sometime, the trick is to be aware of the symptoms of these illnesses and to do all that we can to prevent
their untimely assault on us. The following sections discuss
these major illnesses in terms of what they are, what their
symptoms are and how you can help prevent them. (For
more detailed advice on any one of these illnesses, write to
the appropriate organization listed in *Sources for Further
Information.*)

ARTHRITIS

The word arthritis means "inflammation of the joints." So
virtually any joint irritation will commonly be called "arthritis." The form most common in older people—*osteoarthri-
tis*—covers most joint inflammations for which no other
cause can be found. It can affect any joint, particularly those
subjected to unusual wear over the years. Those who injured

a joint when young may find that it gives them pain in later years; sportsmen or workers who overuse certain joints may be troubled by them later; fat people frequently have pain in their ankle and knee joints. The discomfort is usually comparatively mild, occurring when the affected joint is used. Aspirin or aspirin substitutes are usually effective in controlling the pain.

Three times as many women as men get *rheumatoid arthritis*, the most crippling form of the disease. Its causes are unknown, but it affects chiefly the joints and feet, causing swelling, stiffness, pain and sometimes permanent deformity. General weakness, fever, weight loss, loss of appetite, neck and back pains and tingling or clamminess in the hands and feet are the first symptoms. A less common subtype affects the face, causing shooting pains through the jaws, difficulty in opening and closing the mouth and a constant dull ache in the joints of the jaw. Rheumatoid arthritis usually strikes those between the ages of 20 and 35, so if you haven't got it yet, you probably never will. If you *have* had it, however, you should know that it will never go away. Treatment with aspirin and anti-inflammatory medicines—less and less frequently with cortisone because of this drug's side effects—can reduce the pain considerably, and the disease often disappears of its own accord for months or even years. But don't listen to the fast-buck artists selling copper bracelets or sure cures in the Arizona sun. Arthritis will never kill you, but there is still no cure for it.

Men are subject to a form of arthritis called *gout*. It affects mainly the feet, causing severe pain, inflammation and swelling in the big toe. An excess of uric acid crystals in the body seems to be the cause. Drugs and special diets are usually sufficient to control the disease, and happily, since a large amount of uric acid is passed in the semen, sexual activity helps to mitigate the symptoms.

CANCER

Cancers are malignant tumors, that is, growths or swellings composed of abnormal cells. Unlike benign tumors, which grow slowly and stay in one place, cancers multiply rapidly and sometimes spread from one part of the body to another. The word "malignant"—derived from a Latin term meaning "to do or contrive maliciously" and used to describe cancerous tumors—expresses both their mode of action and the inadequacy of our knowledge about them.

No one knows what causes any cancer. The list of theories and speculations reminds one of Claude Raines' droll remark when Humphrey Bogart murders the Nazi colonel in *Casablanca*, "Round up all the usual suspects." Still, a few of the most responsible theories are worth repeating here since following their advice may help you *prevent* certain cancers.

Occurrence of *lung cancer* shows a very positive connection with cigarette smoking. One sure and easy way to protect yourself from lung cancer is to quit smoking. Remember that lung cancer is one of the most virulent of all cancers, killing nine out of 10 of its victims.

Many *skin cancers* seem to be associated with overexposure, during a period of years, to the direct rays of the sun. Many doctors now recommend that sunbathers wear lotions containing PABA whenever they lie out in the sun, and several over-the-counter suntan lotions contain this sunscreening substance.

Cancers of the colon and rectum have given rise to numerous theories about the best diet for avoiding them. These theories implicate everything from food additives to pesticides to charcoal-broiling as cancer-causing agents. Certain substances whose connection to cancer has been proven—the pesticide DDT, for example—have been banned, and more are being found each year. Controversy over testing methods, hype from both industries and regulators and the sheer expense of eating foods that contain *no* additives make it very difficult for an individual of ordinary means to adjust his or her diet according to the "latest" findings. There are, however, at least two easy-to-make changes in your eating habits that may both reduce your risk

of getting cancer of the colon and rectum and improve your
general health. High-fat diets have been associated in some
studies with increased risk of cancer. Eating too many fatty
foods has also been linked with heart disease. Thus, cutting
your intake of fatty foods may help you kill two birds with
one stone. Lack of food fiber in the diet has also been linked
with colon/rectal cancer. Fiber is provided by such foods as
nuts, whole grains and raw vegetables. The theory is that
fiber, though it provides no nutritional benefits, helps clean
out the colon and is therefore vital to health.

By no means have all of the cancers been mentioned in
this section. The best means of combating the rest of them is
to catch them early, before symptoms appear. Your annual
medical checkup should include a chest X ray, a rectal
examination and a close examination of the mouth. Women
should have a Pap test twice yearly and should perform a
self-examination of the breasts every month as well as have a
doctor perform an examination each year.

There are seven kinds of symptoms that *may* mean
cancer. Often they have nothing to do with cancer, but the
presence of any one of them is a good reason to see your
doctor and find out. These are the symptoms:

1. Unusual bleeding or discharge from such organs
   as breast, penis or uterus
2. A lump in the breast or anywhere else
3. A change in appearance of a mole or a wart
4. A persistent, running sore
5. A persistent hoarseness or cough
6. Persistent indigestion or difficulty in swallow-
   ing
7. A change in bowel or bladder habits

Treatment for cancer ranges from surgical removal of the
tumor to chemical and radiation therapy. Surgery at the
early stage of a tumor's growth may effectively end the
problem by preventing its spread to other organs.

Skin cancer, the slowest moving of the cancers, is often successfully treated by surgery or chemotherapy. A breast cancer, discovered early, can be stopped in its tracks by removal of the affected breast (an operation called a mastectomy). Just how much of the breast should be removed is a subject of controversy, and if you have a breast cancer, you should ask your doctor to explain the surgical options. Chemotherapy is well known for its side effects, among them nausea, loss of hair and reduced ability of the body's healthy cells to fight off disease. Not all anticancer drugs cause the same side effects, however, and the pain and discomfort of the treatment, in many cases, is rewarded by a longer and healthier life.

The good news for elders is that cancers spread far more slowly in us than they do in younger people. Postmortems have discovered cancers in the old that were neither felt nor suspected during life. Having said all this, the best advice for us over-55s is, Don't waste time worrying about cancer. It's not worth the increase in tension and stress.

DIABETES

Diabetes occurs more often in people over 40 than in younger people. Caused by the body's inability to convert sugars (and to a lesser extent, fats and proteins) into usable form, it also appears more frequently in the obese and in people whose parents have had the disease. Its symptoms are so varied that the best preventive measure you can take is to have a regular medical examination, including blood and urine tests.

Diabetes can be controlled in some instances by a special diet (low fat, high carbohydrate) or by a medicine that stimulates the pancreas to produce more insulin, the hormone the body needs to convert sugar into food. More serious cases require regular injections of synthetic insulin to bring the disease under control. Properly treated, diabetes becomes little more than an inconvenience, requiring frequent checkups and careful self-medication. Untreated, it can cause cataracts and hardening of the arteries and can leave the body vulnerable to infection.

HEART DISEASE

Those two words cover several afflictions, each brought on (in most cases) by one or both of the following conditions: *high blood pressure* (or hypertension) and *arteriosclerosis*. *High blood pressure* occurs when the arteries contract, forcing the heart to work harder to pump blood through them. *Arteriosclerosis* (or hardening of the arteries) occurs when the inner walls of the arteries are narrowed by the buildup of cholesterol and other fatty deposits along them. The condition both reduces blood flow to the rest of the body and increases the danger of blood clots, which can block the blood supply to either the heart or the brain.

These two conditions are the major causes of the most serious cardiovascular diseases—heart attack and stroke. They should be of particular concern to elders since our risk is substantially higher than that of younger people. Three-quarters of the six million yearly deaths from heart attack occur among those over 65. Six out of seven deaths from stroke occur in the same age group.

HEART ATTACK

Heart attacks strike when the blood's path to the heart is blocked, usually by a blood clot lodged in an important artery. The heart muscle begins to die from lack of blood. In a mild heart attack, the circulatory system may succeed in compensating for the loss of one artery by sending more blood in through other arteries. An even milder form of this blood starvation—really not a heart attack at all—can be caused simply by constriction of the arteries resulting from, say, physical exertion or emotional stress. The blood supply to the heart drops briefly into the danger zone and the sufferer has chest pains. This kind of episode, called *angina,* can occur repeatedly without actually damaging the heart and medication can control it, but its symptoms are so similar to the onset of a true heart attack that they call for immediate medical attention, at least on first occurrence. Some people who periodically experience angina pains can learn to recognize them and take the appropriate medicine.

The danger signs of heart attack are the following:

1. Prolonged pressure, fullness or squeezing just under the breast bone in the center of the chest
2. Pain spreading through shoulder, neck and arms
3. Fainting, sweating, nausea, shortness of breath, severe pain

If you feel such symptoms, call your local hospital immediately and arrange for an ambulance or friends to drive you there. First aid for heart attacks—cardiopulmonary resuscitation (or CPR)—may help a person who is having a heart attack, but you should perform it only if you've been trained in the technique. Chapters of the American Heart Association (see *Sources for Further Information*) can provide you with information about CPR training in your area.

Recovery from heart attacks is common, providing that they have not been too severe. A combination of medications, proper diet and avoidance of stress can often add years of health to the life of someone who has had a heart attack. In some cases coronary bypass surgery—a procedure whereby a healthy vein is attached to the heart and to the affected artery so as to provide an alternate pathway for the blood—can give lasting relief.

STROKE

Strokes are the other form of cardiovascular disease. They are much like heart attacks, except that they attack the brain instead of the heart. A blood clot may lodge in one of the important vessels leading to the brain, preventing the tissues from receiving an adequate blood supply. In other cases a blood vessel within the brain may become weakened and burst, flooding the tissue with blood. In either case brain cells may be temporarily or permanently damaged, and the sufferer may be left with partial paralysis and difficulty in speaking or understanding language. One distressing habit some stroke victims develop is the tendency to cry out loudly.

The seriousness of such a disease to physical and emotional well-being makes prompt action urgent. If you feel these warning signs of a stroke, consult your doctor immediately:

1. Unexplained headaches
2. Temporary loss of balance
3. Double vision
4. Sudden, temporary loss of vision
5. Trouble speaking or understanding speech
6. Persistent difficulty in thinking straight
7. Numbness in face, arms or legs

The chances are that your fears will be groundless. But it's best to be sure. Early detection can prevent a major stroke.

Contrary to some horror stories, surviving stroke victims are not doomed to a bedridden life of terror. The brain itself is quite resourceful, healing some damaged cells and shifting important cerebral functions out of "dead" cells and into underused ones. Stroke victims may thus recover some of all of the motor and speech functions affected by the disease. In the rehabilitation phase, the key elements are the victim's own desire to improve and the support (not patronizing) of his or her family and friends. Medication and therapy can help restore normal functioning and prevent early recurrence.

Heart diseases are the biggest killers in America today, but taking proper care of yourself can help you *prevent* them. If you smoke, quit. Avoid overeating. Exercise regularly (see section on "Fitness" in this chapter). Have regular checkups, eat a balanced diet that is low in cholesterol and saturated fats, both of which may increase your chance of heart disease.

SOURCES FOR FURTHER INFORMATION

Fitness

The following publications offer helpful suggestions for keeping fit in the later years of life:

Hornbaker, Alice. *Preventive Care: Easy Exercises Against Aging.* New York: Drake Publishers, Inc., 1974.

Christensen, Alice, and Rankin, David. *Easy Does It: Yoga for People Over 60.* Write to Saraswati Studio, Inc., 1249 Cedar Road, Cleveland, Ohio 44106.

Adult Physical Fitness (Consumer Information Catalogue No. 033E). Write to Consumer Information Center, Pueblo, Colo. 81009.

Pep Up Your Life: A Fitness Book for Seniors. Write to The Travelers Insurance Companies, Marketing Services Department, 1 Tower Square, Hartford, Conn. 06115.

Vision

For detailed information about how to prevent vision problems, write to:

National Society for the Prevention of Blindness
79 Madison Avenue
New York, N.Y. 10801

Hearing

If your doctor recommends that you get a hearing aid, make sure that you're fitted with one that will solve your hearing problem at the lowest cost by visiting a nonprofit hearing clinic. For addresses, write to:

National Association of Hearing and Speech Agencies
814 Thayer Avenue
Silver Springs, Md. 20910

For information on deafness, write to:

Deafness Research Foundation
Suite 705
366 Madison Avenue
New York, N.Y. 10017

Teeth

For detailed information about how to prevent teeth problems, write to:

American Dental Association
211 E. Chicago Avenue
Chicago, Ill. 60611

Sex

The following three institutions will give help and advice on sexual matters:

Community Sex Information and Educational Service
P.O. Box 2858
Grand Central Station
New York, N.Y. 10017

Journal of American Medical Association
535 N. Dearborn St.
Chicago, Ill. 60610

Sex Information and Educational Council
New York University
New York, N.Y. 10003

Here is a selection of books and articles on sex:

Comfort, Alex. *Sexuality and Aging* (SIECUS Report vol. 4, number 6, July (1976). Institute for Higher Studies. Santa Barbara.

Dresen, S. E. "The Sexually Active Middle Adult." *American Journal of Nursing*, June 1975, 75:1001–1005.

Masters, William H., and Johnson, Virginia E. *Human Sexual Inadequacy*. Boston: Little and Brown, 1976.

Rossman, I., "Sexual Function During Advancing Ages," in Chap. 29 *Clinical Geriatrics*. Philadelphia: I.B. Lippincott, 1971.

Rubin, Isadore. *Sexual Life After Sixty*. New York: Signet Books, 1965.

——. *Sexual Life in the Later Years*. (SIECUS Study Guide No. 12). New York, 1970.

Arthritis

For detailed information on arthritis, write to:

Arthritis Foundation
3400 Peachtree Rd., N.E.
Atlanta, Ga. 30326

Cancer

For information on cancer, write to:

American Cancer Society
777 Third Avenue
New York, N.Y. 10017

This is the society's national headquarters, which also coordinates the activities of the following groups:

International Association of Laryngectomees
Reach to Recovery (for mastectomy patients)
Stop Smoking Programs

Write to the national headquarters for information about any of these programs. For a publication that explains how women can examine their breasts to detect cancer, write for:

Breast Self-Examination (Consumer Information Catalogue No. 555E). Consumer Information Center, Pueblo, Colo. 81009

For information from an organization that helps families of cancer patients, especially those with leukemia, write to:

Candlelighters
123 C St., S.E.
Washington, D.C. 22223

For information on leukemia, write to:

Leukemia Society of America, Inc.
211 E. 43rd St.
New York, N.Y. 10017

Diabetes

For information on diabetes, write to:

American Diabetes Association
1 W. 48th St.
New York, N.Y. 10020

Heart Disease

The American Heart Association has local chapters throughout the country that sponsor the self-help groups listed below. For information on different types of heart disease and on the activities of the self-help groups, contact your local chapter (you'll find the address in your telephone book) or write to the national headquarters:

American Heart Association
7320 Greenville Ave.
Dallas, Tex. 75231

Self-help groups:

Mended Hearts (for people who've had heart disease and surgery)
Heart-to-Heart (for the spouses of heart patients)

Zipper Clubs (for open-heart surgery patients)
Smoking Withdrawal Programs
Stroke Clubs
Cardiopulmonary Resuscitation (CPR) Training Programs

DIET

HOW MUCH

Sensible diets for those who risk heart disease are the low-fat and low-sodium diets, mentioned in the previous section. "Fad" diets are many and generally not much use. Some claim miraculous results from consumption of sardines; others say we should eat more beets; still others depend on such arcane methods as injections of a serum made from pregnant mares' urine. But the best advice for most people over 50 is to maintain a balanced diet, cutting down slightly on calories to compensate for their decreased physical activity and slower metabolic rate. Calories are nothing but a convenient way to measure the energy value of foods we eat. Caloric needs vary from individual to individual, and the best way to determine your own needs is to find the level of consumption that maintains your normal weight. In general terms, however, a man in his 60s will require only 2,400 to 2,800 calories and a woman only 1,500 to 2,000 calories. These figures represent 200 to 300 fewer calories than we needed when we were young. You can eat a regular, balanced diet, but eat less of each food.

NUTRIENTS

Nutrition is important at all ages. Proteins help maintain body structure and provide energy. Carbohydrates (starch and sugar) and fats provide energy and carry important vitamins. Vitamins and certain minerals further the chemical reactions that keep our organs functioning (see Table 15 on p. 296). A proper diet includes some of each important nutrient.

Table 15

Functions of Important Nutrients

Protein	Preserves and repairs tissues. Forms antibodies to fight infection.
Carbohydrate	Provides Energy. Contains fiber, which prevents constipation.
Fat	Provides energy. Promotes healthy skin.
Vitamin A	Promotes healthy eyes, skin and hair Aids in resisting infection.
Vitamin C	Promotes healthy gums and skin. Helps to heal wounds and bones. Aids in resisting infection.
Thiamin (B_1)	Aids digestion. Promotes a healthy nervous system.
Riboflavin (B_2)	Promotes healthy eyes, skin and mouth. Aids use of oxygen from air.
Niacin	Promotes healthy digestive tract and nervous system.
Calcium	Helps preserve and repair bones and teeth. Aids muscle contraction and blood clotting.
Iron	Aids in building red blood cells to carry oxygen to all parts of body.

Source: National Dairy Council

PROTEINS

Proteins are composed of amino acids. Some amino acids can be produced by the body itself; others—called the "essential" amino acids—must be obtained from food. In other words, all amino acids are not created equal, so not all proteins will have the same nutritional value. Since animals have physical needs similar to ours, the proteins we get by eating foods made from them—meat, fish, poultry, milk, eggs and cheese—are the most "complete" proteins for our bodies. Plant protein sources may be equally high in protein, but the amino acids contained in the plant proteins are less likely to include all those essential for human consumption. A cup of kidney beans, for example, is as high in protein as a cup of beef stew, but the stew is more nutritious because it contains all the essential amino acids.

The fact that animal products are more efficient proteins doesn't mean that vegetable sources should be ignored. The truth is that certain combinations of grains and/or vegetables—particularly of legumes (beans and peas) and cereals (rice and other grains)—provide proteins every bit as complete as meat proteins, provided the plant products are *eaten together*. Why? Because the essential proteins in the one type make up for the lack in the other type and vice versa. This accounts for the popularity of rice and beans in Mexico and Latin America. Bread and peanut butter is another good combination. The advice for vegetarians is to eat a variety of grains and vegetables together; eat plenty of vegetables, since many are lower in protein than meat; and supplement your diet with milk, cheese, eggs or vitamin B_{12} pills, since B_{12} is absent from vegetables.

CARBOHYDRATES

Carbohydrates are abundant in most vegetables and fruits. Because such foods are cheap to produce, they provide 70 percent of the world's calorie consumption. The body converts carbohydrates into glucose, distributes glucose to different parts of the body for energy and stores the rest as fat. Some carbohydrates are among the most efficient food sources we have. Potatoes, for example, though lower in protein than meat, contain abundant carbohydrates, vitamins and 30 important minerals. Potatoes alone will sustain life longer than any other single food, including milk!

FATS

Fat has had bad press in 20th-century America, but the truth is it's just as important a nutrient as any other. After all, we don't get "fat" from fats alone. Excess protein and carbohydrates are also stored in our bodies as what we inaccurately call "fat." True fat provides our most concentrated energy source. A single gram of fat provides more than twice the calories a gram of protein or carbohydrate does. Fat also carries vitamins and the linoleic acid necessary for healthy skin and proper growth. A small amount of fat, however, is sufficient to supply vitamin and acid needs. And since fat is unusually high in calories, it is most likely to end up padding our bellies and hips if we eat too much of it. For this nutrient as for others, moderate consumption is the key.

"Saturated fats" are thought to increase the cholesterol level in the blood and thus to increase our risk of heart disease. Many doctors recommend diets low in these fats. In general, the saturated fats are animal fats—present in large amounts in such products as butter and heavily marbled beef, pork and lamb—but chocolate and palm and coconut oils are also unusually high in saturated fats. "Polyunsaturated fats," on the other hand, may actually decrease the amount of cholesterol in the bloodstream. Safflower, corn, cottonseed, peanut and soybean oils are high in polyunsaturates. Margarines made from these oils are also high in polyunsaturates, though because of the process used to solidify them, they are not as high as they would be in liquid form. Avoidance of animal fats and chocolate will probably reduce your general consumption of fat and also help you keep your weight down.

VITAMINS AND MINERALS

In small amounts vitamins and minerals facilitate many bodily processes. Vitamin C helps maintain the tissue connecting body cells, B vitamins are important to digestion, vitamin D improves the bones and vitamin K helps regulate the blood's clotting. Minerals perform similar functions. The body needs only small amounts of vitamins and minerals. All of these are provided by a well-balanced diet. Therefore most vitamin supplements are unnecessary, unless you have an improper diet. If you're trying to get by on little food plus vitamins, remember this: buying vitamin supplements is the most expensive way to fill your vitamin needs.

THE BASIC FOODS

It's one thing to know what nutrients you need but quite another to learn how to get them. The problem is particularly acute for those elders on fixed incomes, but take heart! Even the poorest need not survive on bread and cat food. Balanced meals are *not* a privilege of the wealthy. If your income isn't sufficient to provide the minimum diet suggested in this section, don't fail to apply for food stamps (see the section on the "Food Stamp Program" in Chapter Three). While you worked, you paid taxes to support the program; now take advantage of its benefits.

The U.S. Department of Agriculture (USDA) distinguishes four basic food groups: meat and other high-protein foods, grains and cereals, milk foods and fruits and vegetables. See Table 16 on p. 300 for the amounts from each group you need daily.

Any way you fill those basic requirements will give you all the nutrients you need for the day. If you want to know more exactly just how much of each nutrient is provided by any food, write the USDA for its book *Nutritive Value of Foods*, an exhaustive listing of foods and their nutritive composition (see *Sources for Further Information*).

Table 16

Basic Food Groups and Servings Needed Daily

Group	Number of Servings Daily	1-Serving Equivalent
Meat	2	2–3 oz. (boneless) poultry, fish or meat 1 cup cooked dried beans, peas or lentils 2 eggs 4 tablespoons peanut butter
Grains	4	1 slice bread (enriched, if white bread) 1 oz. cold cereal ½ to ¾ cup cooked cereal, macaroni, rice, grits, cornmeal, noodles or spaghetti 1 muffin or biscuit 2 graham crackers 5 saltine crackers
Milk	2	8 oz. milk ¾ to 1 cup yogurt 1½ oz. cheddar cheese 1¾ cup ice cream 2 cups cottage cheese
Fruits and Vegetables	4	½ cup vegetable, citrus fruit or fruit juice 1 medium potato 1 medium orange, apple or other fruit ½ cantaloupe or grapefruit (pink grapefruit is more nutritious than white) 1 cup raw green leafy vegetable ½ cup cooked vegetable or fruit

Cutting costs for these basic requirements is largely a matter of careful, comparative shopping. Consumers Union put together a low-cost shopping basket for one person for a month (see Table 17 on p. 301). The foods included are high in essential nutrients and relatively low in cost.

Table 17

A Shopping Basket for One Month

---

15 quarts skim milk or equivalent in instant nonfat dry milk
1 pound cottage cheese and 1 pound natural or pasturized process cheese
(or 2 pounds of either)
1½ dozen eggs
2½ pounds margarine
1 pound ocean perch fillets (fresh, if available)
2 whole chickens or equivalent in chicken parts
2 pounds ground beef
4 cans (6½-ounce or 7-ounce) tuna fish
2 pounds beef liver
1 jar (18-ounce) peanut butter
8 cans (11½-ounce) bean soup
5 cans (6-ounce) frozen orange juice concentrate or 12 pounds citrus fruits
or tomatoes
4 pounds dark-green or deep-yellow vegetables
8 pounds potatoes
· 16 pounds other vegetables and fruits (choose a variety)
2 boxes cereal—Maypo (14-ounce), Cheerios (15-ounce) or Special "K"
(15-ounce)
7 loaves (22-ounce) enriched white bread
1 pound rice
1 pound spaghetti
1 pound flour
2 boxes (16-ounce) crackers or plain cookies
1 box (48 bags) tea or 2 pounds coffee
1½ pounds sugar

Source: Eating Right for Less, published by Consumers Union

FRILLS

Frequently some aids and supplements advertised as beneficial to older people are not necessarily so. Except in cases where your doctor prescribes them, vitamin supplements are superfluous. If you're eating well, you're already getting the vitamins and minerals you need. Vitamin E, in particular, though it's frequently touted as an anti-aging vitamin, has not been shown to have any beneficial effects at all. Mineral supplements like Geritol provide necessary iron, but if your diet is adequate, you don't need the extras.

Laxatives are often pushed on older people as an aid to digestion. Again, you should consult your doctor before embarking on any laxative programs. Usually, eating foods high in fiber will be sufficient to alleviate a constipation problem. Laxatives can be habit-forming, adding an unnecessary expense to your shopping bills.

SOURCES FOR FURTHER INFORMATION

The Consumers Union pamphlet *Eating Right for Less* is a comprehensive and well-written guide to nutrition for older people. It contains many useful suggestions about keeping food costs down. The present 1975 edition was updated in 1977. Order it for $2 plus 25¢ postage from:

Consumers Union
256 Washington St.
Mount Vernon, New York 10550

Detailed information about the nutrients in hundreds of foods is listed in the U.S. Department of Agriculture's *Nutritive Values of Foods*. Order it from:

Superintendent of Documents
U.S. Government Printing Office
Washington, D.C. 20402

HEALTH INSURANCE AND HEALTH COSTS

PUBLIC HEALTH INSURANCE

The United States is the only Western industrial country that does not have a comprehensive health insurance program. What we do have are plans that provide some health aid for the elderly and certain others. The help is limited, but in these days of soaring medical costs, it is, nevertheless, very helpful. The health plans are Medicare and Medicaid, and they are discussed in the following sections.

MEDICARE PART A

Medicare Part A covers anyone who is over 65 and who is entitled to social security or railroad retirement benefits. Notice I used the word "entitled." You are still eligible for Medicare if you are over 65 but not receiving social security. You are also eligible for it if you are less than 65 and have been disabled for 24 consecutive months under social security conditions of disability (see the section on "Social Security" in Chapter One).

Medicare Part A deals essentially with *inpatient* hospital care and *posthospital* care. For the major services that Part A covers when you're a hospital inpatient and when you are in a skilled nursing facility, see Tables 18 and 19 on p. 304.

If you have to be hospitalized, you are responsible for only the first $204, up to 60 days. After that, you must pay $51 a day for up to the next 30 days. If hospitalized for longer than 90 days, you can use up to 60 "reserve" days. These reserve days cost $100 per day, and unlike the first 90 days, the "reserve" days are not renewable. Once used, they're gone forever. Skilled nursing care while in the hospital is covered. Doctors' bills are not. A limited amount of posthospital care is provided for if it is prescribed by a doctor and approved by a certified home health agency.

But of course, as in most government-funded programs, Medicare Part A isn't quite as straightforward as this. In the following sections, I'll discuss some of the main problems under Part A that may confront you—health complications, the restrictive aspect of the program and home-care services—and how to apply for Part A.

Table 18

Major Services Part A Covers for Hospital Inpatients
1. A semiprivate room (two to four beds in a room)   2. All your meals, including special diets   3. Regular nursing services   4. Costs of special care units, such as intensive care unit, coronary care unit etc.   5. Drugs furnished by the hospital during your stay   6. Lab tests included in your hospital bill   7. X-rays and other radiology services, including radiation therapy, billed by the hospital   8. Medical supplies such as casts, surgical dressings and splints   9. Use of appliances, such as a wheelchair   10. Operating and recovery room costs   11. Rehabilitation services, such as physical therapy, occupational therapy and speech pathology

Table 19

Major Services Part A Covers for Those in a Skilled Nursing Facility
1. A semiprivate room (two to four beds in a room)   2. All your meals, including special diets   3. Regular nursing services   4. Rehabilitation services, such as physical, occupational and speech therapy   5. Drugs furnished by the facility during your stay   6. Medical supplies such as splints and casts   7. Use of appliances such as a wheelchair

HEALTH COMPLICATIONS

Suppose that after you've stayed in a hospital, you still require skilled nursing care in some type of skilled nursing facility for the same reason that initially put you into the hospital. For example, suppose you were hospitalized with a broken hip and then required rehabilitation. Nursing-home care for this sort of complication is covered under Part A. But if you got pneumonia in the hospital and were still weak upon discharge, Part A would not cover nursing-home care for that situation. To qualify for posthospital care, you would have to go home.

So if you have a condition that requires care in a skilled nursing facility after your hospitalization, Part A will pay the first 20 days in full, but after that, the cost will be $25 a day for up to a maximum of 100 days. After 100 days, the coverage stops.

RESTRICTIVE ASPECT

Medicare regulations regarding a person's eligibility for skilled nursing care are very restrictive. Restrictive in the sense that frequently, for example, a nursing home will not admit a patient on the grounds that he or she isn't eligible for nursing care under the provisions of Medicare. Quite often, however, if a nursing home or Medicare is challenged on this, the patient will win.

Keep in mind that although Medicare is a government-funded program with an independent individual as the recipient of the benefits, in between the government and the individual are insurance companies, such as Blue Cross, Blue Shield, Group Health Incorporated and Travelers, that actually administer the program. So you're dealing with an insurance company that applies insurance company principles—keeping reimbursements as low as possible.

HOME-CARE SERVICES

Part A also includes home-care services, and here you should know what your rights are. (For a summary of the conditions that you must meet to qualify for services under Part A, see Table 20 on p. 306. And for the type of services that Medicare covers, see Table 21 on p. 306.)

Table 20

Summary of Conditions to Be Met to Qualify for Home-Care Services under Part A
Medicare Part A will pay for home health visits if all of the following six conditions are met: 1. You were in a qualifying hospital for at least three days in a row (not counting the day of discharge). 2. The home health care is for further treatment of a condition that was treated in a hospital or skilled nursing facility. 3. The care you need includes part-time skilled nursing care, physical therapy or speech therapy. 4. You are confined to your home. 5. A doctor determines you need home health care and sets up a home health plan for you within 14 days after your discharge from a hospital or participating skilled nursing facility. 6. The home health agency providing services is a participant in Medicare.

Table 21

Home Health Services Covered by Medicare Under Part A or Part B*

1. Part-time skilled nursing care
2. Physical therapy
3. Speech therapy
If you need part-time skilled nursing care, physical therapy or speech therapy, Medicare can also pay for:
    • Occupational Therapy
    • Part-time services of home health aides
    • Medical social services
    • Medical supplies and equipment provided by the agency

*For a summary of conditions to be met to qualify for home health services under Part A, see Table 20 above. For a summary of conditions to be met to qualify for services under Part B, see Table 24 on p. 311.

Suppose you've been in the hospital for at least the minimum requirement of three days and the home-care services you need are related to the reasons for your hospitalization, as is required to qualify under this part of the program. Then a certified home health agency has to make an assessment of your condition, which involves visiting you at the request of your doctor and deciding what you need.

To be eligible for home care after the required period of hospitalization, you must need *skilled nursing* services. If you require only shopping, cleaning, cooking and social services, you won't qualify.

The important point here is what the agency representatives considers "skilled nursing care." Agency representatives will often speak of rehabilitation and insist that Medicare provides care only for that purpose. But they're wrong. Medicare doesn't require rehabilitation for home-care services. It only requires *maintenance.* So, for example, the question of whether or not you require a physical therapist can be a very "iffy" one. That determination is made by the certified home health agency. But take note, home health agencies are not eager to authorize services that might be denied by the next highest authority because then they will not be paid for whatever services they have already rendered. So you can see that these agencies are very conservative and very cautious.

Home health agencies, such as Visiting Nurse associations and county health departments, must employ registered nurses to be eligible to make the required assessment.

Something to keep in mind should you need home care is that an agency representative will only make an assessment if the hospital discharge planner or your physician or you call and request one. So prevail on the hospital social worker or the hospital discharge planner to make arrangements for home care, call the appropriate agency and ask for an assessment. Your doctor must be advised of what you consider to be the need and must write the proper justification for it. For example, it is not adequate for the doctor merely to state "pneumonia" or "diabetes." An agency will require a description of your functional ability as well as your medical diagnosis.

If an agency turns you down and you think the decision is wrong, you can appeal, but the appeals procedure is quite complex and must be set in motion within 60 days. There are people and organizations that can help, and somebody needing that kind of help should consult a state agency on aging office, which will advise the best way to go through this appeals procedure.

Don't wait until you get sick to apply for Medicare. Apply for it before your 65th birthday.

How to Apply

To apply for Medicare Part A, go to your local social security office or write to them for an application form.

You are eligible for Medicare at age 65 even if you are not eligible for social security because you earn more than the limit allowed. And you should enroll in the program so that if you become ill in your 65th year, you can then apply for Medicare benefits.

There are some exceptions regarding who is and who is not eligible for Medicare. For instance, if you're between 65 and 75 years and are not eligible for social security because you had jobs that were not covered, or worked for exempt institutions, then you can't apply for Medicare. However, at the age of 76, you'll qualify for Medicare regardless of whether you're eligible for social security or not.

Also, if you're under 65 and have been disabled for 24 consecutive months under social security conditions of diability (see "Social Security" section in Chapter One), you are entitled to Medicare. Or if you require kidney dialysis treatment, you're eligible for Medicare.

People who retire as early as social security allows, at age 62, should give some thought to the fact that even though they are receiving social security benefits, they are not yet eligible for Medicare. If you fall into this category, then you should either carry your company's health insurance into retirement, if that's permitted, or you should join some kind of a major medical program or take out some type of health insurance that will cover you through those years, 62 to 65. They are very vulnerable years in a person's life, and at this stage, medical costs can really bankrupt one's finances.

MEDICARE PART B

Medicare Part B is not free; there is a charge. But it is a good idea because, for a rather small monthly payment, a percentage of your doctors' bills is paid by Medicare for the rest of your life. The percentage is supposedly 80 percent of a "reasonable" fee. (This determination can vary, however, and will be discussed in more detail later in the section.) Another extra is that a substantial portion of home care is provided for under Part B.

You have to register for Part B also. So when you file your initial Medicare application, also file for Part B. Unless you have some other special coverage that you've carried over from your employment years, I urge all of you to apply for Part B because its coverage is so good and it costs only about $9.60 a month.

Part B covers a percentage of all doctors' bills incurred over the rest of your lifetime, as long as you continue to pay the premium. On the surface, the proportion is 80 percent of physicians' bills. But the coverage specifies 80 percent of usual, fair and reasonable charges. What really happens is that you go to a doctor and are charged, say, $50. However, the insurance company that administers Part B may decide the charge should be $30. So it will send you 80 percent of $30—or $24—instead of 80% of $50—or $40.

The insurance company is not always being stingy—your doctor may well be overcharging.

Because the first $60 of all medical bills is deductible, or must be paid by you, the 80 percent of the fair and reasonable charge is based on the remainder of the bill. This is especially important with something expensive like surgery. For example, say your surgery bill is $800 and the insurance company decides it should be $600. Medicare will pay only 80 percent of $540, assuming that your $60 deductible comes out of this bill. So, you'll only receive $432 and will be responsible for paying the rest—$368. This is where the appeals procedure can become terribly important.

Part B covers—and this is important to know—wheelchairs, canes, crutches and hospital beds, should you require such things at home. All durable and fixed kinds of equipment are covered. There is some psychiatric coverage— roughly 180 days during the lifetime of a person in case he or she needs institutionalization for short periods of time. (See Table 22 below for the major doctors' services covered by Part B and Table 23 below for the major outpatient hospital services covered by Part B).

Table 22

Major Doctors' Services Covered by Part B

1. Medical and surgical services
2. Diagnostic tests and procedures that are part of your treatment
3. Other services that are ordinarily furnished in the doctor's office and included in his or her bill, such as:
    ● X-rays you receive as part of your treatment
    ● Services of your doctor's office nurse
    ● Drugs and biologicals that cannot be self-administered
    ● Medical supplies
    ● Physical therapy and speech pathology services

Table 23

Major Outpatient Hospital Services Covered by Part B
1. Services in an emergency room or outpatient clinic 2. Laboratory tests billed by the hospital 3. X-rays and other radiology services billed by the hospital 4. Medical supplies such as splints and casts 5. Drugs and biologicals that cannot be self-administered

Part B also covers home care even if you have not been hospitalized. For example, suppose you had pneumonia and got treated at home—never went to the hospital—and now require skilled nursing at home. Under Medicare Part B you can get it by having your doctor write a prescription and then contacting the certified home health agency in your area to apply for home care. (See Table 24 below for a summary of the conditions that you have to meet to qualify for home-care services under Part B. And see Table 21 on p. 306 for the type of services that are covered.)

Table 24

Summary of Conditions to Be Met to Qualify for Home-Care Services under Part B
Medicare Part B will help pay for up to 100 home health visits in a calendar year. You *don't* have to have a three-day stay in hospital in order to qualify for home care under Part B. However, Part B will pay for home health visits only if all of the following four conditions are met: 1. You need part-time skilled nursing care or physical therapy or speech therapy.   2. A doctor determines you need the services and sets up a plan for home health care.   3. You are confined to your home.   4. The home health agency providing services is participating in Medicare.

Part B does not cover eyeglasses, hearing aids or dentistry.

MEDICAID

Medicaid is a supplementary medical insurance program for poor people. For example as an individual living alone, your income has to be roughly less than $300 a month to qualify. Income limits and some other eligibility criteria, however, vary from state to state, and the state of Arizona has no Medicaid program at all. Generally speaking, if you qualify for Supplementary Security Income (SSI) (see Chapter Three), you'll qualify for Medicaid. But 15 states have stricter eligibility standards. So be sure to check with your state's welfare office.

Many people who qualify for Medicaid don't apply for it because they associate it with welfare, because it's too difficult to get to the office to apply or because they're not aware of it.

In some cases, you can qualify for Medicaid even if your income is over the prescribed limit. If you find you have too much income to qualify in your state, begin saving your medical bills for the month, including those for drugs, nursing services, eye examinations and visits to the doctor and the dentist. Add to them your unpaid medical bills from the past (you can only add unpaid bills once). If your total bills for the month are equal to or greater than the amount by which your income exceeds the prescribed limit, then you are eligible for the Surplus Income Program for the coming month.

So let's assume that your income is $340 a month and you spend $40 a month on physicians' bills or prescriptions or *any* kind of health care. You can then be enrolled in the Medicaid program for the coming month. You must reapply each month, showing that your medical expenses remain at or above the amount of your excess income. Most people don't know about this program and it is not publicized. Authorities might also tell you that if you have more than a certain amount in assets, you're not eligible. But what they don't realize is that if you're spending those assets on medical bills, you become eligible when they are spent.

Medicaid covers much more than Medicare. It covers Medicare deductibles, glasses, hearing aids, prescription drugs and, under certain conditions, dentistry. Medicaid usually covers such essential dental treatment as tooth extraction, fillings and routine preventive care, but false teeth and orthodontia may also be included, provided you can show that they were essential to maintaining your health. For the last two, you need to get prior permission from your welfare office. Medicaid covers virtually all health care bills and some ancillary items such as transportation.

To see what Medicaid services each state provides, consult Table 25 on p. 314.

CANADA'S NATIONAL HEALTH INSURANCE PROGRAM

Because not too long ago Canada adopted an all-inclusive national health insurance program, it might be useful to examine just how the program was implemented.

By 1955 several of the provinces, which is where initiatives in Canada tend to begin, got very concerned over the financial problems of their hospitals. They came up with various rescue plans, but it became apparent that the problem was really a national one and required more resources than individual provinces were able to muster. (Incidentally, you can read "state" for "province" in much of this because of resemblances that you will see as we go along.)

At any rate, by 1956 it was decided that the federal government would provide part of the cost to the provinces involved. That portion would come to an average of 50 percent, depending on the wealth of the individual province.

Canada's hospitals then began providing a great deal of medical care to the public for nothing or next to nothing. The program helped many people, and financially, it certainly helped the hospitals and large segments of the medical profession. It did not help the treasuries of the federal government and the provinces. Hospital costs soared. Doctors sent everyone in need of treatment to the hospitals, and of course, the people didn't argue. They could get free or almost free treatment in the hospitals. But they couldn't get any free treatment outside the hospitals.

Something had to be done. Reports outlined the problem and eventually a decision was made. It was an interesting one. Canada would turn to a national health insurance plan.

Table 25

BASIC REQUIRED MEDICAID SERVICES* SEE BELOW	State	Podiatrists' Services	Optometrists' Services	Chiropractors' Services	Private Duty Nursing	Clinic Services	Dental Services	Physical Therapy	Occupational Therapy	Speech, Hearing, and Language Disorder	Prescribed Drugs	Dentures	Prosthetic Devices	Eyeglasses
MEDICAID SERVICES BY STATE — Optional Services in State Medicaid Programs														
•	Alabama		•								•		•	•
•	Alaska		•			•				•				•
•	Arizona													
+	Arkansas		+	+		+	+				+	+	+	+
+	California	+	+	+		+	+	+	+	+	+	+	+	+
•	Colorado	•				•					•		•	
+	Connecticut	+	+	+	+	+	+	+	+	+	+	+	+	+
•	Delaware	•				•					•			
+	D.C.	+	+			+		+			+		+	+
•	Florida										•			
•	Georgia	•				•					•		•	
+	Guam		+			+	+	+		+	+	+	+	+
+	Hawaii	+	+			+	+	+	+	+	+	+	+	+
•	Idaho	•	•	•		•		•			•			
+	Illinois	+	+	+	+	+	+	+	+	+	+	+	+	+
•	Indiana	•	•	•	•	•	•	•	•	•	•	•	•	•
•	Iowa	•	•	•			•	•	•		•	•	•	•
+	Kansas	+	+	+	+	+	+	+	+	+	+	+	+	+
+	Kentucky					+		+	+	+	+		+	
+	Louisiana			+		+					+	+	+	
+	Maine	+		+		•		+	+	+	+		+	
+	Maryland	+	+			+	+				+	+	+	+
+	Massachusetts	+	+		+	+	+	+	+	+	+	+	+	+
+	Michigan	+	+	+		+	+	+	+	+	+	+	+	+
+	Minnesota	+	+	+	+	+	+	+	+	+	+	+	+	+
•	Mississippi						•				•			
•	Missouri		•				•				•	•		•
+	Montana	+			+	+	+	+	+	+	+	+	+	+
+	Nebraska	+	\ +	+	+	+	+	+			+	+	+	+
•	Nevada	•	•	•	•	•		•	•	•	•	•	•	•

MEDICAID SERVICES BY STATE

Optional Services in State Medicaid Programs

SEE BELOW	Diagnostic Services	Screening Services	Preventive Services	Rehabilitative Services	Services for Age 65 or Older in TB Institutions			Services for Age 65 or Older in Mental Inst.			Intermediate Care Facility Services	Intermediate Care Facilities for Mentally Retarded	Emergency Hospital Services	Personal Care Services
					A. Inpatient Hospital Services	B. Skilled Nursing Facility Services	C. Intermediate Care Facility Services	A. Inpatient Hospital Services	B. Skilled Nursing Facility Services	C. Intermediate Care Facility Services				
Alabama					•				•	•	•	•	•	
Alaska								•			•	•	•	
Arizona														
Arkansas					+	•	•	+	•	•	•	•	+	•
California	+	+	+	+	+	+	+	+	+	+	+	+	+	
Colorado								•	•	•	•	•	•	
Connecticut	+	+	+	+				+			+	+		
Delaware								•			•	•	•	
D.C.	+		+	+	+			+			+	+	+	+
Florida					•			•			•	•	•	
Georgia					•	•	•		•	•	•	•		
Guam													+	
Hawaii	+	+	+	+							+	+	+	
Idaho				•						•	•	•	•	
Illinois	+		+	+	+	+	+	+	+	+	+	+	+	
Indiana	•		•	•				•			•	•	•	
Iowa	•	•	•	•				•			•	•	•	
Kansas				+	+	+	+	+	+	+	+	+	+	
Kentucky					+			+	+	+	+	+	+	
Louisiana				+	•			•	•	•	•	•	+	
Maine	+	+	+	+				+	+	•	+	+	•	
Maryland					+			+		+	+	+	+	
Massachusetts	+	+	+	+	+			+	+	+	+	+	+	+
Michigan	+							+	+	+	+	+	+	
Minnesota	+	+	+	+	+	+	+	+	+	+	+	+	+	+
Mississippi					•			•			•	•		
Missouri	•	•	•	•	•			•			•	•	•	
Montana	+	+	+	+				+	+	+	+	+	+	+
Nebraska				+				+	+	+	+	+	+	+
Nevada				•				•			•		•	•

MEDICAID SERVICES BY STATE

Optional Services in State Medicaid Programs

BASIC REQUIRED MEDICAID SERVICES*	SEE BELOW	Podiatrists' Services	Optometrists' Services	Chiropractors' Services	Private Duty Nursing	Clinic Services	Dental Services	Physical Therapy	Occupational Therapy	Speech, Hearing, and Language Disorder	Prescribed Drugs	Dentures	Prosthetic Devices	Eyeglasses
+	New Hampshire	+	+	+	+	+		+	+	+	+		+	+
•	New Jersey	•	•	•		•	•	•	•	•	•		•	•
•	New Mexico	•	•		•	•	•	•	•	•	•	•	•	•
+	New York	+	+		+	+	+	+	+	+	+	+	+	+
+	North Carolina	+	+	+		+	+				+	+		+
+	North Dakota	+	+	+	+	+	+	+	+	+	+	+	+	+
+	N. Mariana Islands		+			+	+	+			+	+	+	+
•	Ohio	•	•	•	•	•	•	•	•	•	•	•	•	•
+	Oklahoma	+					+				+		+	
•	Oregon	•	•		•	•	•	•			•	•	•	•
+	Pennsylvania	•		+		+	+				•	•	•	
+	Puerto Rico					+	+	+	+	+	+			
+	Rhode Island	+	+				+				+	+	+	+
•	South Carolina	•		•		ċ					•		•	
•	South Dakota			•		•	•	•	•		•	•	•	
+	Tennessee						+				+		+	
•	Texas	•	•	•							•		•	•
+	Utah	+	+		+	+	+	+		+	+	+	+	+
+	Vermont	+				+					+		+	
+	Virgin Islands					+	+	+	+	+	+	+	+	+
+	Virginia	+	+			+		+	+	+	+			+
+	Washington	+	+	+	+	+	+	+	+	+	+	+	+	+
+	West Virginia	+	+	+	+	+		+			+	+	+	+
+	Wisconsin	+	+	+	+	+	+	+	+	+	+	+	+	+
•	Wyoming		•										•	
20	•	14	13	10	5	14	10	9	7	6	19	10	15	11
34	+	25	25	17	14	31	24	26	19	23	33	24	30	26
54	Total	39	38	27	19	45	34	35	26	29	52	34	45	37

MEDICAID SERVICES BY STATE

	Diagnostic Services	Screening Services	Preventive Services	Rehabilitative Services	Services for Age 65 or Older in TB Institutions			Services for Age 65 or Older in Mental Inst.			Intermediate Care Facility Services	Intermediate Care Facilities for Mentally Retarded	Emergency Hospital Services	Personal Care Services
					A. Inpatient Hospital Services	B. Skilled Nursing Facility Services	C. Intermediate Care Facility Services	A. Inpatient Hospital Services	B. Skilled Nursing Facility Services	C. Intermediate Care Facility Services				
New Hampshire	+	+	+	+				+			●	●	●	+	+
New Jersey	●	●	●	●	●				●	●	●	●	●	●	
New Mexico											●	●	●	
New York	+	+	+	+	+	+	+	+	+	+	+	+	+	+
North Carolina	+	+	+	+	+			+		+	+	+		
North Dakota	+	+	+	+				+			+		+	
N. Mariana Islands					+	+		+	+				+	+
Ohio								●	●	●	●	●	●	
Oklahoma			+					+			+	+		+
Oregon	●		●					●	●	●	●	●	●	
Pennsylvania								+	+	+	+	+	+	
Puerto Rico	+	+	+	+	+								+	
Rhode Island								+			●	●		
South Carolina			- - -		●			●			●	●	●	
South Dakota				●					●	●	●	●	●	●
Tennessee					+	+	+	+	+	+	+	+	+	
Texas				●	●						●	●	●	●
Utah								+			+	+	+	
Vermont								+			+	+	+	
Virgin Islands														
Virginia					+			+	+	+	+	+	+	
Washington	+		+	+	+	+	+	+	+	+	+	+	+	
West Virginia					+	+		+	+		+	+	+	
Wisconsin	+	+	+	+	+	+	+	+	+	+	+	+	+	+
Wyoming				●								●		
●	5	3	4	10	9	2	2	14	9	12	24	22	18	4
+	17	13	16	20	18	10	8	29	18	17	26	25	28	10
Total	22	16	20	30	27	12	10	43	27	29	50	47	46	14

Optional Services in State Medicaid Programs

Although many services would continue to be provided within hospitals, the plan would do two very, very important things: change the system for financing and, where possible, use its payment system to encourage treatment in other, less-expensive institutions, like nursing homes of various kinds, and at home.

The old financing system, providing about half of all costs depending on the financial situation of the individual province, had led to an out-of-control situation. In one province, for instance, the federal government's subsidy ran to 80 percent of the cost. There was no incentive to hold costs down, as there is none here in the United States. But now the Canadian federal government would, over a period to be concluded by 1980, change the system: it would pay each province 50 percent of the *national average* for treatment of medical care multiplied by the number of patients each province had.

This system seems to have been a big incentive to save, and so has been the fact that under the new law (which has the glamorous name of C-37) federal money would be made available to the provinces for those other kinds of programs that I mentioned, programs aimed at providing alternatives to care within hospitals. In addition other kinds of medical professionals were gathered under C-37's coverage—podiatrists, dental surgeons (for care within hospitals, in this case), optometrists and even the MDs'cherished enemies, chiropractors.

What I'm giving you here is shorthand of course. But it should be emphasized that unlike Medicare and Medicaid in the United States, the Canadian system includes just about *everyone* in the country needing the kinds of care covered. The overall rule is that the costs should be for medically required services. There are no limitations. Rich as well as poor and middle-income people qualify. There are no deductions, as there are under Medicare, and there are no charges to patients, none at all.

Not *all* services are covered by *all* provinces. For example, at this time only a few cover routine dental care. Almost all cover outpatient prescriptions. And there are differences among the provinces as to whether they will or will not pay for eyeglasses for the elderly and so on. But all the basics are covered in Canada. As I said, there are no deductions; no provisions whereby after a specified number of days you, the patient, must pay a certain amount; no limitation on the length of time for treatment; and no careful differentation between what is *acute* care (covered here by Medicare) and what is *chronic* sickness (covered here only by Medicaid). (See "Canadian Sources" under *Sources for Further Information* for addresses to write to obtain detailed information on Canada's health insurance program.)

Much of the assistance provided is aimed at keeping people out of institutions, which is, as we know, a lot cheaper. Canada pays less of its gross national product to the medical profession and related fields than does the United States. And Canadians do not, as many of them have testified, live in dread of being financially destroyed by catastrophic illness.

PRIVATE HEALTH INSURANCE

Over the last 15 years, health-care costs rose 400 percent. During the same period, the proportion of expenses paid by Medicare declined to around 38 percent. Americans spent $200 billion on health care in 1979 alone. In short, if you have no private health insurance, you stand to incur greater and greater out-of-pocket expenses for health care in the coming years.

With Medicare coverage, the longer you are sick, the greater the proportion of hospital or nursing home costs you must pay. And you always pay 20 percent of doctor bills, plus any amounts that Medicare formulas deem above and beyond "reasonable charges." (Actual doctor bills are often more than Medicare's "fair and reasonable" estimates.) In addition, Medicare gives you no coverage at all for outpatient prescription drugs and long-term custodial care in a nursing home, expenses that together account for almost half of an older person's unreimbursed medical bills.

The solution isn't to dismantle Medicare. Indeed, your low-premium Part B Medicare coverage is probably the best buy you'll ever make in insurance. Since it's government-subsidized, it offers good services for a minimal premium. Moreover, if you use medicine wisely, you can keep your copayments to a minimum. If, for instance, you and your doctor decide that after 60 days in the hospital you can be transferred to a nursing facility, you'll avoid the high copayment for your first 20 days in a nursing home. Regardless, since you can't plan your illness to fit the coverage, what you need to do is find private insurance to cover what Medicare does not. (The "Medicare Gaps Checklist" below is designed to help you determine what you need in the way of private health insurance.) No private policy or combination of policies can cover all Medicare's gaps, but there are several reasonable alternatives that can take care of most of them. They are all discussed in the following sections.

Medicare Gaps Checklist

Not Covered by Medicare°	Covered by My Private Insurance Plan
$204 deductible for first 60 days in hospital	
$51 per-day copayment for 61st to 90th day in hospital	
$100 per-day copayment for up to 60 "reserve" days in hospital	
$25.50 per-day copayment for 21st through 100th day in skilled nursing facility	
$60 deductible plus 20% copayment for medical/surgical bills	
$60 deductible plus 20% copayment for psychiatric services (up to $250 per-year maximum)	

Not Covered by Medicare	Covered by My Private Insurance Plan
Private nursing costs	
Long-term custodial care in nursing home	
Outpatient prescription drugs	
Routine checkups or dental care	
Health aids (eyeglasses, dentures, hearing aids etc.)	

*Dollar amounts are those in force in January 1981.

IF YOU'RE UNDER 65

Some beneficial policies are very hard to join after you retire. Bright actuaries realize that people past retirement age are going to need more medical care, on the average, than people under 65. They are therefore reluctant to offer similar policies to both the lower- and higher-risk groups. If you join while you're still working, however, some companies will permit you to carry on with the policy even after you retire.

GROUP INSURANCE

According to the Health Insurance Institute, an industry-sponsored organization, there is a trend among insurers to allow members of group plans to continue their insurance after retirement. Continuing your group plan can be beneficial to you because group plans tend to be cheaper than individual policies and because your employer may keep subsidizing the cost of your group policy after you retire. Before you agree to continue a group policy, however, go to your personnel department and find out just how well your group policy will mesh with Medicare. Take a copy of the "Medicare Gaps Checklist" with you. If the company policy duplicates Medicare without filling the gaps, the continuing cost won't be worth it. But if it does fill Medicare gaps, then of course, continuing the policy is probably a good idea.

MAJOR MEDICAL

Major medical policies are often carried by individuals to supplement their group plans. These policies frequently have high deductibles and a coinsurance feature whereby you pay part of costs incurred (typically you pay 20 percent). They are useful as protection against catastrophic illnesses because they offer a much higher maximum benefit than do ordinary policies. If you have a major medical policy, check to see if it is "guaranteed renewable for life." If it is, ask your insurance agent about the benefits the policy will bring you when you're over 65. Some major medical policies can be used to cover the usual hospital copayments under Medicare and to pay for some of the outpatient costs that Medicare does not cover. Even if you intend to convert to another type of policy when you reach 65, you may be wise to continue your major medical until the new policy's "waiting period" is over. Most policies bought after age 65 include a period (between three months and two years) during which pre-existing illnesses are not covered. Continuing your major medical can keep you from having to pay for very large expenses until your new policy takes effect. The drawback to major medical is that it's relatively expensive to keep. Though a few companies will issue major medical policies to people over 65, such policies usually offer reduced benefits at a high price.

HEALTH MAINTENANCE ORGANIZATIONS (HMOs)

These organizations are just right for the health needs of older people, providing preventive care, diagnosis, hospitalization benefits and nursing, all for an annual fee. The problem is that very few HMOs will accept new members over age 65, and when they do, the price is high. The best way to join an HMO is through your group policy before you retire. Most group health plans automatically give you the right to join an HMO. But before you join, check to see that the organization will accept payment from Medicare as well as from your group policy. Fees for HMOs are typically quite high, but Medicare and your group policy can pick up part of the tab.

IF YOU'RE OVER 65

Occasionally, people over 65 can get major medical insurance or join an HMO, but the more popular option is a "Medigap" policy. Such policies are sold by Blue Cross/Blue Shield, some insurance companies and two retirement groups (AARP and NCSC). Medigap policies are specifically intended to fill the "gaps" in Medicare, but no two policies are alike. In general, however, there are two types: hospital indemnity policies and wrap-around policies.

HOSPITAL INDEMNITY POLICIES

These provide a fixed dollar benefit (usually between $10 and $80) for each day spent in the hospital, up to a prescribed limit. Appropriately enough, such plans are also known as "hospital income policies." But regardless of which name you call them, they are *not* the best idea for older people. In the first place, they only pay for days spent in the hospital and not for any other medical expenses. Theoretically, since Medicare covers most of your hospital bills for the first 60 days, the holder of a hospital indemnity policy can save his or her daily cash benefits and apply them later to other medical costs. This, however, seems an inconvenient and insecure way of accumulating dollars for outpatient expenses. Also, since the daily benefit is fixed, it effectively shrinks with inflation.

If you do consider a hospital indemnity policy, I strongly advise you to follow these suggestions.

● Avoid mail-order policies. They're not tailored

to the needs of older people, and they're sometimes difficult to collect on.

- Make certain that the exclusion for pre-existing
  illnesses isn't too long. Some are as long as a year
  or two. Though longer exclusion periods mean
  lower premiums, you could end up paying out of
  your pocket for serious complications resulting
  from a minor pre-existing condition.
- Find out how many days you must spend in the
  hospital *before* the policy begins paying benefits. Some policies have an "elimination period"
  during which no benefits are paid.
- Make sure you know how long you'll receive
  benefits if you stay in the hospital. Some policies
  provide benefits for two years, but others may
  pay for less than one year.

WRAP-AROUND POLICIES

This kind of coverage is, in general, the best widely
available to people over 65. It's specifically designed to
supplement Medicare, though the details of coverage vary
widely among policies. Most of them pay for the deductible
amounts in Medicare plus the copayments for extended
hospital care and physician's services. A smaller number will
cover such expenses as prescription drugs, private nurses and
unlimited hospital care. Of course the more payments
provided the higher the premiums, but wrap-around policies
are far more cost-efficient than hospital indemnity plans.
The former return an average of 70¢ for every dollar in
premiums, while the latter pay back only around 40¢ per
premium dollar. Moreover, the greatest advantage of wrap-
around policies is that they pay all (or a given precentage) of
the *actual expenses* you incur, instead of a fixed dollar
amount.

When you're shopping for a Medigap wrap-around policy, you should consider the same questions appropriate to
consideration of any policy. Make sure the exclusion for

pre-existing illnesses isn't longer than six months. Do comparison shopping to find out who offers the cheapest premiums for the best coverage with the smallest deductibles and copayments. If the policy offers coverage of "extras"—nursing care, for example—make sure that all the "extras" can be included under the same policy. Avoid buying more than one policy whenever you can.

CUTTING HEALTH COSTS

Cutting health costs means staying out of hospitals and nursing homes as much as possible. So do all you can at home or in your doctor's office. That way you'll not only avoid large expenses (which, even with insurance, will begin to use up your benefits), but also escape the usually depressing and dehumanizing atmosphere of institutional care.

LIMITING INSTITUTIONAL CARE

If possible, stay out of emergency rooms. They cost two or three times what your doctor will charge you, and especially in congested urban areas, they may keep you waiting for hours. Of course, if your condition is acute and no doctor is available, the emergency room is your only alternative. But if it's not a matter of life and death and your doctor *is* available, go to his or her office for diagnosis and treatment. You'll save money and have the advantage of getting immediate advice from a professional who knows your situation and cares about you.

If you do need minor surgery and you're in good health otherwise, ask your doctor about same-day surgery. You may be able to have preoperative tests done at your doctor's office or the hospital's outpatient clinic on the day before your operation. You enter the hospital only for the surgery itself plus a few hours afterwards for recovery and observation. You'll sleep in your own bed that night. Some of the types of operations appropriate for same-day surgery are the following: biopsies, cyst removals, hernia operations and minor plastic surgery. Even a few more serious operations can be done on a same-day basis. If a skin cancer requires removal, the procedure can often be accomplished in a single day, using only a local anesthetic. Be aware, however, that if your doctor is thinking of your general health and the possible complications that may result from surgery, he or she may hesitate to recommend same-day surgery.

If you anticipate staying more than a day in the hospital, there are still things you can do to keep costs down. First, try to choose a voluntary, nonprofit teaching hospital instead of a for-profit hospital or a public municipal hospital. The care will be more reasonable in price but still of a high quality. The Joint Committee on Accreditation of Hospitals (JCAH) puts its seal of approval on hospitals that live up to its standards for care. Find an accredited hospital in your area (see *Sources for Further Information*). Second, get as many of the necessary tests as possible done *before* you enter the hospital. That way, you won't have to pay for nights spent simply sleeping off a day's tests or preparing for the next day's tests. Third, don't take services like a private room, telephone, television or air-conditioning without first finding out what costs these will add to your bill. And finally, ask your doctor about the possibility of getting low-cost convalescent care *at home*, instead of in the hospital or at a nursing home. Some states and communities administer low-cost services, including nursing care, household maintenance and meals-on-wheels, all of which can help take care of you at home. Certain areas even offer long-term "nursing home without walls" programs, in which home care is coordinated according to your own doctor's plan. Such home-care arrangements can save up to 75 percent of the cost of hospital or nursing-home care. One 89-year-old with heart disease lived five years under a home-care program that cost him $500 per year. Nursing-home care in his community would have cost $24,700 each year! Contact your city or county health department to find out what services are available in your community.

SELF-CARE

We can all take our own temperature, and many of us can take our own pulse. Diabetics often learn to measure their own blood sugar and are taught to keep their blood sugar in balance by injecting insulin or taking sugar tablets. Angina sufferers learn to recognize their symptoms and medicate themselves. Increasingly, local chapters of the American Red Cross and American Heart Association are offering classes in such important first-aid procedures as artificial resuscitation, cardiopulmonary resuscitation and the Heimlich Maneuver (a procedure for saving choking victims). Though nothing can replace a physician's expertise in diagnosis and treatment, certain simple procedures can be usefully performed by individuals.

What is called activated patient courses are now available in many states. They offer classes on such topics as hypertension, common injuries, foot care and proper use of drugs. They also provide students with instruction in the use of such common medical tools as an otoscope for examining the ears, a stethoscope for checking heart rate and pulse, a sphygmomanometer for measuring blood pressure and a low-reading thermometer for discovering hypothermia. Such training helps the patient to become an active partner in maintaining his or her own health. Increased self-knowledge may also help reduce the "panic" calls that can lead to a needless and expensive visit to the doctor. To find out more about activated patient courses, see *Sources for Further Information*.

SOURCES FOR FURTHER INFORMATION

Public Health Insurance

The Department of Health and Human Services offers a number of basic information pamphlets on Medicare. All of the following are available from the Superintendent of Documents, U.S. Government Printing Office, Washington, D.C. 20402:

Medicare and Medicaid: Which Is Which?
Your Medicare Handbook
Home Health Care Under Medicare
Medicare Coverage in a Skilled Nursing Facility
Medicare Coverage of Kidney Dialysis and Kidney Trans-
plant Services

Information about Medicaid in your state is available from your state department of social services or your county welfare department.

Private Health Insurance

A useful discussion of policies for people over 65 is contained in the January 1976 edition of *Consumer Reports,* available in your local library. Your local social security office can give you the government publication *Guide to Health Insurance for People with Medicare.*

Cutting Health Costs

A directory listing home-care opportunities in your area can be obtained from:

National Home Caring Council
67 Irving Place
New York, N.Y. 10003

Information on "activated patient" and other self-care programs in your area is available from:

National Health Information Clearinghouse
P.O. Box 1133
Washington, D.C. 20013
Tel.: (800) 336-4797

Further information on self-care is available in the quarterly magazine *Medical Self-Care: Access to Tools.* The publishers can also provide information on self-care courses in your area. Write the magazine at:

Box 717
Inverness, Calif. 94937

The following up-to-date book on self-care is available for $8.95 at your local bookstore:

Ferguson, Tom. *Medical Self-Care*. New York: Simon and Schuster, 1980.

Canadian Sources

Dept. of National Health and Welfare (Catalogue Number E52-8/18) 1979. The publication describes each province's health plan coverage. It can be obtained by writing to:

Department of Health and Welfare
Information Directorate
Brooke Claxon Building
Turney's Pasture
Ottawa, Ontario K1A OK9

For more specific information on health insurance, write to one of the following offices:

	Medical Care	*Hospital Insurance*
Newfoundland	Newfoundland Medical Care Commission Elizabeth Towers Elizabeth Avenue St. John's, Newfoundland A1C 5J3	Hospital Services Division Department of Health Confederation Building St. John's, Newfoundland A1C 5T7
Prince Edward Island	Health Serices Commission P.O. Box 4500 Charlottetown, P.E.I. C1A 7P4	Hospital Services Commission of Prince Edward island P.O. Box 4500 Charlottetown, P.E.I. C1A 7P4
	Medical Care	*Hospital Insurance*
Nova Scotia	Health Services and Insurance Commission P.O. Box 760 Halifax, Nova Scotia B3J 2V2	Department of Health P.O. Box 488 Halifax, Nova Scotia B3J 2RB

	Medical Care	*Hospital Insurance*
New Brunswick	Department of Health Insured Services Division Box 5100 Fredericton, New Brunswick E3B 5G8	Department of Health Insured Services Division Box 5100 Fredericton, New Brunswick E3B 5G8
Quebec	Quebec Health Insurance Board P.O. Box 6600 Quebec, Quebec G1K 7T3	Department of Social Affairs Joffre Building 1075 chemin Ste-Foy Quebec, Quebec G1A 1B9

Ontario   Ontario Health Insurance Plan (Medical Care and Hospital Insurance)

HAMILTON	KINGSTON
25 Main Street W. LBP 4P9	1955 Princess Street K7L 5A9
LONDON 227 Queens Avenue N6A 5G6	MISSISSAUGA 55 City Centre Drive L5B 3M1
OSHAWA 44 Bond Street W. L1G 1A4	OTTAWA 75 Albert Street K1P 5Y9
SUDBURY 295 Bond St. P3B 2JB	THUNDER BAY 435 James St. S. P7C 5G6
TORONTO 2195 Yonge st. M5W 1A0	

	Medical Care	*Hospital Insurance*
Manitoba	Manitoba Health Services Commission 599 Empress St. Winnipeg, Manitoba R3C 2T6	Manitoba Health Services Commission 599 Empress St. Winnipeg, Manitoba R3C 2T6
Saskatchewan	Saskatchewan Medical Care Insurance Commission Provincial Health Building 3211 Albert St. Regina, Saskatchewan S4S 5W6	Saskatchewan Hospital Services Plan Provincial Health Building 3211 Albert St. Regina, Saskatchewan S4S 5W6

	Medical Care	*Hospital Insurance*
Alberta	Alberta Health Care Insurance Commission P.O. Box 1360 Edmonton, Alberta T5J 2N3	Alberta Department of Hospitals and Medical Care, Hospital Services P.O. Box 2222 9945–108 St. Edmonton, Alberta T5J 2P4
	or Alberta Health Care Insurance Commission J. J. Bowlen Building 620–7th Avenue S.W. Calgary, Alberta T2P 0Y8	
British Columbia	Medical Services Commission 1515 Blanshard St. Victoria, B.C. V8W 3C8 Insurance contract may be obtained from the Medical Services Plan of British Columbia, 1515 Blanshard St. Victoria, B.C. Mailing Address: P.O. Box 1600 Victoria, British Columbia V8W 2X9	Hospital Programs Ministry of Health Parliament Buildings Victoria, British Columbia V8V 1X4
Northwest Territories	N.W.T. Health Care Plan Government of the N.W.T. Yellowknife, N.W.T. X1A 2L9	N.W.T. Health Care Plan Government of the N.W.T. Yellowknife, N.W.T. X1A 2L9

	Medical Care	*Hospital Insurance*
Yukon	Yukon Health Care Insurance Plan P.O. Box 2703 Whitehorse, Yukon Y1A 2C6	Yukon Hospital Insurance Services P.O. Box 2703 Whitehorse, Yukon Y1A 2C6

A summary of all health plans, medical benefits and costs is included in Chapter Five of the *Canada Year Book*, available at all libraries.

NURSING CARE AND OTHER CONSIDERATIONS

A Japanese legend tells about the *obasuteyama*, or old-woman-throwing-away-mountain. In the bad old days, the legend says, old people didn't die at home in bed. They left their village and went to die of exposure on the *obasuteyama*. Young and old alike are horrified by the tale. But if you say the words "nursing home" to an American today, he or she will likely feel as revolted as though you'd mentioned the *obasuteyama*.

Scandals rocked the nursing home industry repeatedly during the 1970s. Patients died as a result of fires, malnutrition and suffocating heat. Doctors charged for patient visits when all they did was look at charts and renew medications. In some homes the only medical care was provided by untrained orderlies. Patients were tied to their beds with cloth or ropes or kept heavily sedated. Industry spokesmen asserted that these horror stories applied to less than five percent of all nursing homes. Even so, it seems probable that serious, though less spectacular, inadequacies have existed at many more.

It's not that nursing homes are a bad idea in themselves. The popular notion that they are repositories for elders discarded by their children is false. Only one of five nursing home residents is "put" there by a family member. Most are placed directly out of a hospital, by a doctor or social worker. Fully half have either no living relatives or none with whom they are in contact. For such people especially, a nursing home can provide renewed social contacts in addition to health care and housekeeping. Too often, however, the poverty and loneliness of incoming nursing home patients has made them vulnerable to exploitation by quick-buck artists. Even those who have both money and caring relatives may find themselves in institutions where they get little privacy, no respect and barely adequate services.

Alternatives to nursing-home care do exist. Many older people who might formerly have been "dumped" into nursing homes now have several noninstitutional alternatives. Home-care services (see section on "Cutting Costs" earlier in this chapter) are being successfully implemented in some communities; congregate housing is expensive to maintain but helps elders keep their independence (see section on "Congregate Homes" in Chapter Three); and senior day-care centers are also on the rise (see section on "Day Care" later in this chapter). Still, for those who do need regular nursing care, a nursing home is probably the best idea. The trick is choosing the right one.

HISTORY OF THE NURSING HOME

To understand the difference between types of nursing homes and the root of certain abuses, you have to understand how our present nursing home industry came about. Before the Social Security Act of 1935, most old people either stayed at home or were sent to county poorhouses. The few old age homes that existed were run by churches, charities and fraternal organizations. Social security payments gave older people the money to stay out of the poorhouse. Instead, they began to end up in boarding houses, apartments or informal nursing homes, often run by widows themselves.

Thirty years later, with the advent of Medicare and Medicaid, the nursing home grew from a cottage industry to big business, practically overnight. Voluntary, nonprofit nursing homes—run by churches, charities, fraternal organizations and occasionally the government—continued to exist, but they nearly disappeared from sight in the flood of for-profit nursing homes.

The reason for the boom isn't hard to find. Shrewd business people quickly discovered that the government insurance programs could provide a high, guaranteed income for inpatient facilities housing Medicare and Medicaid recipients. Medicare payments to qualifying institutions were equal to costs plus a profit margin tied to the interest rate on treasury bonds! And since the number of old people was growing steadily, business was likely to keep growing too. Nursing homes full of government-sponsored patients were like money in the bank. Though today Medicaid has replaced Medicare as the main source of government insurance payments to nursing homes, the dollar amount of direct payments is still high. In 1979 Medicaid payments alone accounted for half of the nursing-home profits.

NONPROFIT OR FOR-PROFIT?

There are some who would like to see all nursing homes run on a nonprofit basis. The vast majority of the abuses, they point out, have occurred at the for-profit homes. That's true, but to claim therefore that all for-profit homes should be eliminated is rather like saying that because the sun has been shown to cause skin cancer, you should always stay in the shade. But just as you exercise care when you spend a lot of time in the sun, so you should be very careful, if you choose a for-profit home, to choose a good one.

Nonprofit, voluntary homes have a long tradition. Indeed, one of the benefits of membership in a church or fraternal organization was that you could depend on it for help and guidance as you grew older. Church, fraternal and charitable homes are now supplemented by a limited number of government homes. A significant proportion of the best nursing homes are nonprofit homes, though they account for less than one-quarter of all nursing homes in the country. Staff-patient ratios are often better in the nonprofit homes. Visitors and some voluntary staff may be drawn from the ranks of the church or fraternal organization, adding a caring group of regular helpers to the paid staff. The people who run the home, moreover, are accountable to the leaders of the church or fraternal groups, rather than to a group of stockholders.

The scarcity of such homes and their reputation for high-quality care means that they are, as a rule, more expensive than for-profit homes. In 1979, the average for-profit facility charged about $640 per month, compared with the $720 monthly fee at the average nonprofit home. Not only are nonprofit homes more expensive, but they also tend to have long waiting lists—and some may require a hefty entrance fee.

Another problem with nonprofit homes is that most are classed as "intermediate care facilities," that is, they emphasize personal and not medical care. If you become seriously ill, the home may ask you to transfer to a "skilled nursing facility," better equipped to handle serious medical problems. Most skilled nursing facilities are for-profit homes.

"Life-care communities" (see section on "Retirement Villages" in Chapter Three) are most often nonprofit facilities offering the amenities of a retirement community together with the services of a nursing home. All of what has already been said about nonprofit homes' costs and waiting lists is just as true of life-care facilities. It used to be common in such communities to have residents trade their homes and all other assets to the life-care home in exchange for lifetime care. But because of consumer complaints and because it's no longer really cost effective, this practice has declined in recent years.

For-profit homes account for between 75 and 80 percent of all nursing homes in the country. These homes may be either "intermediate care facilities," offering chiefly personal and custodial services, or a "skilled nursing facility," offering more medical care. Many are qualified to serve as both.

Most Medicaid patients end up in for-profit homes, though some of the better ones may try to keep Medicaid patients out, holding beds empty in anticipation of the higher rates private patients can pay. Courts in at least two states—Pennsylvania and Massachusetts—have struck down this practice, but it still occurs in many places. The best advice about finding a good for-profit nursing home is to shop and shop and shop, until you find the right one. Not every operator is squeezing dollars out of the elderly, and not every better home turns a cold shoulder to the poor.

FINDING THE RIGHT NURSING HOME

Whether you're looking at a nonprofit or for-profit home, be choosy. Once you've decided on a location, you can find out what the alternatives are in several ways:

- Ask your friends or a physician you trust which homes in the community they would recommend.

- Contact the local senior center and find out if they sponsor or know of citizens' groups that visit and rate the community's nursing homes.

- Ask for referrals from your church or club, from the state or county health department and from the two nursing home industry associations (see *Sources for Further Information*).

From the list of possibilities you compile, develop a tentative ranking of your own, taking into account recommendations, location and suitability of the facility for your particular needs. Then you can begin to visit the homes yourself.

The Nursing Home Checklist, on pp. 339, which is taken from the U.S. Department of Health and Human Services *How to Select a Nursing Home*, is a useful companion for your visit to the homes. A "No" checked anywhere on the list is an indication that you should look elsewhere.

Many experts emphasize, however, that you should try to get as much first-hand information as possible. Don't depend on asking the director of the nursing home all your questions. As one source put it, "Don't just look at the menu. See what's on the table." Does the food taste good? Is it what the menu advertised? Do patients find it varied and tasty? Does a patient who has trouble feeding himself or herself get help before the meal is stone cold?

What about the physical and occupational therapy rooms? Are they spacious and above all, are they in use? Are scheduled activities in progress at the scheduled time? Are the patients participating? One of the most frequent complaints about nursing homes is that they treat all patients as "custodial" patients, downgrading the activities and rehabilitation that might allow some of them to leave the home.

Talk to patients about their lives at the home. When did they last see their doctor? What are their favorite activities? Have they had a fire drill recently? Some patients won't have very good memories, but their cheerfulness and willingness to talk is a good sign. If the majority of patients are lying listless and immobile in their rooms, watch out.

Talk to the staff. Are they pleasant and informative? How long has the average staff member been there? Fast turnover may mean an inferior home. How do staff members themselves talk to patients? Are they friendly and respectful? Or surly? Or do they treat the patients like babies? Do they knock before they enter a patient's room? If you push the nurse's call button in a room, how long does it take for someone to respond?

Finally, you might ask the director these tough questions: how many patients does he or she release each year? Does he object to showing you any areas of the facilities? Does he resist your talking to patients? If an administrator is willing to explain, it's a good sign. If he or she is surly, huffy or evasive, beware! The how-dare-you-ask-such-a-question attitude usually hides some deficiency.

One last matter to check out thoroughly with the administrator is the financial arrangements. Monthly charges usually include at least basic room and board, housekeeping, nursing care and recreational activities. Make sure they do. "Extras" include doctors' care, drugs, tests, physical therapy and amenities like haircuts and telephone calls. If the extras are charged directly through the home, find out what the charges are.

DAY CARE

Studies show that anywhere from 10 to 40 percent of the patients in nursing homes don't need to be there. But while almost 75 percent of all Medicaid money is spent on hospitals and nursing homes, only one percent goes to home-based care. Home-care services themselves are nonetheless on the rise. Another alternative—halfway between home care and institutional care—is the adult day-care center.

Pilot day-care programs are in operation across the country. They provide elders with a pleasant social environment, including companionship and supervised recreational activities. They also serve a participant's physical needs, serving at least one meal per day and providing transportation to and from medical appointments. Programs are designed to keep people healthy and alert, not simply to entertain them. Exercise classes are popular, as is an oral history program, in which the elders record their significant life experiences for use in the classroom or for storage in public libraries and historical societies.

NURSING HOME CHECKLIST

The following is a checklist of important points to consider in selecting a nursing home. You should find the checklist helpful in several ways: for brushing up on things to look for and ask about before you visit a home, for referring to as you talk with staff members and tour a home and for sizing up a home after a visit and comparing it with other homes you have visited.

There are many items on the list, because nursing homes are complex operations. To cover all the items, you may have to make additional visits or follow-up telephone calls.

Some of the items will be difficult to find out on your own, so you will probably have to ask personnel of the home.

This checklist is offered to serve as a reference guide:

The name of nursing **Home A** is _____

The name of nursing **Home B** is _____

The name of nursing **Home C** is _____

	HOME A	HOME B	HOME C
	Yes/No	Yes/No	Yes/No
1. Does the nursing home have the required current license from the state or letter of approval from a licensing agency?	☐ ☐	☐ ☐	☐ ☐
2. Does the administrator have a current state license or waiver? (Required for nursing homes operating under Medicaid.)	☐ ☐	☐ ☐	☐ ☐
3. Is the home certified to participate in the Medicare and Medicaid programs?	☐ ☐	☐ ☐	☐ ☐
4. If the person you are placing requires special services, such as rehabilitation therapy or a therapeutic diet, does the home provide them?	☐ ☐	☐ ☐	☐ ☐
5. Is the general atmosphere of the nursing home warm, pleasant and cheerful?	☐ ☐	☐ ☐	☐ ☐
6. Is the administrator courteous and helpful?	☐ ☐	☐ ☐	☐ ☐
7. Are staff members cheerful, courteous and enthusiastic?	☐ ☐	☐ ☐	☐ ☐
8. Do staff members show patients genuine interest and affection?	☐ ☐	☐ ☐	☐ ☐

	HOME A	HOME B	HOME C
	Yes/No	Yes/No	Yes/No

9. Do patients look well cared for and generally content? ☐ ☐ ☐ ☐ ☐ ☐

10. Are patients allowed to wear their own clothes, decorate their rooms and keep a few prized possessions on hand? ☐ ☐ ☐ ☐ ☐ ☐

11. Is there a place for private visits with family and friends? ☐ ☐ ☐ ☐ ☐ ☐

12. Is there a written statement of patient's rights? As far as you can tell, are these points being carried out? ☐ ☐ ☐ ☐ ☐ ☐

13. Do patients, other visitors and volunteers speak favorably about the home? ☐ ☐ ☐ ☐ ☐ ☐

GENERAL PHYSICAL CONSIDERATIONS

1. Is the nursing home clean and orderly? ☐ ☐ ☐ ☐ ☐ ☐

2. Is the home reasonably free of unpleasant odors? ☐ ☐ ☐ ☐ ☐ ☐

3. Are toilet and bathing facilities easy for handicapped patients to use? ☐ ☐ ☐ ☐ ☐ ☐

4. Is the home well lighted? ☐ ☐ ☐ ☐ ☐ ☐

5. Are rooms well ventilated and kept at a comfortable temperature? ☐ ☐ ☐ ☐ ☐ ☐

SAFETY

1. Are wheelchair ramps provided where necessary? ☐ ☐ ☐ ☐ ☐ ☐

2. Is the nursing home free of obvious hazards, such as obstacles to patients, hazards underfoot, unsteady chairs? ☐ ☐ ☐ ☐ ☐ ☐

3. Are there grab bars in toilet and bathing facilities and handrails on both sides of hallways? ☐ ☐ ☐ ☐ ☐ ☐

4. Do bathtubs and showers have nonslip surfaces? ☐ ☐ ☐ ☐ ☐ ☐

5. Is there an automatic sprinkler system and automatic emergency lighting? ☐ ☐ ☐ ☐ ☐ ☐

6. Are there portable fire extinguishers? ☐ ☐ ☐ ☐ ☐ ☐

	HOME A	HOME B	HOME C
	Yes/No	Yes/No	Yes/No

7. Are exits clearly marked and exit signs illuminated? ☐ ☐ ☐ ☐ ☐ ☐

8. Are exit doors unobstructed and unlocked from inside? ☐ ☐ ☐ ☐ ☐ ☐

9. Are certain areas posted with no-smoking signs? Do staff, patients and visitors observe them? ☐ ☐ ☐ ☐ ☐ ☐

10. Is an emergency evacuation plan posted in prominent locations? ☐ ☐ ☐ ☐ ☐ ☐

MEDICAL, DENTAL AND OTHER SERVICES

1. Does the home have an arrangement with an outside dental service to provide patients with dental care when necessary? ☐ ☐ ☐ ☐ ☐ ☐

2. In case of medical emergencies, is a physician available at all times, either on staff or on call? ☐ ☐ ☐ ☐ ☐ ☐

3. Does the home have arrangements with a nearby hospital for quick transfer of nursing home patients in an emergency? ☐ ☐ ☐ ☐ ☐ ☐

4. Is emergency transportation readily available? ☐ ☐ ☐ ☐ ☐ ☐

PHARMACEUTICAL SERVICES

1. Are pharmaceutical services supervised by a qualified pharmacist? ☐ ☐ ☐ ☐ ☐ ☐

2. Is a room set aside for storing and preparing drugs? ☐ ☐ ☐ ☐ ☐ ☐

NURSING SERVICES

1. Is at least one registered nurse (RN) or licensed practical nurse (LPN) on duty day and night? ☐ ☐ ☐ ☐ ☐ ☐

	HOME A	HOME B	HOME C
	Yes/No	Yes/No	Yes/No

2. Is an RN on duty during the day, seven days a week?   ☐ ☐   ☐ ☐   ☐ ☐

3. Does an RN serve as director of nursing services?   ☐ ☐   ☐ ☐   ☐ ☐

4. Are nurse call buttons located at each patient's bed and in toilet and bathing facilities?   ☐ ☐   ☐ ☐   ☐ ☐

5. Are occupational therapy and speech therapy available for patients who need them?   ☐ ☐   ☐ ☐   ☐ ☐

SOCIAL SERVICES & PATIENT ACTIVITIES

1. Are there social services available to aid patients and their families?   ☐ ☐   ☐ ☐   ☐ ☐

2. Does the nursing home have a varied program of recreational, cultural and intellectual activities for patients?   ☐ ☐   ☐ ☐   ☐ ☐

3. Is there an activities coordinator on the staff?   ☐ ☐   ☐ ☐   ☐ ☐

4. Is suitable space available for patient activities? Are tools and supplies provided?   ☐ ☐   ☐ ☐   ☐ ☐

5. Are activities offered for patients who are relatively inactive or confined to their rooms?   ☐ ☐   ☐ ☐   ☐ ☐

6. Look at the activities schedule. Are activities provided each day? Are some activities scheduled in the evenings?   ☐ ☐   ☐ ☐   ☐ ☐

7. Do patients have an opportunity to attend religious services and talk with clergymen both in and outside the home?   ☐ ☐   ☐ ☐   ☐ ☐

8. Are a barber and beautician available?   ☐ ☐   ☐ ☐   ☐ ☐

PATIENTS' ROOMS

1. Do all the rooms open onto a hallway?   ☐ ☐   ☐ ☐   ☐ ☐

2. Do they have a window to the outside?   ☐ ☐   ☐ ☐   ☐ ☐

	HOME A	HOME B	HOME C
	Yes/No	Yes/No	Yes/No

FOOD SERVICES

1. Is the kitchen clean and reasonably tidy? Is food needing refrigeration not left standing out on counters? Is waste properly disposed of? □ □ □ □ □ □

2. Ask to see the meal schedule. Are at least three meals served each day? Are meals served at normal hours, with plenty of time for leisurely eating? □ □ □ □ □ □

3. Are no more than 14 hours allowed between the evening meal and breakfast the next morning? □ □ □ □ □ □

4. Are nutritious between-meal and bedtime snacks available? □ □ □ □ □ □

5. Are patients given enough food? Does the food look appetizing? □ □ □ □ □ □

6. Sample a meal. Is the food tasty and served at the proper temperature? □ □ □ □ □ □

7. Does the meal being served match the posted menu? □ □ □ □ □ □

8. Are special meals prepared for patients on therapeutic diets? □ □ □ □ □ □

9. Is the dining room attractive and comfortable? □ □ □ □ □ □

10. Do patients who need it get help in eating, whether in the dining room or in their own rooms? □ □ □ □ □ □

REHABILITATION THERAPY

1. Is a full-time program of physical therapy available for patients who need it? □ □ □ □ □ □

2. Does each patient have a reading light, a comfortable chair and a closet and drawers for personal belongings? □ □ □ □ □ □

3. Is there fresh drinking water within reach? □ □ □ □ □ □

4. Is there a curtain or screen available to provide privacy for each bed whenever necessary? □ □ □ □ □ □

	HOME A	HOME B	HOME C
	Yes/No	Yes/No	Yes/No
5. Do bathing and toilet facilities have adequate privacy?	☐ ☐	☐ ☐	☐ ☐

OTHER AREAS OF THE NURSING HOME

	HOME A	HOME B	HOME C
1. Is there a lounge where patients can chat, read, play games, watch television or just relax away from their rooms?	☐ ☐	☐ ☐	☐ ☐
2. Is a public telephone available for patients' use?	☐ ☐	☐ ☐	☐ ☐
3. Does the nursing home have an outdoor area where patients can get fresh air and sunshine?	☐ ☐	☐ ☐	☐ ☐

FINANCIAL AND RELATED MATTERS

	HOME A	HOME B	HOME C
1. Do the estimated monthly costs (including extra charges) compare favorably with the cost of other homes?	☐ ☐	☐ ☐	☐ ☐
2. Is a refund made for unused days paid for in advance?	☐ ☐	☐ ☐	☐ ☐
3. Are visiting hours convenient for patients and visitors?	☐ ☐	☐ ☐	☐ ☐
4. Are these and other important matters specified in the contract?	☐ ☐	☐ ☐	☐ ☐

The trouble with day care is that it's expensive, more expensive even than nursing homes themselves. Expansion of day-care centers will depend upon the availability of funds to run them. To find out if there's a program in your community, call your state or county welfare department.

A NURSING HOME THAT WORKS

Some time ago, we at WNBC's "Prime of Your Life" show were looking for a really well-run private nursing home located nearby. There had been a spate of exposes about certain homes run at substantial profit to the owners but with sickening disregard for the welfare of the patients, thanks both to the owners' indifference and their influence with important political figures. People had written in claiming it isn't always like that. There are good nursing homes. Such as which ones? we asked. The Kingsbridge Nursing Home was the reply. So we sallied forth to take a look.

We saw two red brick buildings, each five stories high, filling a large part of an odd-sized city block. Surrounding the home were private houses on three sides and a fairly large apartment house on the fourth. The neighborhood seemed pleasant. The streets were clean. Children were able to play on them with apparent safety because traffic was quite light. The small lawns were well kept, as were the homes themselves. The architecture of the nursing home was undistinguished, two squarish buildings with lots of windows but no attempt at ornamentation. The buildings were connected by a covered runway under which a number of clearly quite elderly people were sitting in wheelchairs against that side of the building where the fading sun of an autumn day could still feed some warmth.

We walked into an open lobby with a counter and a switchboard on one side. The receptionist greeted us with a smile and asked us to wait a moment. We did. Now, I must confess to having felt some apprehension. I didn't know *what* to expect. Some months earlier a reporter with a camera crew working on a documentary I was supervising had been harshly turned away from another nursing home. What little he had been able to see did nothing to make me expect anything other than a miserable day ahead. The fact that I was more aware of my own distaste for nursing homes than of the plight of the elderly patients I had come to see left me somewhat ashamed but no less apprehensive. Right there I learned something from my own reactions about why old people are so often

mistreated. As I got my first glimpse of a couple of very
old people sharing the lobby with me, I found myself
unconsciously building up a protective mental barrier,
willing myself to make a distinction between them and
me, trying to deny their equal share of humanity. For
if I could successfully dehumanize the people in this
place, then I would not have to feel any personal
concern about the way in which they were treated.

I could have spared myself the effort. The people
were old, it's true. But even when just sitting, most
were active. Certainly there was plenty of activity
around us. From down a wide, uncluttered hallway
could be heard the sound of a piano. Chopin, I thought.
Not well played, but Chopin nevertheless. Voices
bounced happily off one another. Women in white
uniforms bustled back and forth.

A voice called my name, and I turned to be greeted
by a rather small, sturdy figure. This was Mrs. Rose
Boritzer, the owner and director. She smiles a lot and
doesn't seem to conceal any ogreish tendencies. With
her as our guide, we spent the afternoon filming and
talking to patients. We filmed exercise classes and
ladies in the beauty shop. We filmed a bingo game and
my friend the piano player, an almost elfin figure of a
man, a retired pharmacist who had taken up the piano
not much more than a year ago. And playing Chopin!
So it wasn't great, but still—! His heart was not good.
He had other ills as well, but each week he went to his
lesson on the outside and then came home to practice.
And how he did practice! But nobody else in the large
living room seemed to mind.

We took a film of the kitchen and of a dining room
where tablecloths of different colors signified different
diets for some of the diners. We were learning about
nursing homes without even knowing that we were
learning. I remember a bulletin board telling of a
meeting on a political issue, of a house committee and
of other events, including a party. We sat in on a session

with a psychologist: a number of people discussed visits from family and their own living preferences. They told how often they wanted to see their kids, and how often they actually did. Some were full of resentment, some quite happy with things as they were.

Then to another floor, in one of two commodious elevators. A lady in a room for two looked smilingly over some family pictures and gave an equally happy look to her portable typewriter. She is the editor of the home's paper and prides herself on her job. Would she rather be with her daughter, outside? She thought not. Here she had friends, things to do. When she wanted to visit, to shop or whatever, she could and did. Not often now because the leg is bad. She needs a walker to make her way along.

Things, events, crowded in. There was a solarium, a room for watching TV. In this large room people were making things, some of them for charity. A cloth clown doll was pressed on me. It still sits on my mantlepiece at home. I talked to a painter, a creator of primitive ethnic scenes and tableaux, but no Grandfather Moses, this one. He is an angry man, an unreconstructed old radical, unhappy with the way the world is arranged and as determined as ever (at age 82) to do what he could to change it.

What was it? What was the important perception? Why, this place where I had expected nothing but doddering forms in various stages of decomposition was *vital!* Oh, people weren't playing basketball in the hallways, but they were not (for the most part, let's be honest) simply waiting for the end. They were living their lives and getting something out of it.

DRUGS

We spend around $16 billion annually on medicine, and—largely because of strict government regulation—

much of it is well spent. According to the U.S. Food and Drug Administration (FDA) standards, a drug must be shown to be safe and therapeutically valuable before it can be sold. The two main risks the American drug consumer runs are overmedication and overpayment for brand-name prescription drugs.

OVER-THE-COUNTER DRUGS

Over-the-counter drugs are widely advertised in the national media, often claiming to be "more effective than the leading pain reliever" but seldom identifying that pain reliever. Drug labeling laws are therefore quite useful to consumers. They require that each over-the-counter product list all of its active ingredients, together with directions for use and a caution about any possible side effects. The ingredients can help you avoid buying, say, what amounts to four kinds of aspirin because each was marketed under a different name, claiming benefits in fighting a different malady. Ingredients lists are also useful to those who may be allergic to certain medicines.

PRESCRIPTION DRUGS

When your doctor writes you a prescription, be sure that he or she tells you the following:

- If there are any medicines that shouldn't be taken together with the drug being prescribed.
- Whether the drug should be taken on a full or an empty stomach—some drugs may cause nausea if taken at the wrong time.
- If you can refill the prescription yourself, and if so, how many times you can refill it.

One question to be sure to discuss with your doctor is whether or not he or she can fill your prescription with a *generic* version of a given drug instead of with a brand-name version. The brand name is often much more expensive, and according to the FDA, it is no more safe or effective than the generic. A 1979 survey done in Brooklyn, New York, for example, showed price differentials like these: $1 or more between the generic and brand-name version of the same antibiotic; $4 to $8 between the two versions of one tranquilizer; and 50¢ to $2 between two versions of penicillin. Only 60 or 70 of the 200 commonly prescribed medicines are available generically, but that minority includes most of the antibiotics and some painkillers. Table 26 on p. 350 the 14 most frequently prescribed drugs showing both their generic names and the brand-name versions.

Getting a generic prescription isn't the only key to saving money on drugs. You should also shop around for the pharmacy with the lowest prices. On the other hand, you'll want to find a pharmacy that will care about keeping you as a regular customer. The store should keep a record of the medicines you buy and also advise you about drugs that should not be taken together.

LAETRILE

Every generation has its wonder drug, guaranteed to rid the body of that generation's most feared disease. Laetrile is the current "wonder" supposed to kill cancer with its "magic bullets" made of cyanide. However, no medical evidence has yet been advanced to demonstrate that laetrile is of any use at all in the treatment of cancer.

Some states have nevertheless legalized the use of the drug (sometimes advertised as a "vitamin," though it isn't one), reasoning that even if it does only psychological good, it isn't harmful to take and does make the patient feel better. The argument sounds good on the surface, but it ignores the possibility that, once legalized, the drug could be used to the exclusion of other, proven drugs or therapies, thereby letting patients die who might have lived. Laetrile therapy is certainly less painful than some chemotherapy; the only other difference is that chemotherapy sometimes works, while we don't know that laetrile ever does.

Table 26

Frequently Prescribed Drugs
(with General and Brand Names) and Their Purpose

Generic Name	Commonly Prescribed Brand Names	Purpose of Drug
Ampicillin	Amcill Omnipen Polycillin Principen	To fight infection (antibiotic)
Tetracycline	Achromycin V Panmycin Sumycin Tetracyn	To fight infection (antibiotic)
Acetaminophen/ codeine	Tylenol with Codeine	To relieve pain, fever and cough
Hydrochlorothiazide	Esidrix HydroDiuril Oretic	For hypertension and edema (diuretic)
Penicillin V-K	Pen-Vee K V-Cillin K Veetids	To fight infection (antibiotic)
Chloridiazepoxide hydrochloride	Librium	To relieve anxiety and tension
Propoxyphene hydrochloride, aspirin, phenacetin and caffeine	Darvon Compound-65	To relieve pain (analgesic)
Erythromycin	Erythrocin Stearate	To fight infection (antibiotic)
Amitriptyline	Elavil Endep	To relieve symptoms of depression

Frequently Prescribed Drugs
(with General and Brand Names) and Their Purpose

Diphenhydramine hydrochloride	Benadryl	Antihistamine (also for motion sickness and parkinsonism)
Diphenoxylate hydrochloride with atropine sulfate	Lomotil	To help control diarrhea
Meclizine hydrochloride	Antivert	To control nausea and vomiting and dizziness from motion sickness
Chlorothiazide	Diuril	For hypertension and edema (diuretic)
Erythromycin ethyl succinate	E.E.S.	To fight infection (antibiotic)

PSYCHOLOGICAL PROBLEMS

Imagine your husband died of a heart attack, sitting in his favorite chair, and you found him. Imagine you had major surgery, were forced to stay in bed for over a month and developed bed sores. Or you're losing control of your bladder, say, twice a week. Or sometimes you start crying in the middle of a sentence and forget what you were saying, only to come to yourself after a moment, realizing you've behaved like an idiot. Or you've been placed in a nursing home whose main concession to recreation is an orderly who wheels you outside to watch cars on the freeway. Or the medication you're taking gives you dizzy spells, but the doctor says it's normal. Or your relatives take control of your assets and dole out allowances to you as though you were a child. If only two of the above happened to you, how would you feel? Depressed? Confused? Disoriented?

No one denies that older people can have serious psychological problems. After all, elders suffer such shocks of loss,

illness and sudden powerlessness as would make most young
college graduates drop dead of anxiety before they could
reach their therapists' office. Many of us are surprised to
hear that a quarter of all suicides are people over 65, but
what people should also know is that many psychologically
troubled elders can recover completely if they are treated
promptly and adequately. Dr. Robert N. Butler, in his
Pulitzer prize-winning *Why Survive? Being Old in America*, reports that according to studies done in private mental
hospitals 75 percent of patients over 65 were able to improve
and return to their homes after only two months of treatment. The nightmare vision of a ward full of old people
staring eternally and vacantly into space is more the product
of the inadequate care offered by some state mental hospitals and nursing homes than of any "inevitable senility" in
the old.

Elders may suffer from either organic brain syndrome or
purely psychological disturbances (or both). The worst thing
that frequently happens to them is to have organic problems
mistaken for mere "senility." Brain syndromes can be
caused by malnutrition, congestive heart failure, anemia and
even certain medications. The patient may act withdrawn
and confused or may have nervous twitches. If organic brain
syndrome is diagnosed early, many symptoms can be
reversed and the patient can recover completely. If the
symptoms turn out to have no apparent physical cause, then
therapy is probably in order, just as it would be for someone
younger.

The ingrained American notion that "if the pipes aren't
broken, then the thing must work" makes it hard for older
people to get psychological help. The Medicare plan that's
willing to put thousands of dollars into a medical doctor's
pocket limits reimbursements for outpatient psychiatric
treatment to a mere $250 per year.

One source of low-cost psychological help for elders are
the Community Mental Health Centers located in cities and
towns across the country. They have generally been underfi-
nanced, and some critics charge that they have been slow to

develop programs for older people and their staffs are frequently only minimally trained. Still, they do offer treatment on a sliding-scale payment schedule, bringing regular therapy within the reach of elders. To find out about centers in your area, write the National Institute of Mental Health (see *Sources for Further Information*).

A better idea may be to contact your state agency on aging, local senior center or church organization. Such groups may be able to refer you to clinics or individual practitioners who are qualified to offer treatment to older people. A few pilot clinics specializing in geriatric psychiatry have opened around the country, but their further development awaits adequate funding.

Sources for Further Information

Nursing-Home Care

A cogent critique of the nursing home industry is Chapter Nine of Robert N. Butler's *Why Survive? Being Old in America* (1979), published in New York by Harper and Row and available at your bookstore or library.

The Department of Health and Human Services offers the pamphlet *How to Select a Nursing Home*. Order it from:

Superintendent of Documents
U.S. Government Printing Office
Washington, D.C. 20402

The two industry nursing home associations are the following: the first represents nonprofit nursing homes; the second represents commercial nursing homes:

American Association of Homes for the Aging (AAHA)
1050 17th St., N.W.
Washington, D.C. 20036

American Nursing Home Association
(aka American Health Care Association)
1025 Connecticut Avenue, N.W.
Washington, D.C. 20036

Drugs

If you want to understand all the effects and side effects of
the drugs you take, you can check the following handbook,
available for $8.95 at your bookstore or from your local
library:

Long, James W. *The Essential Guide to Prescription Drugs.*
    New York: Harper and Row, 1977.

Psychological Problems

A list of Community Mental Health Centers in your area
is available from:

National Institute of Mental Health
5600 Fishers Lane, Rm. 214–21
Rockville, Md. 20857

INDEX